# MULTICULTURAL EDUCATION SERIES

### JAMES A. BANKS, *Series Editor*

*(continued)*

# RACE, EMPIRE, AND ENGLISH LANGUAGE TEACHING

## CREATING RESPONSIBLE AND ETHICAL ANTI-RACIST PRACTICE

### SUHANTHIE MOTHA

TEACHERS COLLEGE PRESS

Teachers College, Columbia University
New York and London

Published by Teachers College Press, 1234 Amsterdam Avenue, New York, NY 10027

This book incorporates elements from the following published works:

"Afternoon tea at Su's: Participant voice and community in critical feminist ethnography" by S. Motha, 2009, In S. Kouritzin, N. Piquemal, & R. Norman (Eds.), *Qualitative research: Challenging the orthodoxies* (pp. 103–120), New York, NY: Routledge. © 2009 Taylor & Francis Group. Republished with permission.

"Racializing ESOL teacher identities in U.S. K–12 public schools" by S. Motha, 2006, *TESOL Quarterly, 40*(3), 103–118. © 2006 TESOL International Association. Republished with permission of John Wiley and Sons.

"Decolonizing ESOL: Negotiating linguistic power in U.S. public school classrooms" by S. Motha, 2006, *Critical Inquiry in Language Studies, 3*(2&3), 75–100. © 2006 Taylor & Francis. Republished with permission.

*Library of Congress Cataloging-in-Publication Data*

Motha, Suhanthie.
  Race, empire, and English language teaching : the light cast by someone else's lamp / Suhanthie Motha.
      pages cm. — (Multicultural education series)
  Includes bibliographical references.
  ISBN 978-0-8077-5512-9 (pbk. : alk. paper) —
  ISBN 978-0-8077-5513-6 (hardcover : alk. paper) —
  ISBN 978-0-8077-7271-3 (ebook)
    1. Linguistic minorities—Education—United States. 2. English language—Study and teaching—United States—Foreign speakers. 3. English language—Social aspects. I. Title.
  LC3731.M685 2014
  371.8290973—dc23                                                                2013044862

ISBN 978-0-8077-5512-9 (paper)
ISBN 978-0-8077-5513-6 (hardcover)
eISBN 978-0-8077-77271-3

For Alexandra, whose gutsy foregrounding of uncomfortable themes made it impossible to ignore silences in which oppression grows

For Jane, who kept my attention on student success and access within the long-term project of transformative pedagogy

For Katie, who helped me to understand how the fluidity of difference is connected to epistemology

For Margaret, who taught me to seek compassion, ethics, and beauty in pedagogical moments

# Contents

# Series Foreword

This illuminating and timely book challenges the idea that English teaching is a neutral and apolitical endeavor and describes the ways in which it is interwoven in complex ways with race, empire, colonization, deculturalization (Spring, 2010), modernization, and language loss. In describing the complex ways in which English teaching is related to power, race, and other variables, Motha's goal is to help teachers of English as a second language practice their craft with keen and critical insights into the ways in which English teaching is situated within the political, cultural, and economic contexts of school and society. This book is also designed to help teachers to acquire the knowledge and skills needed to teach English to students from diverse cultures and language groups in ways that honor—rather than denigrate—their first languages and cultures.

Alexandra, Jane, Katie, and Margaret—the four first-year ESOL teachers on which the study reported in this book is based—describe the myriad ways in which their students and their classrooms were marginalized within their schools and how their students became double victims because they internalized many of the negative conceptions of their languages and groups that were institutionalized within the school and that were held not only by many teachers but also by some parents. Motha describes ways in which the marginalization of language minority students in U. S. schools today is a continuation of the ways in which colonized nations and cultures have been historically victimized, oppressed, devalued, and viewed as the "Other." Through the voices of Alexandra, Jane, Katie, and Margaret, Motha describes creative and ingenious ways in which teachers can resist the institutionalized structures in schools that deprecate students who are learning English as a second language. ESOL teachers will find the interventions that were used by these four insightful, creative, and diligent teachers inspiring and helpful.

This book will help teachers and other educational practitioners to examine and to better understand the ways in which race, language, power, and learning are interrelated. It will also provide them with innovative ideas about ways to conceptualize and implement interventions and teaching strategies that will enable students to maintain their cultural integrity, linguistic pride, and skills in their first languages while learning English. Reforming

the structure of schools to make them more linguistically and culturally empowering will greatly benefit students from diverse groups who are rapidly
increasing in the nation's schools.

American classrooms are experiencing the largest influx of immigrant
students since the beginning of the 20th century. Almost 14 million new immigrants—documented and undocumented—settled in the United States in
the years from 2000 to 2010. Less than 10% came from nations in Europe.
Most came from Mexico, nations in Asia, and nations in Latin America, the
Caribbean, and Central America (Comarota, 2011). A large but undetermined number of undocumented immigrants enter the United States each
year. The U.S. Department of Homeland Security (2010) estimated that in
January 2010, 10.8 million undocumented immigrants were living in the
United States, which was a decrease from the estimated 11.8 million that re-
sided in the United States in January 2007. In 2007, approximately 3.2 million children and young adults were among the 11.8 million undocumented
immigrants in the United States, most of whom grew up in this country (Perez, 2011). The influence of an increasingly ethnically diverse population on
U.S. schools, colleges, and universities is and will continue to be enormous.

Schools in the United States are more diverse today than they have been
since the early 1900s when a multitude of immigrants entered the United
States from Southern, Central, and Eastern Europe. In the 20-year period
between 1989 and 2009, the percentage of students of color in U.S. public
schools increased from 32% to 45% (Aud et al., 2011). If current trends
continue, students of color will equal or exceed the percentage of White
students in U.S. public schools within one or two decades. In 2010–2011,
students of color exceeded the number of Whites students in the District of
Columbia and in 13 states (listed here in descending order of the percentage of ethnic minority students therein): Hawaii, California, New Mexico,
Texas, Nevada, Arizona, Florida, Maryland, Mississippi, Georgia, Louisi-
ana, Delaware, and New York. (Audet al., 2012). In 2009, children of undocumented immigrants made up 6.8% of students in grades kindergarten
through 12 (Perez, 2011).

Language and religious diversity is also increasing in the U.S. student
population. The 2012 American Community Survey estimated that 21%
of Americans aged 5 and above (61.9 million) spoke a language other than
English at home (U. S. Census Bureau, 2012). Harvard professor Diana L.
Eck (2001) calls the United States the "most religiously diverse nation on
earth" (p. 4). Islam is now the fastest-growing religion in the United States,
as well as in several European nations such as France, the United Kingdom,
and The Netherlands (Banks, 2009; Cesari, 2004). Most teachers now in
the classroom and in teacher education programs are likely to have students
from diverse ethnic, racial, linguistic, and religious groups in their classrooms during their careers. This is true for both inner-city and suburban

teachers in the United States, as well as in many other Western nations such as Canada, Australia, and the United Kingdom (Banks, 2009).

The major purpose of the Multicultural Education Series is to provide preservice educators, practicing educators, graduate students, scholars, and policymakers with an interrelated and comprehensive set of books that summarizes and analyzes important research, theory, and practice related to the education of ethnic, racial, cultural, and linguistic groups in the United States and the education of mainstream students about diversity. The dimensions of multicultural education, developed by Banks (2004) and described in the *Handbook of Research on Multicultural Education* and in the *Encyclopedia of Diversity in Education* (Banks, 2012), provide the conceptual framework for the development of the publications in the Series. The dimensions are content integration, the knowledge construction process, prejudice reduction, equity pedagogy, and an empowering institutional culture and social structure.

The books in the Series provide research, theoretical, and practical knowledge about the behaviors and learning characteristics of students of color, language minority students, low-income students, and other minoritized population groups, such as LGBT youth (Mayo, 2014). They also provide knowledge about ways to improve academic achievement (Au, 2011; Gay, 2010; Lee, 2007) and race relations in educational settings (Howard, 2006; Stephan & Vogt, 2004). Multicultural education is consequently as important for middle-class White suburban students as it is for students of color who live in the inner city. Multicultural education fosters the public good and the overarching goals of the commonwealth.

This book is timely and significant not only because students who speak a language other than English are the fastest-growing population in the nation's schools, but also because many of the practices within schools are stigmatizing the languages and cultures of language minority students and are not giving them recognition for their linguistic gifts and talents. The nurturing of the linguistic knowledge and skills of the diverse groups of students who attend U. S. schools will facilitate their learning of English as well as enrich our nation. I hope that the incisive research and wisdom about the relationship between race, language, power, and learning that are revealed in this sobering book will enable teachers and other educators to envision actions they can take to help preserve the rich linguistic diversity that students bring to the nation's schools.

—James A. Banks

# REFERENCES

Au, K. H. (2011). *Literacy achievement and diversity: Keys to success for students, teachers, and schools.* New York, NY: Teachers College Press.

Aud, S., Hussar, W., Johnson, F., Kena, G., Roth, E., Manning, E., Wang, X., & Zhang, J. (2012). *The condition of education 2012* (NCES 2012-045). Washington, DC: U.S. Department of Education, National Center for Education Statistics. Retrieved from nces.ed.gov/pubsearch

Aud, S., Hussar, W., Kena, G., Bianco, K., Frohlich, L., Kemp, J., & Tahan, K. (2011). *The condition of education 2011* (NCES 2011-033). U.S. Department of Education, National Center for Education Statistics. Washington, DC: U.S. Department of Education, National Center for Education Statistics. Retrieved from nces.ed.gov/programs/coe/pdf/coe_1er.pdf

Banks, J. A. (2004). Multicultural education: Historical development, dimensions, and practice. In J. A. Banks & C. A. M. Banks (Eds.), *Handbook of research on multicultural education* ( 2nd ed., pp. 3–29). San Francisco, CA: Jossey-Bass.

Banks, J. A. (Ed.). (2009). *The Routledge international companion to multicultural education.* New York, NY: Routledge.

Banks, J. A. (2012). Multicultural education: Dimensions of. In J. A. Banks (Ed). *Encyclopedia of diversity in education* (vol. 3, pp. 1538–1547). Thousand Oaks, CA: Sage Publications.

Camarota, S. A. (2011, October). A *record-setting decade of immigration: 2000 to 2010.* Washington, DC: Center for Immigration Studies. Retrieved from cis.org/2000-2010-record-setting-decade-of-immigration

Cesari, J. (2004). *When Islam and democracy meet: Muslims in Europe and the United States.* New York, NY: Pelgrave Macmillan.

Eck, D. L. (2001). *A new religious America: How a "Christian country" has become the world's most religiously diverse nation.* New York, NY: HarperSanFrancisco.

Gay, G. (2010). *Culturally responsive teaching: Theory, research, and practice* (2nd ed.). New York, NY: Teachers College Press.

Howard, G. R. (2006*). We can't teach what we don't know: White teachers, multiracial schools* (2nd ed.). New York, NY: Teachers College Press.

Lee, C. D. (2007*). Culture, literacy, and learning: Taking bloom in the midst of the whirlwind.* New York, NY: Teachers College Press.

Mayo, C. (2014). *LGBTQ youth and education: Policies and practices.* New York, NY: Teachers College Press.

Perez, W. (2011). *Americans by heart: Undocumented Latino students and the promise of higher education.* New York, NY: Teachers College Press.

Stephan, W. G. & Vogt, W. P. (Eds.). (2004). *Education programs for improving intergroup Relations: Theory, research, and practice.* New York, NY: Teachers College Press.

Spring, J. (2010). *Deculturalizaiton and the struggle for equality: A brief history of the education of dominated cultures in the United States* (7th ed.). New York, NY: McGraw-Hill.

U.S. Census Bureau. (2008, August 14). *Statistical abstract of the United States.* Retrieved from www.census.gov/prod/2006pubs/07statab/pop.pdf

U.S. Census Bureau. (2010). *2010 American community survey.* Retrieved from factfinder2.census.gov/faces/tableservices/jsf/pages/productview.xhtml?pid =ACS_10_1YR_S1603&prodType=table

U. S. Census Bureau (2012). *Selected social characteristics in the United States: 2012 American Community Survey 1-year estimates.* Retrieved from factfinder2.census.gov/faces/tableservices/jsf/pages/productview.xhtml?pid =ACS_12_1YR_DP02&prodType=table

U.S. Department of Homeland Security. (2010, February). *Estimates of the unauthorized immigrant population residing in the United States: January 2010.* Retrieved from www.dhs.gov/files/statistics/immigration.shtm

# Acknowledgments

I am deeply indebted to many, many intellectual companions, more than I can mention here.

Alexandra, Jane, Katie, and Margaret held my hand as I struggled to understand what it means to know, to learn, and to transform. They continue to teach me and to awe me with their pedagogical practice (in Jane's case, in a substantially different form). This book is not only my work, it is theirs, and I am grateful to them for sharing it with me.

My heartfelt thanks goes to Shelley Wong, Manka Varghese, Stephanie Vandrick, and Ryuko Kubota for reading the entire manuscript although they didn't have to and for giving me careful and helpful feedback. I thank Shelley for indefatigable cheerleading and for shaping in wondrous ways my imaginings of the possibilities for my own future—just by being herself. Manka, my constant and generous friend and mentor, helped me to clear away a workable and thinkable path. Stephanie believed in the goals of the book, engaged me in conversations when I was unsure of myself, and always modeled a graceful and balanced academic persona. Ryuko inspired me to persevere and offered steady encouragement. I have received warm, unflagging, and humorous support far beyond any reasonable call of duty from my department chair, Gary Handwerk. I thank my program director, Sandra Silberstein, for characteristically insightful comments and for creating the type of intellectual space at the University of Washington in which I truly felt comfortable exploring my line of research, no matter how politically laden. Sherrie Carroll, my dear partner-in-crime and encouraging grad school comrade, made sure all along the way that I didn't mistake the finger pointing at the moon for the moon.

This book serves as a testament not only to the value of the mentorship and support I have been fortunate enough to receive, but also to the tremendous power of collaborative intellectual communities. I have been blessed with many communities to thank. I am indebted to my fairy godmothers, the Sister Scholars: Rachel Grant, Ryuko Kubota, Angel Lin, Gertrude Tinker Sachs, Stephanie Vandrick, and Shelley Wong. What a wild ride this has been. I couldn't have done it without you. I'm grateful for the Quotable Quills: Kara Blank-Gonzalez, Sherrie Carroll, Noriko Ishihara, Melinda Martin-Beltran, Gloria Park, and Megan Peercy, with whom I escaped for soothing and productive writerly Saturdays.

I cannot imagine a more vibrant and stimulating intellectual home than the one the University of Washington has been for me, and I am thankful for whatever random (and not so random) turns of events had me land there.

My WIRED Sisterhood were lamplighters and spirit guides. For wise, intentional, and loving guidance, I thank Rachel Chapman, Angela Ginorio, Michelle Habell-Pallan, Alexes Harris, Habiba Ibrahim, Janine Jones, Ralina Joseph, LeiLani Nishime, Sonnet Retman, Ileana Rodriguez-Silva, Stephanie Smallwood, Alicia Wassink, and Manka Varghese. I was enriched by numerous, often unexpected, conversations with Julia Aguirre, Raquel Albarrán, Sareeta Amrute, Dafney Blanca Dabach, Kiki Jenkins, Hedy Lee, Naomi Murakawa, Jessica Sullivan, Carolyn Pinedo-Turnovsky, Sasha Welland, and Joy Williamson-Lott.

A warm thank you goes out to Juan and Diane Guerra for their caring social, intellectual, and institutional support and to generous and wise Habiba Ibrahim for her ongoing and reassuring demystification of many academic processes. Thank you to my program colleagues, Priti Sandhu and Mary Nell Sorenson, for being lovely to work with.

My Language and Rhetoric colleagues, Anis Bawarshi, Nancy Bou Ayash, George Dillon, Juan Guerra, Colette Moore, Candice Rai, Gail Stygall, and John Webster, welcomed me warmly into their fold.

I've benefited greatly from the ongoing mentorship from other departmental colleagues: Carolyn Busch, Eva Cherniavsky, Gillian Harkins, Habiba Ibrahim, Charles LaPorte, Kathy Mork, Chandan Reddy, Caroline Simpson, Anu Taranath, and Alys Weinbaum. I am grateful for serendipitous and well-timed conversations in hallways and stairwells, in grocery stores and on islands, with Bob Abrams, Carolyn Allen, Linda Bierds, Kathleen Blake, the late Herb Blau, Laura Chrisman, Louis Chude-Sokei, Kate Cummings, Tom Foster, Laurie George, Kimberlee Gillis-Bridges, Sydney Kaplan, Monika Kaup, Michelle Liu, Carrie Matthews, Mona Modiano, Brian Reed, Juliet Shields, Elizabeth Simmons-O'Neill, Henry Staten, Maya Sonenberg, Míćeál Vaughan, Rob Weller, Shawn Wong, and Kathy Woodward.

My Writing On Site Group helped to keep my writing warm during a time when a heavy frost was forming over it: Beth Kalikoff, Theresa Ronquillo, Betty Schmitz, Anu Taranath, and Joanne Woiak.

I was fortunate to belong to an exhilarating and thoughtful gathering, the Simpson Center Society of Scholars for 2012–2013: Kathy Woodward, Miriam Bartha, George Behlmer, Stephanie Camp, Annie Dwyer, Ben Gardner, Gillian Harkins, Celia Lowe, Louisa Mackenzie, LeiLani Nishime, Maria Quintana, Christine Sunardi, Anjali Vats, and Patrick Zambianchi.

Many conversations with stimulating and caring doctoral students furthered my thinking: Tae Youn Ahn, Avram Blum, Grace Chen, Julie Dykema, Norah Fahim, Chris Featherman, Ron Fuentes, Sunao Fukanaga,

I-Chen Huang, Rashi Jain, Jitpicha Jarayan, Hee-Seung Kang, Laura Kusaka, Wanda Liao, Natasha Merchant, Thuong Pham, Yasmine Romero, Bonnie Vidrine, Kerry Soo Von Esch, Xuan Zheng, Wei Zhou, Dan Zhu, and Jennifer Zinchuk.

I learned a great deal hunkered down in the basement of the Art Building with the community of my Race and Empire class in the Spring of 2011. A huge thank you to Olivia Connor, Jed Domigpe, Norah Fahim, Sunao Fukanaga, Brandi Hair, Johnica Hopkins, Jitpicha Jarayapun, Wanda Liao, Alex Schiff-Bellabiod, Veronica Villarreal, Elinor Westfold, Sasha Yanak, Brett Yarnton, and Jennifer Zinchuk.

The Diversity Pedagogies Group helped me to knit connections between pedagogy and epistemology: founders Miriam Bartha, Beth Kalikoff, Betty Schmitz, and Anu Taranath, and companions Cherry Banks, Jeannette Bushnell, Rachel Chapman, William Daniell, Bill Erdly, Karen Friesem, Juan Guerra, Brinda Jegatheesan, Kanta Kochhar-Lindgren, Linda Martin-Morris, Ratnesh Nagda, LeiLani Nishime, Joanne Woiak, and Manka Varghese.

The ever-inspiring Sarah Benesch has introduced me to the ideas of numerous interesting people. I am particularly grateful for a late-night conversation on a beach in a tropical country about Sarah Ahmed.

Other members of the TESOL and applied linguistics community have been encouraging and exciting to think alongside: Theresa Austin, Gulbahar Beckett, Diane Belcher, Suresh Canagarajah, Chris Casanave, Carla Chamberlin-Quinlisk, Christian Chun, Graham Crookes, Deborah Crusan, Andy Curtis, Doug Fleming, Christine Higgins, Alan Hirvela, Awad Ibrahim, Roumi Ilieva, Rashi Jain, Lia Kamhi-Stein, Yasko Kanno, Sandra Kouritzin, Ena Lee, Guofang Li, Enric Llurda, Ahmar Mahboob, Aya Matsuda, Elizabeth Miller, Brian Morgan, Cynthia Nelson, Bonny Norton, Brian Paltridge, Aneta Pavlenko, Matt Prior, Vai Ramanathan, Davi Reis, Mary Romney, Ali Fuad Selvi, Shawna Shapiro, Hyunjung Shin, Sue Starfield, Yilin Sun, Tsegga Tecle, Ana Wu, Aiden Yeh, and Lawrence Zhang.

Thank you to the late Arthur Whiteley, who passed away during the writing of this book, for establishing the Whiteley Center, to Kathy Cowell for her support and friendship, and to all the lovely folks at Whiteley. I wrote most of this book there and would not have been able to write it otherwise. Thank you to the Board of the Whiteley Center for opening its doors to me.

Thank you to the Simpson Center for the Humanities and the Royalty Research Fund for funding and, in particular, Kathleen Woodward and Miriam Bartha for their lively and stimulating support.

At Teachers College Press, my series editor Jim Banks listened to a 30-second conversation, recognized a nugget worth pursuing, and followed up actively. Thank you for your faith in the project. Thank you also to Brian Ellerbeck for helping me to reconceptualize my audience; to John Bylander for being so efficient, reliable, and flexible; to Dave Strauss for his commitment to my ideas for the cover design; and to Tara Tomczyk for careful reading.

My enduring gratitude goes to the patient and dedicated Jeremy Price, and deep thanks go to William DeLorenzo, Shelley Wong (again!), Linda Valli, Francine Hultgren, and Rebecca Oxford on whose watch this work originated.

Most importantly, I thank my first, best, wisest, most long-term and steadfastly committed teachers and most inspiring models of true scholarship, Guy and Cecilia Motha, who unrelentingly believed that their daughters could achieve anything. I'm not sure how one says thank you for a lifetime of support of every imaginable level. Thank you for your unshakeable faith in me, for decades of unbelievable sacrifice, for modeling lives filled with goodness and concern for ethics and justice, and more recently for countless transcontinental plane journeys to provide childcare so that I could write.

I am grateful to Ayuska and Sonali Motha, my oldest, most cherished, and most *katchaka* traveling partners.

Valerie Tourikian, my dearest friend, helped me to seek balance and to remember whom I wanted to be throughout the process.

Finally, there are no words that can adequately express my heartfelt gratitude to Nishan de Silva, who cheerfully and enthusiastically made colossal sacrifices. Who was it who said that the most important professional decision you'll ever make is your choice of a life partner? Thank you also for the metaphor of the lamp, which guided me throughout the writing. I am grateful for our two extraordinary daughters, Minola and Nikhela, who have never had a Mummy who wasn't writing this book in one form or another. Thank you for helping me to see the world through your sweet little eyes, for making the familiar strange, and for all of the surprising wisdom you shared with me as I wrote. Thank you for accompanying me to a remote island off the coast of Washington state again and again so that I could write, and for your merry encouragement throughout. I hope that this book will be a small slice of a much-larger-scale, concerted effort to make the world a better place for you and your generation.

# Prologue

As I sit at the handsome pine desk in the Whiteley Writing Center, surrounded by almost obscenely stunning island beauty and feeling nourished by the energy of the creative artists who have occupied this space before me, ready to embark upon the book that I believe must be written, it hits me: The last thing that I want to do is to write this book. I struggle against my emotions until my phone, set to silent mode, flashes at me. It is my friend and anthropologist colleague, Rachel Chapman. Grateful for a temporary reprieve, I slide through the French doors to stand in the silent tall grasses by the water's edge and hit the answer button.

"But you *want* to tell this story," Rachel exclaims. "What's going on? Is there something getting in the way of the story you want to tell? Do you feel some kind of conflict?"

And there it was. I am, indeed, deeply conflicted. I am conflicted, as every English teacher, teacher educator, school administrator, and language policymaker should be, about my participation in the project of the global spread of English. I am conflicted about contributing to the international dominance of English, associated as it is with Whiteness, wealth, power, and cosmopolitanism, arousing in all of us around the world acute and entrenched desires for all that it has come to represent—and stirring these desires surreptitiously, so that we often don't even quite know what our longings are for or from where they emerge. The teaching of English is frequently represented as a neutral enterprise or even a benevolent one, one that promotes equity and access, arming learners with skills that allow them to escape poverty, to deploy identities of privilege and power, to move ahead socially. These representations bear truth, and the proliferation of English does indeed open doors and further futures. It is undeniable that around the world, English and opportunity walk hand in hand. However, I have begun to see that as English is spread, it carries other effects. It reinforces colonial divisions of power and racial inequalities. As English is increasingly commodified, racialized, and globalized, it is implicated in the persistence of racial inequalities, in cultural and economic domination, in heritage language loss, in the extinction of less-commonly-spoken languages and their inherent epistemologies, and in inequitable distribution of global wealth and resources. English changes the ways in which we view the world. So now, more than ever before, I am struggling with the question of how I as an English-teaching professional come to terms with my practice.

I wasn't always conflicted. When I started teaching immigrants on a voluntary basis, as a late-night escape from the fast pace and acquisitive culture of wealth accumulation that I lived at my day job at an economic consulting firm, I experienced the imparting of English as unequivocally valuable, munificent, even generous. The ways in which the profession mimicked patterns of colonization escaped my attention. I frequently taught my students turns of phrase accompanied by comments such as "This is how you can sound more like a native speaker" and "This is how an American would say it" without giving any critical thought to the assimilationist effect of my words. I often tried to help my students be more American-like without giving thought to the fact that for many of them, it was American-like political action, economic practices, or military intervention that had made it necessary for them to leave, or even flee, their homes and immigrate to the United States. In my later work at a community center for undocumented immigrants, after having quit my job and returned to graduate school to embark upon a career teaching English, I constructed the learning of English on an individual level as a crucial process and separated it, to some degree, from the more global effects of wide-scale English teaching, the English teaching industry, and unequal distribution of capital. Who knows? Perhaps it might even have sounded far-fetched to me to hear it suggested that the teaching of English is somehow tied up with the inequitable allocation of resources internationally. Even after developing some awareness of these patterns, supported by the work of, among many others, Vandrick (2002), Grant and Wong (2004), Kubota (2004), Lin (2008), Tinker Sachs and Li (2007), Varghese and Johnston (2007), Canagarajah (1999), Morgan (2004), Kouritzin (2000), Pennycook (1998, 2001), and Phillipson (1992, 2009), I was comfortable with my constructed argument: "The spread of English is inevitable. That train has already left the station. English is going to continue to gain power, either way, and at this juncture our task as educators is to equip students with a critical awareness of not only the benefits of learning English but also of the larger-scale, global effects of English language spread so that they are in a position to make their own decisions about their own acquisition." My prepackaged argument also made a distinction between contributing to the importation of English in postcolonial or English-as-a-lingua-franca contexts and teaching English in, say, my current context, the United States, where its acquisition seems to be more of an unquestionable necessity.

Then, last spring, I taught a special topics class that I titled Race and Empire in TESOL (teaching English to speakers of other languages) to a group of particularly thoughtful, principled, smart graduate-level students who were mostly teacher candidates. We read a range of TESOL work relating to race, empire, and postcolonialism. We read about Alexandra, Jane, Katie, and Margaret, the four first-year teachers you will meet shortly within the pages of this book (their names, like the names of all other participants, teachers, and students in this book, are pseudonyms). We spent hours grappling with our own and each other's ideas about racial formation, globalization, language minority rights, English as a lingua franca, native-speaker supremacy, evangelism and religious identity, and media representations. As I taught this class, I sought to heed Vai Ramanathan's (2002) call for TESOL teacher education to support in teacher candidates what she calls a "meta-awareness"—that is, a "heightened awareness of how their thinking evolves as they are being socialized into their disciplines" (p. 2). Ramanathan notes that "you cannot, after all, address problems in your existing condition unless you have reflected on them and recognized your own participation in this condition" (p. 2). On the last day of class, as we looked back on our quarter together, huddled in a basement classroom of the Art Building on my campus, one student asked me: "I have a question for you, Su. What sustains *you?*" I had a response ready, the one I've been revisiting and fine-tuning since I began teaching. The phrases emerged from my mouth and hovered in the air—"changing the world," "social justice," "critical consciousness"—but they rang hollow and sounded trite and unconvincing in my own ears. Students nodded, but I found myself wondering fleetingly whether they could read what was beginning to feel like insincerity and were simply being kind, concealing doubt in their eyes.

As I made my way back to my office, the exchange stayed in my mind. I began asking myself questions about the degree to which English language teaching (ELT) professionals participate in creating a market for and desire for English—in producing a lack that we then move in to remediate. I realized, sitting down that evening with a leaden sensation inside my ribcage to continue writing my book, that my speeches weren't working anymore, that I was no longer convinced.

Writing this book has somehow changed me. The terrain of English language teaching can no longer seem benign. However, because English will continue to spread, teaching it remains important, life-changing work. Must empire and racism necessarily inhabit the teaching of English? The challenge I face, the same challenge faced by the participants in my study, is the question of how to participate in English language teaching in a way that is responsible, ethical, and conscious of the consequences of our practice. It is to this question that this book seeks to respond.

# CHAPTER 1

# Introduction

So I got the book *Counting in Korea.* . . . On the cover, there's a picture of a [boy wearing a] traditional Korean outfit. All the kids looked at it and said, "He looks like you." So he looked at it and said, "He's stinky! Stinky boy." And he pushed it away.

—Margaret, Afternoon Tea, November 1
[Names are pseudonyms chosen by participants.]

Yesterday in the lunchroom [two teachers] were talking about a student who's obviously struggling in class, and Geraldine said that she could spot from a mile off that he has a learning disability, and Mr. Berwick's first question was, "Well, is he Black?"

—Katie, Afternoon Tea, June 19

This one kid flipped through [the school newspaper] and said, "Ms. Fitzpatrick, this paper is racist!" I said, "Okay, why?" . . . And he said, "It doesn't reflect anything about the Hispanic kids; it's all about the American Black kids and their music."

—Jane, Afternoon Tea, April 10

One of my students who's Chinese started making fun of his own language. The Korean student was asking him how to pronounce something in Chinese, and he started mimicking some of the kids who make fun of his language. I said, "Why are you making fun of your language?" . . . He's picked on an awful lot. His accent is very heavy.

—Alexandra, Interview, May 21

## LOOKING AT THE LIGHT

The quotes above represent a glimpse into some of the different challenges faced by K–12 ESOL (English for speakers of other languages) teachers Alexandra, Jane, Katie, and Margaret as they journeyed through their first year of teaching. Many conversations and much of the coursework and literature within their preservice experiences had focused on discovering the most appropriate teaching methods and on understanding the mechanics of language. However, during their first year of teaching, the four teachers found themselves negotiating an unfamiliar set of questions: What does it mean to become an English teacher in a global context in which English(es) carry tremendous cultural and social capital and economic power? How do teachers support their students' access to privileged forms of English while maintaining a critical eye toward the legacy of colonization and racialization in which the profession is embedded? How is the broader international terrain of the profession relevant to practices within the walls of one individual classroom (and vice versa)? How can teachers negotiate the racialized nature of the English language as they are teaching it, remaining mindful that the historical connection between the spread of the English language and the international political power of people who were identified as "White" has resulted in a messy intertwining of English and Whiteness? How does teachers' consciousness of their own racial identities become salient in their practice? These were not the questions that Alexandra, Jane, Katie, and Margaret had contemplated during their teacher education program, but as the teachers passed through their first year of teaching, they found themselves needing to consider them as they addressed complicated questions about assimilation and racial identification, media representations of language-minority students, shame, and language and accent hierarchies.

In spite of its complex sociopolitical terrain, as the English language has spread around the globe, assuming steadily increasing international political power, the teaching of English has historically most frequently been represented within language teacher education as a race-neutral, apolitical, ahistorical endeavor in which learners work to produce appropriate sounds, master correct grammatical structures, and acquire larger vocabularies. Such a focus on accuracy and form has contributed to the invisibility of the language's complicated history and has made it possible for teachers to complete their teacher-education programs without ever having an opportunity to engage with the broader social, racial, economic, and political implications of their practice.

If you are entering the English-teaching profession and wondering about the relevance of race in your practice, this book is for you. This book is also for you if you have been teaching for a while and find yourself wanting support in thinking about race and coloniality in ways that are complex, constructive, and practical. I wrote this book for you if you, like me, find yourself wondering, here and there, about differential achievement between language learners and "native speakers," about hierarchies of languages and language varieties and their connectedness to historical colonial patterns, about the difference between an accent identity and an incorrect pronunciation, about the use of students' first languages in English classes, about which curricular arrangements should be used in what situations, and about what advocacy for students learning English might look like. Almost every time I have a conversation about race, I worry that something I say will not sound the way I wanted it to. I am writing this book in the hope that it will be helpful for those of us who want to find more-effective ways of talking about race without fear of appearing ignorant or saying "the wrong thing." In the United States, the starkly polarized reactions of different racial groups toward high-profile media stories, such as the 1995 O. J. Simpson trial, the 2009 arrest of Henry Louis Gates for breaking into his own home, and the recent trial in which George Zimmerman was found not guilty of murdering Trayvon Martin, have prompted me to think about the divergent ways in which we all read the same reality depending on our racial identity. Through this book, I have attempted to create a space for thinking about how these contradictory worldviews shape our responsibility when we teach students who don't share our racial identification. This book is written for you if you are looking for, not a list of directions or black-and-white answers about how to teach, but rather a guide for thinking knowledgeably and judicious-ly through the individual particularities of your practice and making well-informed, agentive decisions about your students and your own personal and professional identities in thoughtful ways.

Developing English-teacher identities and practices that are consistent with the mores and conventions of public schools is an important part of becoming a language teacher. However, an elusive space exists between com-petently developing expertise within the culture of schooling and becoming unwittingly indoctrinated into it. In Singhalese, there is a phrase to describe the appropriation of knowledge that feels alien to the learner: අනුන්ගෙ එළියෙන් ජහන බලනවා, or "looking at the light cast by someone else's lamp." The metaphor is ambiguous and captures a tension within the process of learning to teach. It can refer to compliant and prescribed learning, in which teachers are forced to gaze upon knowledge that someone else wants them to see, for instance, representations of English teaching tied to particular dis-ciplinary ideologies, knowledge generated by administrators or researchers and disseminated to novice teachers in public schools, knowledge that might be referred to by Belenky, Clinchy, Goldberger, and Tarule (1997) as *knowl-edge-received*. Alternatively, it can refer to knowledge created in collabora-tion with others, light cast by the supportive scaffolding of fellow teachers, a former graduate community, compassionate mentors, or provocative stu-dents and then generated by teachers as *knowledge-constructed* (Belenky et al., 1997). This book draws from the stories from the first year of teaching of four teachers who, in the face of increasing demands for strict account-ability and a context of stifling top-down management of their schools and school systems, sought to generate their own knowledge together, to draw on their own experiences and voices, to embrace their own identities, to light their own lamps. Their process of doing so illuminates for educators the importance of safe spaces removed from institutions for teachers, positioned as they are as "subordinates at the bottom of the educational hierarchy" (Webb, 2002, p. 47), coming to terms with the messiness and inequities that become evident through the project of teaching English.

## ENGLISH AS A "CONTRADICTION"

"The light cast by someone else's lamp" also serves as a metaphor for the multiple possible ways for us to think about the acquisition of English. Let's pause for a moment to consider the variety of meanings that are associated with English and consequently English acquisition. When you close your eyes and think about English, what images and ideas come to mind? Whom do you imagine when I say "English speaker"? The language is more than a collection of words and phrases that get stuck together in instrumental and possibly grammatical ways so that we might convey meaning, as in "Pass the salt." It is imbued with a history and undertones and associations that reach far beyond the actual mechanics of the system. I've always been a little bemused by the wide variety of attitudes that I see expressed (and indeed experience myself) toward English learning: commitment, hostility, desire, ambivalence, resistance, longing—sometimes within the same individual, sometimes at the same time. And no wonder, with the multitude of meanings, positive and negative and everything in between, that are ascribed to English itself.

On one hand, the English language carries enticing meanings and is connected to social advancement, opportunity, modernity, wealth, enlightenment, Whiteness, and cosmopolitanism. Those learning English do so with the assumption that the language will allow them access to certain possibilities and identities. English comes to take on positive meanings in many ways. For instance, for many years in the United States, immigrant parents were encouraged to speak only English with their children so that this new language would replace heritage languages and increase the children's chances for success. It seems that these efforts were particularly successful with English learners in the United States, who acquired the language wholeheartedly—Alejandro Portes and Rubén Rumbaut (2006) note that more bilingual immigrants have moved to the United States than any other country in the world over the past 3 centuries, but for a variety of reasons, while immigrants to other countries often managed to maintain their bilingualism, most language minority immigrants to the United States lose their heritage languages rapidly, typically within two generations, despite ample research evidence detailing the benefits of bilingualism (Cook & Bassetti, 2011). Another attractive characteristic of the idea of English is the associations it carries with class status around the world. For instance, the South

Korean mothers in So Jin Park and Nancy Abelmann's (2004) study wanted their children to learn English because they perceived the language to be representative of class prestige, cosmopolitan identity, and educational opportunity. English is often related to the trendy, the up-to-date. For the teen-aged Arjun Appadurai (1996) living in Bombay, English language books and movies represented modernity and seemed to promise to help him realize his wish to become modern. In my own family history, my great-grandparents living in Sri Lanka understood English monolingualism to open up opportunities, and they made the decision to use English with their children and loosen their hold on our heritage language, Tamil, several generations ago. Although not everyone thinks of the English language as raced, Gail Shuck (2006) helps us understand that English is evocative of racial identity through her analysis of discursive processes that associate Caucasian identity with English and that mark nonnative speakers of English as non-White and for-eign. English's tight connections to Whiteness are also made evident by the frequency with which language schools in non-English-dominant countries advertise for teachers who are "White, native-English speakers." The female Japanese sojourners in Sydney in Kimie Takahashi's study (2013) associated the English language with their imaginings of desirable "Western" identity, often represented by a *gaijin* (foreign) boyfriend. Ryuko Kubota's (2011a) participants, students at informal conversation schools in Japan, saw the learning of English as allowing them proximity to internationalization and global identities. As the language travels around the globe, it is imbued with a variety of meanings and connotations, many of which present English as attractive and desirable and promising to rescue those who might otherwise be doomed to provincial lives of ignorance and poverty.

At the same time, I can think of numerous ways in which the spread of English has been conceived of as having adverse consequences or as shaping identities and futures in negative ways. These are complicated representations but are also worth contemplating. Researchers have asked whether English contributes to the gap between the rich and the poor globally, whether it somehow manages to transmit messages through its teaching, whether it makes promises it then fails to deliver on. The term *linguistic imperialism*, coined by Robert Phillipson (1992), describes the dangers inherent in the global dominance of English, including its role in increasing economic disparities and in the extinction of other languages, especially those languages spoken by only a small number of individuals. Pattanayak (1996) has highlighted the role of English in maintaining inequalities around the world, noting the ability of the language to accentuate the divide between rural and urban populations and to underscore the dependence of "non-English cultures" on "English and English-speaking countries." (p. 150). The economic effects of the increasing dominance of English are highlighted by Yan Guo and Gulbahar Beckett (2007), who point out that the spread of English increases class inequalities because in most contexts worldwide, access to high-quality or effective English instruction requires wealth. In numerous countries, including Pakistan (Tamim, 2013), Egypt (Warschauer, El Said, & Zohry, 2004), and India (Sandhu, 2013), students typically receive more-effective English instruction in private schools than public schools, and wealthy parents are better able to afford private schools, after-school "cram lessons," and a period of immersion in an English-dominant context, all of which often lead to admittance at English-medium universities or colleges. Joseph Sung-Yul Park (2011) describes the ways in which workers in South Korea learn to internalize the logics of capitalist markets as they invest in English competence, which is typically required for white-collar positions and therefore shapes the investments and motivations of individuals despite the fact that they will rarely or perhaps never use English on the job. He critiques the ideal image of the neoliberal worker, committed to constantly upgrading skills and accepting personal blame when he or she falls short of the standard of proficiency, the criteria for which are an unattainable moving target, increasing every year.

A common assumption in the United States is that children from homes in which English is not the first language are less likely to make it to college. Although it is true that English language learners (ELLs) in U.S. high schools participate significantly less frequently in any postsecondary education than do non-ELLs, Yasko Kanno and Jennifer Cromley (2013), using a detailed quantitative analysis of a 12-year study sponsored by the National Center for Education Statistics, demonstrated that it is not so much inadequate English proficiency that holds learners back as other disadvantages, including academic underpreparation resulting from schooling that provides inequitable experiences for ELLs and non-ELLs and the absence of effort by schools to involve immigrant parents. Researchers including Jacqueline Widin (2010) have reproached universities and nongovernmental organizations (NGOs) in English-dominant countries for marketing English as a key to social mobility while developing systems that ensure that revenue to be made by the English-teaching industry is generated for the profit of what Kachru (1990) has termed "inner circle countries" (p. 3) such as Australia, the United Kingdom, Canada, and the United States. If the loss of heritage languages follows the learning of English, it also implies the loss of epistemologies and philosophies particular to the language. Harbert, McConnell-Ginet, Miller, and Whitman (2008) highlight the numerous ways in which English operates in a complicated relationship with indigenous languages around the world, with opportunities to move away from poverty being connected to competence in English.

Why does this matter? If languages aren't widely spoken, why don't we just let them die out? Seonaigh MacPherson (2003) explains that languages carry within them worldviews, ways of conceptualizing reality, and that the loss of a language may be more far-reaching than most linguists can understand. She offers by way of example the introduction of a medical psychiatric discourse to a community of refugee Tibetan Buddhist nuns, some of whom had been tortured. The language used by health workers visiting the monastery, including terms such as "post-traumatic stress disorder" and "biochemical," was incompatible with the mind-science-based language underlying Tibetan monastic education, which relied more on meditative technologies and viewed the relationship between the mind and the body in more-proximal terms. Language shift to the English terms would have implied a parallel shift to new ways of thinking about health. MacPherson thus illustrates that as English replaces other languages, it can also replace other, perhaps deeply valuable, ways of understanding the world. The desirability of nonnative-English-speaker identity, too, is shaped by the social meanings attributed to the category. Carla Chamberlin-Quinlisk (2012) notes that depictions of nonnative English speakers in U.S. media, including newspapers, popular television shows, and Hollywood films, portray them most frequently as "laughable," "disempowered," "menial," "unmotivated," and "lazy," constructing accented and nonnative-English identities as shameful and undesirable. The widespread nature of these images contributes to the embarrassment that students in this study experienced about their placement in ESOL, including a student of Margaret's who pretended not to know her when he passed her in the presence of classmates in the school hallway in an effort to disassociate himself from ESOL, and a class of Alexandra's who asked that the blinds be drawn in order to conceal their presence in the classroom that was known to house ESOL students. (Both of these incidents will be examined in further detail in Chapter 3.) Ofelia García and Leah Mason (2009) have noted the ways in which the shaping of Spanish as a language of poverty serves to create a foil for English, constructing it in contrast as a language associated with wealth and spoken by people with financial means.

The teaching of English has, in recent years, been connected to neoliberalism. David Block, John Gray, and Marnie Holborow (2012) deplore education's shifting priorities around the world and the presumption that the primary purposes of schooling to be the individual's upward economic and therefore social mobility and the promotion of capitalist ideologies. For instance, they focus on the domination of United Kingdom–produced materials within the lucrative ELT textbook industry, demonstrating with text analyses the ways in which textbooks circulate capitalist values and "construct English as a condensation symbol of wealth, individualism and extraordinary professional success" (p. 11). Christian Chun (2009) has similarly examined the articulation of neoliberal discourses in marketing and curriculum materials from an intensive English program in the United States, critiquing the ways in which these materials present English as a commodity to be sold, associated through subtle means with leisure and a high-end lifestyle, and promoting as obligatory for success within the broader global economy particular "inter-actional norms" such as communications skills and emotional intelligence. Kubota (2011b) has questioned the legitimacy of discourses of linguistic in-strumentalism (Wee, 2008), which promote English language skills as essen-tial for economic and social advancement globally. Linguistic instrumentalism was not confirmed by the learners and managers in her study, who found that other factors, such as gender and geography, were more likely to determine professional success than was English proficiency.

Sometimes representations of English are presented as an unequivocal muddle. For the Tamil-speaking teachers in Suresh Canagarajah's (1999) study, learning English was a complicated affair, with the language repre-senting both power and wealth on one hand and a history of colonialism on the other. Despite having made a deliberate choice to study English lan-guage and literature, the Moroccan university students in Abdellatif Sella-mi's (2006) study nonetheless associated the language with decadence and veneration of sex, alcohol, and money. Kenyan writer Ngũgĩ wa Thiong'o, who wrote for many years in English, in fact has called for African authors to abandon English because it strengthens historical ties to a colonial past and extinguishes creativity in African languages and therefore the develop-ment of African language literature.

On one hand, "the light cast by someone else's lamp" could represent the bestowing of English upon those who would otherwise be trapped in lives of poverty in order to illuminate a shining world of opportunity and social mobility. On the other hand, "someone else's lamp" could describe the col-onizing effects of English-language spread and might well refer to the magic lantern said to have been brought along by explorer David Livingstone on his travels in order to "blind his African audiences with science" (Holmes, as cited in Willinsky, 1998, p. 3) and to reinforce the impression that he hailed from a civilization that was superior, technologically and otherwise.

These two faces of English have led Kandiah (as cited in Skutnabb-Kangas, Phillipson, Mohanty, & Panda, 2009) to label the learning of the language a "contradiction." English is arguably indispensable to those seeking to participate in a global economy, but at the same time "English is accom-modating to and constituting a neoimperial, U.S.-dominated world, leading possibly to a global linguistic apartheid." (p. 9). Does either of these "fac-es" of English resonate with you? As an English-teaching professional, I ask myself what lesson I might take from these contested meanings of English's positioning on the global landscape. Is the lesson that we should choose which "face," which version of English teaching is correct? It would appear that both "faces" hold truth simultaneously. Could the lesson be that we should stop teaching English, learning English, speaking English? Would this not simply create a situation in which those who already know English hold unearned and greater power than those who don't? Perhaps the lesson instead relates to the importance of a deliberate consciousness that the learning of English remains always situated within and limited by the possibilities and boundaries of the context in which it is taking place. This includes the immediate context—the moment, the conversation, the classroom, the school—and also the broader historical level at which it has taken place (that is, a history of English language spread that has been inseparable from coloniality and racial inequality). In order to ensure that Kandiah's "contradiction" is amenable to analysis, it must be viewed within the historical terrain in which it developed—that is, in the context of English's colonial and racialized past.

The relevance of colonialism (or empire—we'll explore the distinctions between the two shortly) to the teaching of English appears at first glance to be most pressing in postcolonial nations, not so much in the United States. Much of the literature linking the teaching of English to colonialism explores English language teaching in postcolonial contexts or in what Braj Kachru (1990) has termed "expanding circle countries" (p. 3)—that is, in nations in which English has no historical or official role but is nonetheless used widely as a lingua franca. For instance, Angel Lin and Peter Martin's (2005) important volume *Decolonisation, Globalisation: Language-in-Education Policy in Practice* offers astute analyses of colonial processes in many contexts, including India, Hong Kong, Singapore, Malaysia, Iran, Turkey, Kenya, South Africa, and Tanzania. Hyunjung Shin (2006) has offered ways of rethinking knowledge production through an epistemology of the colonized informed by indigenous knowledge and local practices in the South Korean context. Problems of pedagogical ethics and appropriateness arise when "Western"-trained English teachers import foreign practices to, for instance, Bangladesh, as described by Raqib Chowdhury and Phan Le Ha (2008). This focus on postcolonial and English-as-a-lingua-franca (ELF) contexts can contribute to the impression that it is primarily within postcolonial contexts that processes of colonization and empire are playing themselves out in English-language classrooms. This belief, however, obscures the essential role played by ELT practices within nation-states that are themselves considered "empires" (sometimes called neo-imperial or neocolonial contexts), such as Alexandra, Jane, Katie, and Margaret's context, the United States. Within the interconnectedness of today's networked world, it is not possible for empire and colonization to evolve in a vacuum in schools within one nation-state. Rather, colonial processes are part of a larger web in which media and events and consumption within one site inevitably shape and are shaped by those in others.

ELT practices within the United States merit further exploration. Alexandra's Chinese student, described mocking his own language at the beginning of this chapter and discussed in greater detail in Chapter 4, is significant not only in his classroom in a middle school in the suburbs of a large city in the United States but also in the historical context of the relationships that different nations (and accents) have with each other globally and of the dynamics that various groups within the United States have shared histori-cally. The tradition of schooling within the United States has had a compli-cated history, tangled as it has been with the country's evolving ideas about race, nationhood, gender, cultural identity, foreign policy, religious freedom, and property rights, including ownership of land, material goods, and oth-er human beings. National policies and philosophies, both historically and contemporaneously, play a role in determining the practices and character of today's classrooms, including ESOL classrooms.

For example, assumptions about the racial and cultural superiority of Americans of European descent undergird some of the more disturbing and oftentimes most difficult-to-talk-about chapters of U.S. history—those most deeply anchored by violence or domination, both internally (domestically) and externally (beyond its borders), and by racism in its most brutal and exploitative configurations. It was by conceptualizing Native Americans as culturally inferior that British settlers were able to rationalize the murder of Native Americans, the taking of their lands, their containment on reser-vations, and the establishment of schools intended to replace First Nations cultural and linguistic resources with the English language and with cultural traditions that were understood to be related to English. Similarly, consider-ing Africans to be inferior made it possible to kidnap, harm, and extract labor from them, to first deny them any education and then to enforce racial seg-regation of African Americans from Americans of European descent. These processes are part of what Joel Spring (2004) refers to as "deculturalization," which he defines as "the educational process of destroying a people's culture and replacing it with a new culture" (p. 3), claiming that the new culture is better. The United States does not hold exclusive rights to such phenomena as the genocide of indigenous people, slavery, boarding schools intended to assimilate aboriginal children, racially segregated schools, and other practices related to deculturalization such as international invasions and occupations, internment camps for selected ethnic groups, and the denial of citizenship or voting rights on the basis of race. Nonetheless, ideas about racial and cultural superiority are part of the particular combinations of ideas and principles that have given rise to these historical moments in U.S. history and are there-fore part of the country's foundation, its ideological genealogy, the formation of its educational systems, and the ways in which all disciplines, including English, are taught and learned within its school walls. As an example, Jane needed to make decisions about what varieties of English to affirm when her English learners asked her about language associated with African American Vernacular English. More than 70% of students at her school were Afri-can American, but her decisions were undergirded by an acknowledgment that ideas about cultural superiority resulted in African American forms of English being accorded a lower level of legitimacy than varieties of English associated with White Americans.

It was within the U.S. historical terrain that the four teachers in this study practiced and were called upon to craft pedagogies that helped their students develop English speaker identities while simultaneously resisting Spring's (2004) "deculturalization." They were charged with teaching their students English while supporting their critical understandings of the ways in which English acquisition, language hierarchies, and accentedness would position them within their school settings and beyond.

Because the historical processes of colonialism were so dependent on racial divisions, to speak of colonialism is to speak, whether explicitly or not, of race. The spread of the English language across the globe was connected for many centuries to the international political power of people who are constructed as White, so that English and Whiteness are thornily intertwined (Motha, 2006a). Racialization is inevitably salient in language teaching. It is important that the racial roots of English language teaching be clear and visible to teachers if they are to carve out pedagogies that are well informed and conscious of the consequences of their practice. However, throughout the year of this study, the dominant discourses surrounding race in the ESOL teachers' contexts supported silences about racial identity, which created a challenge for teachers seeking to craft antiracist pedagogy. Through the lens of snippets from the experiences of Alexandra, Jane, Katie, and Margaret, this book examines the interconnectedness of race, empire, and language ideologies and engages with the process of becoming an English language teacher with an eye to the inherently racialized and colonial nature of the terrain within which English language teaching is embedded. It engages with the ways in which the racialized and colonial nature of English teaching becomes and remains invisible, drawing from the experiences of four teachers who used an informal space removed from their schools as a site for shaping and crafting their emergent transformative pedagogical practices during their first year of teaching.

This work rests upon the simple assumption that teachers are theorizers, transformative intellectuals (Giroux, 1988), and the most knowledgeable and sensitive analysts of their own classrooms. My aim was not to examine the teachers' practice and evaluate it from the outside but rather to learn from Alexandra, Jane, Katie, and Margaret. The book therefore seeks to privilege teachers' knowledge and perspectives of their own classrooms, offered in their own voices and within their own communities, above the analysis of other observers, researchers, or administrators. In line with this belief, this book draws on a year of not only classroom observations and interviews but of transcriptions of "afternoon teas" held every 2 or 3 weeks over the course of a school year—unplanned and informal gatherings that began to take place when first Alexandra and then Katie expressed a desire to spend time with their peers, with Margaret and Jane soon echoing the suggestion. When the four teachers graduated from their master's programs and embarked upon their first year of teaching English learners in public schools, they did not anticipate the tangled and strangely invisible navigation of connections among empire, race, and linguistic-minority status that they were soon called upon to negotiate. The afternoon teas became a space in which they could seek support from each other, in which they could work together to explore broad questions about how power and privilege circulate in language education, about how inequitable distribution of local and global resources is related to the construction and dissemination of English, and about the ways in which the teaching of English is a racialized practice. (See Appendix for further discussion of the afternoon teas.) As they generated knowledge for themselves and each other, they were also claiming a space within the study, a space in which they had increased agency in the representation of themselves, in the telling of their own stories. In the context of the afternoon teas, the teachers' theorizing was made explicit, theory and practice had a meeting place, and a window was opened onto the crafting of the teachers' praxis (Motha, 2009).

In this exploration I do not provide, nor did I set out to develop, facile solutions to any of the challenges the teachers faced, and I did not expect them to resolve the numerous dilemmas they encountered. The stories that follow are therefore neither victim nor victory narratives (Motha, 2006a). This study does not focus on how the four teachers could have or should have addressed the tensions they encountered. Rather, I sought to explore from the inside out how the knowledge they constructed from their experiences could inform current understandings of language teaching. In this vein, I do not presume to suggest alternative pedagogical practice. I simply sought deeper insight into the teachers' experiences as they struggled with and negotiated the complexities nestled at the nexus of race, language, power, and learning in their teaching lives with the hope that the sense they made of their own experiences might inform other TESOL professionals, including myself.

## "A GENERAL RUPTURE"

An important argument to be made in this book is that the current period is a moment of great opportunity for English-teaching professionals. Appadurai (1996) describes what he terms "a general rupture in the tenor of intersocietal relations" (p. 2), most likely brought about primarily by faster and more easily achieved connectedness between individuals and communities. Today, many more individuals are communicating with each other over longer distances, and without any time delay between the moment that a message is spoken or sent and the moment it is received or heard, through technologies that were not available previously, such as email and social media, or technologies that were previously too expensive to be used without inhibition, such as telephones. These patterns of communications are changing pretty much everything about modern life: the ways in which we trade stocks, interact socially, buy groceries, run businesses, perform surgery, speak, learn in classes, perform, and fall in love. They are calling into question our definitions of fundamental social concepts, such as war, friend (which has now become a verb), nation, economy, sex, and government. And they are changing the ways in which English is used, taught, and learned. English often becomes the medium of communication when only one person in an exchange uses English as a primary language, and often when neither interlocutor does if two different languages are involved and English is the lingua franca. The position occupied by English in trade, socially, and in the global social imaginary therefore looks quite different from the way it did 1 or 2 or even 3 decades ago. A larger number of people speak English worldwide, posing a challenge to understandings of English ownership as limited to those from what Holliday (2005) has referred to as BANA countries—that is, Britain, Australasia, and North America. English is a compulsory part of public education in numerous non-BANA nations, such as China, Brazil, and Cameroon. Appadurai (1996) draws our attention to recent changes in global arrangements, noting that "the new global cultural economy has to be seen as a complex, overlapping, disjunctive disorder that cannot any longer be understood in terms of existing center-periphery models" (p. 32).

Other theorists have advanced parallel arguments. Although some of the substance of their theorizing is controversial, as will be discussed further in Chapter 5, Hardt and Negri's (2000) description of this moment as an era of rapidly changing political and economic arrangements is valuable in supporting us as we contemplate the ways in which the teaching of English has metamorphosed in recent decades to become quite a different, more complex process. Hardt and Negri, like Appadurai, make a distinction between the circulation of power globally in the past and modern-day configurations. In the past, the international promotion of European culture (and, relatedly, languages) was an intentional effort led by the governments of colonizing nation-states, including Great Britain. For instance, during the 1800s, the British government ensured that English was taught in schools in British colonies around the world and that it was used instead of indigenous languages in government communication. Today, however, Hardt and Negri perceive global power relationships taking on different shapes. The valuing of some cultures, ideologies, economic and social practices, and languages over others emanates not from government coercion but from multiple sources working together—powerful media messages, transnational corporations, the United Nations and its affiliated organizations, religious bodies, nongovernmental organizations, universities—rather than from a single site such as the government of one nation-state. Hardt and Negri perceive domination becoming less of an intentional endeavor and more of simply an unconscious, unplanned, even incidental reproduction of the status quo, with the boundaries between colonizer and colonized becoming less visible and the range of identities and relationships considered acceptable becoming more dynamic and hybridized. This means that boundaries between nations, cultures, races, and languages have become less defined. According to Mignolo (1995), "Colonization is not behind us but has acquired a new form in a transnational world" (p. 1).

What are some examples of this hybridity and blurring of boundaries? For one, multilingual and multiracial characters appear in mainstream media more frequently today. Of course, multilingual and multiracial individuals are not new to human society, but they have been unrecognized as such within broader social consciousness. They have not figured largely in literature and media, and when they have, their hybridity has been represented as abnormal or Other, has not been represented (for instance, a Black/White biracial character presented simply as Black), or has been their defining characteristic (such as the character Clare Kendry in Nella Larsen's [1929/1997] *Passing*). In today's world, these boundaries are becoming less fixed. In 2000, the U.S. Census acknowledged the possibility of multiracial identity by allowing respondents to select more than one racial identification. The boundaries between many nation-states have become more porous; for instance, most border crossings between countries of the European Union are no longer staffed by immigration officials, and in recognition of the globalized and transnational character of today's citizens, an increasing number of nation-states grant dual-nationality status. For many years, until a change in Australian citizenship law, I lived in the United States but could not become a U.S. citizen without renouncing my Australian citizenship. Underlying the denial of dual citizenship is the assumption that national identity and allegiance cannot be hybrid. With contemporary changes comes a greater visibility within the social imaginary for possibilities for moving away from black-and-white dichotomies.

Because language is inseparable from racial and national identity, the concept of linguistic hybridity is also gaining favor. Although Hardt and Negri do not specifically discuss the English language, English is deeply implicated in the changes they describe and indeed in any possible transformation of current global relationships, both within ESOL classrooms in the United States and, on a broader level, in English classrooms around the world. In today's world, multiple varieties and accents of English are acknowledged, and the one variety that was historically considered to be "correct," the British received pronunciation (RP), is no longer the guiding standard internationally. The possibility of more than one "correct" form of English exists in the modern world, with the BBC now employing anchors with Indian and Jamaican accents, with internationally successful authors (for instance, Junot Díaz and Earl Lovelace) winning high-profile awards for writing in varieties of English considered nonstandard. The NNEST (nonnative English-speaking teachers) movement, an organized effort to critique the imprecise term *nonnative* and to end discrimination against teachers labeled "nonnative," has provided awareness and political action and increased the professional legitimacy of individuals with a wide range of accents and varieties of English around the world (Braine, 1999; Moussu & Llurda, 2008).

This changing linguistic landscape opens up possibilities for a broader range of legitimate racial and linguistic identities and related language varieties, for greater attention to be paid to ownership of English and control of the ways in which it is commodified and distributed, and for critical attention to representations of the language's various speakers within the broader social imaginary. Although it is indisputable that linguistic and racial identities are becoming conceptualized as less stable, these changes are far from uncontested. Complex practices alter the degrees and forms of hybridity permissible. Blatant impediments to linguistic hybridity are evident—movements toward English-only, monolingual education, and the delegitimization of particular forms of English (especially those associated with racial groups coded as non-White). These are related to a form of globalization that reinforces differences in wealth and power in relation to individual racial, colonial, and linguistic histories. But less obvious practices, too, can shape the ways in which English and the profession change and the role English plays in the world. Some examples are the configurations of ESOL programs, placement policies, ESOL policies surrounding English varieties, error-correction practices, ideologies of teacher education, and the language used (lexical choices) to describe individuals in schools, and these will be discussed throughout the pages of this book. The teachers, administrators, policymakers, and teacher educators who make up the ELT industry are implicated in these practices, although the significance of our role may not be obvious. If we are able to be open-eyed, intentional, and conscious and can harness the exciting possibilities offered by this moment of transition, we might find this to be a moment of magnificent transformation, a time for challenging patterns of racial and linguistic inequity on global and national levels. It seems to me that English-teaching professionals play a vital, deeply underestimated role in this process and have the potential to influence the ways in which relations of global power change. The responsibility of English in maintaining the current inequitable global economic order has been taken too lightly. The first step toward that change is to ensure that all ELT professionals have a conscious awareness of the political, racial, and colonial underpinnings of the project of teaching English and of the desires and purposes that accompany the acquisition of English.

This book aims to interrupt and enter into conversations that represent English language learning in primarily linguistically mechanistic terms, as a mission to transmit words and information about syntax and word order

and master pronunciation. Such a focus on accuracy and form has contributed to the invisibility of the ways in which English functions within a
larger communications-and-knowledge-production industry with a variety
of political and social effects. This book offers examples drawn from the
first year of teaching of four K–12 ESOL teachers, Alexandra, Jane, Katie,
and Margaret, highlighting associations between English on one hand and
Whiteness, prestige, and privilege on the other and interpolating explicit
analysis of the ways in which constructions of race and language work together to exclude racial minorities and ex-colonial subjects from ownership
of and even access to the English language. This book is not the story of a
study in the traditional sense. It is instead an argument for a reframing of the
historical foundation of English language teaching to acknowledge its rootedness in racialization, globalization, and empire. It offers a retheorizing of
the project of English teaching and consequently an attendant re-envisioning
of its goals and intentions. To do so, it draws on fragments of everyday life—
mundane, unremarkable occurrences drawn from the everyday experiences
of first-year teachers.

Although attention has been paid to the effects of ideologies of race
and empire in postcolonial contexts (Lin & Martin, 2005; Ramanathan,
2006; Shin, 2006), these effects have been less visible within the teaching of
English in schools in the United States. Race and empire are, however, unquestionably present in U.S. K–12 public schools, although perhaps not so
easily visible. They become apparent when we examine the disproportionate
number of children of color in ESOL classrooms in the United States, patterns of differences in the quality of education between students who have
received ESOL services and those have not, the differential ways in which
postcolonial varieties of English are legitimated within U.S. schools, and the
social status of ESOL students and ESOL departments within school hierarchies. Suárez-Orozco and Sattin (2007) note the necessity for educational
systems to be responsive to a changing contemporary context, remarking
that "these new global realities are challenging schools everywhere and in
multiple ways" (p. 7). This book is intended to illustrate, through clear
examples from actual classroom practice, the imprudence of attempting to
conceptualize the English language as racially neutral, the inextricability of
the teaching of English from the postcolonial terrain in which it is embedded, and the complicated nature of the politics of Global Englishes. I offer
numerous examples to demonstrate how invisibly the political nature of
English teaching functions. The reader will notice that these are not stories
of extraordinary schools nor of exceptional classrooms. They are, in fact,
notable for their ordinariness. The events described in the vignettes in this
book could have taken place anywhere in the country; these are scenes that
play themselves out every day in classrooms around the United States and
other neo-imperial contexts. Throughout the study we see teachers going to

astonishing lengths to reorganize inequitable relations of power within their schools and communities. Although their efforts usually yield some results, the effects of their work are almost always limited by the unseen effects of empire and race, which I argue form the basis of our profession. For instance, you will read shortly about Jane's attempts to present as legitimate to her class the variety of English spoken by her Ghanaian student, Terrell, whose first language was listed by the school district to be "World English." Her ability to argue that Terrell's language variety does actually constitute English is limited by assessment policies that have placed Terrell in her ESOL class to, in fact, learn English. The logics that determine which varieties of English count as English are rooted in racial and colonial ideologies, with varieties associated with postcolonial contexts and higher non-White populations often being considered less valid. However, these patterns are easy to overlook and remain outside consciousness unless TESOL professionals are actively engaged in noticing them. In fact, it was several months before I myself noticed the contradiction of Terrell's placement in ESOL. In this book, I seek to demonstrate the importance of moving from unconscious to conscious planes (Motha & Lin, 2013) the role played by race and empire in the teaching of English.

## ACCIDENTS AND INTENTIONALITY

One issue that arises frequently when I speak about how race functions within school walls is the issue of intentionality. The ways in which racial inequality is sustained through English teaching are largely unwitting or accidental and exist only because of patterns established before any of the current-day actors in U.S. schools were even born. It is a rare adult in the school system who is actively in pursuit of racial or colonial inequality. However, we nonetheless end up with inequality, what Bonilla-Silva (2013) calls "racism without racists." How does this happen?

I once heard a wise fellow-playgroup parent explaining to her son that there are two types of accident: the accidents that are part of life and are largely unavoidable and the accidents that happen because we're not paying attention and are careless. These latter accidents can be prevented, and she impressed upon her son that watching for and preventing them is actually part of his responsibility when he plays with other children. Her son was the oldest, biggest child in the playgroup, and he was therefore the one who was least likely to be hurt in a mishap. Because of his size, he was also most likely to cause damage if, say, he collided with a much smaller child. This meant that he had less of an investment in preventing mishaps but, his parent argued, more of a responsibility in preventing them. She taught him that if being careful not to harm other children is a low priority for him and an accident occurs because of his carelessness, he is culpable regardless of intentionality. Her words raise a question for me. If patterns of racial and colonial inequality are unwitting and accidental, what responsibility do we have for noticing and preventing them? Is it enough for us to say that because racial, colonial, or linguistic inequality is not our intention we are therefore not implicated? How is the responsibility different for those of us (individuals, teachers, institutions, nation-states) who are bigger—or who have more economic power or more unearned privilege because of our colonial or racial identities or who have less to lose or perhaps even something to gain in the short term from inequality (such as greater employment potential because of a prestige accent)? Some accidents are not truly accidents but reflect (sometimes unconscious) individual and social priorities. If we believe on some level that we profit from inequality, we might be less inclined to move social justice to the top of our list of priorities. At a minimum, if we are not the direct recipients of discrimination, we may have less of a motivation to spend our time fighting against it rather than on another task. To what degree are we called upon to be conscious and mindful of the potential for mishaps, such as the widening of the gap between rich and poor, the extinction of indigenous languages, the perpetuation of racism, or linguistic and racial minority students' lower achievement and lack of access to college? To what degree are we culpable if we do not act?

Watching Alexandra, Jane, Katie, and Margaret and listening to them make sense of their teaching lives helped me think through many of these questions. In this book I share with you what I learned from them.

## ALEXANDRA, JANE, KATIE, AND MARGARET SIPPING TEA

I see Margaret, a willowy flash of lavender, moving up the driveway, and I open the front door. She smiles her characteristically serene smile, hair the color of clover honey and dark-lashed, bottomless eyes the same shade. I feel the urge, as I always do when I see her, to put my arms around her protectively. Margaret has an unflagging belief in the inherent goodness of all humans, and as long as I have known her, I have felt a guarded but persistent certainty that humans are about to let her down. We've been friends for many years now and it hasn't happened yet, but my impulse to shield remains. Margaret embraces me, then proffers a delicately painted Japanese bowl filled with her lentil salad. The kettle whistles, beckoning us back into the kitchen, and she settles onto the carpet in the adjacent living room, leaning against the sofa and tucking her toes under her, while I slosh water over the dark, heady tea leaves, scalding deep flavor out of them.

The next to arrive is the other elementary-level teacher in the study, perpetually smiling Katie, swirling warmth into the front foyer, an eddy of animated energy. She carries handouts in her hands, resources to share with the rest of us, and spills over with animated stories of the first days of school. "Tea, yes, please!" she sighs with a "hit-the-spot" exhalation. She sinks to the floor, flipping her long, straight black hair behind her. Her vitality is infectious, and we sit up straighter and listen to her tale. She begins to tell us about a conversation that has just taken place between her sister, who like Katie was adopted from Korea in infancy, and her parents, Americans of German-Irish descent, humorously describing her own intervention into the family conversation. Katie is the only teacher in the study who does not identify as White.

The doorbell interrupts the unfolding story. Alexandra arrives, her hands full of entertainment for her solemn 4-year-old, Daniel, who wanders in beside her. Alexandra remains, to this day, the most unflappable person I know. She juggles numerous duties simultaneously, multitasking with aplomb, maintaining a quietly self-assured manner in her middle school classroom and the appearance of composure under the most chaotic of circumstances. She comes from a family of educators and has deep and time-consuming commitments to political action within schools while navigating a long-distance marriage to a pilot. I wonder whether I'm imagining that her bright blue eyes look tired as she slips off her shoes and lowers herself to the carpet. Although none of us knew it that bright autumn day, not even Alexandra, she was pregnant with her first biological child at that moment.

The last to arrive was cheerful, commonsensical Jane, who worked in a neighboring, poorly resourced district, James District, where salaries were quite a bit lower than in Bennett District, where the other three teachers worked. Jane's salary was therefore the lowest of the four teachers, and during her busy first year of teaching high school, she moonlighted at night as a waitress in a movie house. She was skilled at steering herself through what would otherwise have been a frenzied and muddled year. Long and slender, hair the color of glossy dark chocolate, faint freckles across her nose, she telegraphed liveliness as she reached for her cup of steaming tea and joined the huddle around my oversized coffee table.

The afternoon teas formed the basis of a study that drew from the traditions of critical feminist ethnography (Behar, 1996; Carspecken, 1996; Fine, 1992; Madison, 2012) to explore the pedagogy and perspectives of four women who were K–12 public school ESOL teachers during their first year of teaching. They were recent graduates of an MEd in TESOL program at the institution at which I was a PhD student, a large publicly funded land-grant institution in the suburbs of an ethnically diverse metropolis in the Mid-Atlantic region of the U.S. East Coast. I had known Alexandra, Jane, Katie, and Margaret for 2 or 3 years before the study began, having served as the graduate-student advisor for incoming MEd students, a teaching assistant in their classes, the supervisor of their student teaching, and the supervisor of Alexandra's, Katie's, and Margaret's master's theses. Each teacher had been in at least one class that I cotaught. They were similarly closely connected to each other; each teacher had taken at least two classes with each of the others. I was familiar with their pedagogical practice, conducting observations on their teaching and providing them with feedback, meeting with cooperating teachers, and gathering with the teachers in a seminar context every 2 weeks during their student-teaching semesters. Margaret and Jane were first-semester teachers when we began the study, while Katie and Alexandra had graduated a semester earlier and were beginning their second semester of teaching. We had developed friendships before the study began, socialized out of school, and faced professional doubts together. We had met each other's families and attended each other's weddings.

The nature of this history together created a power imbalance in our relationship. I took all steps I could think of to diminish the effects of the hierarchy—reiterating that they should not feel obligated to have me in their classrooms or to come to the afternoon teas, repeating in every email and phone call that they should not feel compelled to respond, discussing openly and repeatedly with them my concerns about exploiting them. I tried to make the afternoon teas a place of support and camaraderie for the teachers, rather than a site of data collection. However, none of these steps could have erased the hierarchy among us, and this story should be read as such.

## FOUR DIFFERENT SCHOOL CONTEXTS

The study was carried out in four separate schools, which represented a range of demographics. Katie, Margaret, and Alexandra taught in Bennett District, whose majority population was White. Jane taught in neighboring James District, in which 86% of K–12 public school students were racial minorities.

I use the district's terminology to describe student categories, including racial categories. (Percentages do not always add up to exactly 100% because they have been rounded up or down.) Katie's elementary school, which served children in grades K–6, was located in one of the highest-income regions of the district. Of the student population of 317 students, 28% were classified by the district as Limited English Proficient and receiving ESOL services, the highest percentage of the four schools, and most of these students were Asian/Pacific Islanders. The school population receiving free or reduced-price meals was 13.9%. The racial composition of the population was predominantly White (not of Hispanic origin) at 66%, followed by 15% Asian/Pacific Islanders, 13% Hispanic, and 7% African American. Margaret's school, also a K–6 institution, was larger, with 489 students, although only 9.1% of the school population was defined as Limited

English Proficient. It was also a poorer school, with almost a third (30.9%) of children receiving free or reduced-price meals. Margaret's school's African American population was much larger, at 35%; the Hispanic population at 13.1% was essentially the same, and the White (not of Hispanic origin) and Asian/Pacific Islander populations were smaller, at 46.8% and 5.9%, respectively. Margaret's school also had a 0.4% American Indian/Alaskan Native population. Alexandra taught in a large and diverse 6th- through 8th-grade middle school. Of the 903 students, 37% received free or reduced-price meals, and 6.3% were considered to be Limited English Proficient. The student population was predominantly African American (41.5%), 25% White (not of Hispanic origin), 17.4% Hispanic, 15.6% Asian/Pacific Islander, and 0.3% American Indian/Alaskan Native. Jane's dauntingly big high school, the only study school in James District, was by far the largest school in the study, at 2,100. It had a large African American population (70.5%) and also the largest Hispanic population of the study schools (21%). It had relatively small numbers of White (6.6%) and Asian/Pacific Islander (3%) students and no American Indian/Alaskan Native students. At this school, 6.5% of students were defined as Limited English Proficient.

## ABOUT THE STUDY OF FIRST-YEAR TEACHING

My ideas about school-based research were shaped by my early readings of educational researchers I admire—for instance, Deborah Britzman (1991), Annette Lareau (2000), and Signithia Fordham (1996)—passing in and out of the school communities they were learning about, observing, and interviewing along the way. I carried these images with me as I embarked upon the first days of this study. As I designed the study, I imagined that I would rely heavily, as did the researchers I sought to emulate, on observational and interview data, which have always seemed to me to be mainstays of work informed by ethnographic methods. However, over the year of the study I found myself on a complicated journey, one that called into question my ideas about the relationships among representation and voice, objectivity and objectification, power, humanity and the nature of being human, praxis, community, validity, agency, and the politics of telling other people's stories.

Spradley (1980) has suggested that ethnography should rely primarily on observations, and as I set out to learn from these four women, I concurred. I was attracted to ethnographic methods for their richness, their ability to talk to the situatedness of language learning and language teaching. Observations appeared to me as somehow organic; they seemed to offer a chance to see the teachers living their lives in natural, authentic contexts. I initially imagined myself quietly observing classrooms with a video recorder, tape recorder, pen and notebook, and that is indeed how I started out my study year, surreptitiously tucking myself into a quiet corner at the back of each teacher's classroom, silently scribbling and diligently avoiding eye contact with curious students in order to minimize my influence on classroom events. However, two things happened along the way: one relating to participant voice and the other to community, both of which troubled my wholehearted commitment to an observational study. First, as I began my ongoing data analysis during the first few weeks of the study, I started to sense that my fieldnotes and consequently my representation of my participants were suffering from a gaping absence of the teachers' voices. Instead, I had the impression that as I was telling the teachers' stories, I was interpreting their actions, cloaking their practices with my perspectives, and in the process appropriating their lives. My first effort to counteract this effect was to extend the length of my interviews, asking the teachers for detailed elucidations of classroom incidents that I'd observed, as if by gathering enough of their words to serve as a proxy for my own, I could somehow neutralize my own presence and diminish the volume of my voice. The second important happening, also during the first few weeks of the school year, was that Alexandra and then Katie expressed a desire to meet regularly with their former classmates as they had while they were student teaching. Imagining something reminiscent of the kitchen table conversations of the early feminist movement, I offered my home, which was a geographical midpoint among the four schools.

And so began the afternoon teas. The five of us would sit on my family room floor, clustered around the coffee table, drinking strong tea and munching cucumber sandwiches, scones, and Sri Lankan *mas-paan* (meatbread). We gathered together in the afternoon after the last school bell rang, sometimes rushing off to prepare lessons or put children to bed, more often talking late into the night. By the second semester of the study, the afternoon teas had grown into dinners, although we always drank tea as we chatted. Alexandra, Katie, Jane, and Margaret were seeking support from each other out of personal need, but in doing so they claimed a space within the study. The afternoon teas transformed the study, which I had initially designed as a collection of four cases. I had intended to explore the experiences of four individual beginning ESOL teachers during their first year of teaching, following the portraits with cross-case analysis (Yin, 1994). However, with the afternoon teas an unanticipated element surfaced: the element of *community*. I was no longer exploring four cases of individual teachers but rather was now studying one group of four teachers, a community of practice (Lave & Wegner, 1991) of teachers who came together and developed their meanings of teaching in a socially and culturally fertile context. As I became increasingly appreciative of the constructs supported by the afternoon teas, such as connection, legitimization of participant voice, community, and the sociocultural nature of identity construction, I simultaneously began to see some of the shortcomings of an exclusive focus on observations and in-terviews, both of which had initially formed the methodological backbone of the study. Observations and fieldnotes did not adequately capture the participants' voices, and one-on-one interviews lacked the richness of com-munity. Mindful of Harding's call to rectify the androcentrism of research (1987) and Reinharz's (1992) suggestion that a feminist perspective on data analysis includes flexibility and creativity in format, I made the decision to modify commonly used qualitative research methods in order to foreground the afternoon tea transcriptions over all other data sources, including ob-servations and fieldnotes. Further information about the methodological orientation of the study is included in the appendix.

Just as English represents a contradiction, so too, for me, does tea. Over the years, tea has come to take on complex meanings in my day-to-day life. I have been offered tea or have brewed tea for those I cherish in response to heartache or illness or tears, as an expression of caring and welcome, and as a commemoration of friendship. I serve it during my practicum classes, my office hours, upon returning home with my young daughters after picking them up from school, and in gatherings of my writing collective. Tea has come to represent for me comfort, community, contemplation, consolation, camaraderie, and creativity. But I add other troubling Cs to my associations with tea—for instance, in the context of Sri Lanka: colonization. Anoth-er C is ceremony, evoking the ways in which obfuscated social knowledge surrounding formal teas has served to reinscribe social hierarchies. In her wonderful book, *Interrogating Privilege*, my friend and mentor Stephanie Vandrick (2009) similarly connects tea with various notions, including, she tells us, "my childhood in barely post-colonial India, my Anglophilia, my beloved English novels, women's groups" (p. 18), and expresses misgivings that resonate with my own: "It is also a source of ambivalence because of its postcolonial and social class associations" (p. 18).

## OUTLINE OF THE BOOK

Following this introductory chapter, Chapter 2, "Operating in Concert: Em-pire, Race, and Language Ideologies," explores the interconnectedness of ideologies of race, empire, and language ideologies and situates the ideas contained within this book in relation to other significant conversations, drawing from a range of disciplinary traditions. In Chapter 3, "Teaching Empire or Teaching English?" I take up themes of empire, imperialism, and decolonization in relation to English, engaging specifically with the construction of the category ESOL as a school and institutional construct within the broader context of globalization. Chapter 4, "English, Antirac-ist Pedagogies, and Multiculturalism," focuses on the racialization of the

English language in general and English language teaching specifically, exploring the ways in which school and classroom practices provide terrain for the dynamic and continuous construction and renegotiation of racialized identities. Chapter 5, "Producing Race and Place: Language Varieties and Nativeness," engages with the concept of English, exploring the range of ways in which English was defined in the various study contexts, the tension between heterogeneity and homogeneity of language varieties, and the language hierarchies teachers found themselves subscribing to or questioning. In Chapter 6, "Toward a Provincialized English," all of the preceding discussion is brought together in an exploration of the central notion of how language, race, and empire meet. Here are posed perhaps the most profound and complex questions in the book, all of which center around one fundamental issue: How might teachers' practice be shaped by their deep understanding of the complex racialized and postcolonial terrain of English language teaching? This chapter considers the implications of this analysis for classroom teaching, for educational policy, for the administration of schools and programs, for the practice of teacher education, and for research on second language education. It further explicates and elaborates upon the theoretical implications of the book.

When my graduate student teacher candidates at the University of Washington (and previously at the University of Maryland) walk into my classes, they are sometimes confused to see mention of race or colonialism on my syllabi. "What's teaching English got to do with race?" "How is it related to colonialism?" they ask. This book is for them; my primary audience is preservice teachers at the graduate and undergraduate levels who will be using English in any form as they teach, including those preparing to become ESOL teachers. This is the book I wish we had to read together as they begin their teacher education journeys. This work assumes teaching to be intellectual practice and views teachers as transformative intellectuals (Giroux, 1988). As such, it approaches its topic not as a how-to manual seeking to offer simple solutions to everyday teaching challenges nor as an easy guide to "teacher-proof" and "scripted" curricula—indeed, it offers no solutions at all. Rather, its point of departure is that it is only through the intellectual engagement of teachers that these changes can take place. This work is intended to bring together everyday challenges of teaching with what we understand of the theoretical terrain of empire, race, and linguistic ideologies so that teachers might find support in analyzing their own local circumstances and developing individual context- and moment-specific responses accordingly.

The book's audience is not limited to teacher candidates. It is also for scholars of English linguistics, English language pedagogy, and TESOL; for teacher educators reflecting on their practice; for inservice teachers trying to make sense of their practice in messy and inequitable linguistic terrain; and for critical race scholars whose focus is not necessarily on English language teaching but who are interested in how the teaching of English is shaped by race. I further intend this work to also be of interest to scholars of multicultural education, critical race theory, postcolonial studies, globalization studies, second language acquisition and applied linguistics, educational critiques of neoliberalism, and social scientific critiques of colorblind racism.

Throughout this work I seek to begin and end each idea with the classroom, while never shying away from intellectually engaging process. Teaching requires knowledge, analytical skills, a talent for deep reflection, and an ability to connect the events within classroom walls to the larger sociohistorical context of our world. No one—not teachers, not students, not communities—is served by a positioning that assumes teachers to be in need of nothing more than quick and easy instructions on how to teach without regard for teachers' own understandings of the peculiarities of their own local classrooms. For this reason, I close each section with a set of concrete pedagogical Reflection Questions. The Reflection Questions are designed to support the reader in thinking about how the concept being described is relevant within familiar classroom contexts. For faculty members using the Reflection Questions in teacher education classrooms, I offer a caution. The questions might require students to reveal uncomfortable thoughts, opinions, or information. I therefore suggest that students decide whether to participate and then choose the question on a list they would like to discuss, rather than being asked to discuss a specific question.

My writing buddy and departmental colleague, Anu Taranath, a scholar of postcolonial literature, shared with me a quote by Toni Morrison, who wrote, "If there's a book you really want to read, but it hasn't been written yet, then you must write it." This book is my response to her charge. I hope that it will be picked up by practicing and future teachers in all disciplines who have contact with linguistic-minority students in public schools, in university intensive English programs, and at universities around the world.

# CHAPTER 2

# Operating in Concert: Empire, Race, and Language Ideologies

Three primary themes run through the core of this book, and in this chapter I pause to reflect on each and to think about the almost puzzling ways in which they become invisible as they connect English language teaching to ideologies of empire and racism. The themes are (1) the reproduction of historical connections between English language spread on one hand and colonization, imperialism, and *empire* on the other, (2) the repeated underscoring of English language teaching's embeddedness within a context of inequitable *racial relations*, and (3) the role played by *language ideologies* in perpetuating racism and linguistic discrimination. These themes have been examined separately, but it is their interrelatedness, the complex ways in which they perform in concert with each other, that is the focus of this book. The three themes are tightly connected to each other, in the fashion of the overlappings of a three-circled Venn diagram. They cannot be cleanly disentangled from each other; in fact, they originate from and nurture each other. I examine them separately not to indicate in any way that they are separable, nor to represent English language teaching in any symbolic way. Rather, they are examined individually in order to demonstrate clearly the relevance of each within a matrix of complicated relationships. The connections among the three are then explicated.

## THEORETICAL SITUATEDNESS

These three main foci of the book are informed by three primary, interconnected bodies of theoretical work, those examining: (1) empire, globalization, and post/coloniality; (2) the connections between race and English language teaching; and (3) linguistic ideologies, most notably language variation and language hierarchies. In this next section, I summarize each of these areas and each one's relevance to English language teaching. I then go on, throughout the book, to explain the imprudence of attempting to conceptualize any one of these three as separate from the others.

## Empire (Colonialism, Postcoloniality, and Imperialism)

The opening line of *The Empire Writes Back*, written by three post-colonial theorists, reads, "More than three-quarters of the people living in the world today have had their lives shaped by the experience of colonialism" (Ashcroft, Griffiths, & Tiffin, 1989, p. 1). I was surprised when I read those words. Three-quarters? I would argue that no one on this planet is untouched by the lasting effects of European colonialism. Even the miniscule number of individuals living in isolated communities who have never seen a television nor accessed the Internet have been touched by colonial legacies—a change in air quality because of deforestation a thousand miles away and 200 years ago, or a change in diet because the creatures previously consumed were trapped to extinction by colonists or because a water source was dammed far down the river by conquerors. These are not random and unexpected butterfly effects (Lorenz, 1993) but rather a persistent and widespread pattern.

Just as I need to understand something of a student's personal history and current environment in order to teach him or her effectively, I also need to understand something of English's history and current environment in order to teach it effectively—how colonialism and English came to be inter-woven and, just as important, how the current environment allows them to remained connected. English carries particular accountability within colonial processes. The spread of the English language historically accompanied colonial endeavors, as colonists sought to acquire territory that didn't belong to them and to kill, displace, or control the people who lived on that land. The insertion of English into the mouths and hearts of the population was often an inherent part of the project, although it represented itself rather as a project of discovery, exploration, civilization, progress, and munificence. So a colonial imprint is stamped into our profession and remains there in-delibly even in a modern-day context in which English is presented as in-tensely desirable through global media and the English-teaching industry. All schooling, not only the teaching of English, has been shaped by the histori-cal legacy of colonialism (Willinsky, 1998) and its contemporary offspring, imperialism (Phillipson, 1992, 2009), postcolonialism (Lin & Luke, 2006), and Empire (Hardt & Negri, 2000). A distinction needs to be made here be-tween *empire* with a lowercase *e*, for the most part used synonymously with *imperialism*, which was historically a deliberate domination and expansion usually performed intentionally by a government, and *Empire* (Hardt & Negri, 2000) with an uppercase *E*, representing a modern-day and more complicated power relationship. It is useful to employ in this exploration the lenses of theories of Empire, decolonization, neoliberalism, transnation-alism, diaspora and hybridity studies, and globalization theory. Because it may seem at times that I am using some of these terms interchangeably, par-ticularly these five—*colonialism, coloniality, postcolonialism, imperialism,* and *Empire*—I will spend a moment briefly disentangling the five from each other all the while remaining mindful that all five are the ideological spawn of the same parent. I am arguing that modern-day epistemologies of empire rose from various millennia-long efforts at widespread domination and exploitation, several centuries of English language spread as part of the violence and exploitation of post-Renaissance colonialism, the epistemic violence that accompanied decolonization and attempts at postcolonial healing, and the contemporary imperialism of nation-states that are no longer under military or governmental control of dominant powers.

**Colonialism and English Language Teaching.** Willinsky (1998) has explored imperialism's influence on ideologies cultivated during times of imperial expansion:

> We need to learn again how five centuries of studying, classifying, and ordering humanity within an imperial context gave rise to peculiar and powerful ideas of race, culture, and nation that were, in effect, conceptual instruments that the West used both to divide up and educate the world. (pp. 2–3)

Broadly, the word *colonialism* refers to the domination of one group of people by another. More specifically and for the purposes of this book, the word refers to the period extending from the 1500s to the 1900s during which various European countries, most notably Spain, Britain, the Netherlands, Germany, France, and Portugal, occupied and controlled in a variety of ways the largest part of the rest of the planet including most of Africa, the Middle East, the Americas, Asia, and Australia for a variety of reasons. The reach of British colonialism was particularly vast, and an intentional, explicitly hegemonic propagation of the English language accompanied the expansion of the British Empire. This propagation was part and parcel of a specific form of cultural exploitation. John Willinsky (1998) notes the power of European colonization across the planet to change the ways in which the human population understood and viewed the world:

> Britain was the largest of a series of European empires that in the last five centuries managed to annex the Western Hemisphere, foster a global slave trade, divide the African continent, and create a revolution in the arts and sciences. (p. 2)

The terrain of English language teaching in particular is indelibly marked with the stain of British colonialism, leaving us to wonder about the effects of having our understanding of the world so intrinsically shaped by our having conquered it or by having been conquered in it. How do these consequences play themselves out in contemporary English language classrooms in the United States?

One of the primary arguments being made in this book concerns not only the effects of colonial ideologies and influences of Empire within English language teaching, but the invisibility of these influences within ELT. Willinsky (1998) cautions us that "given the enormity of imperialism's educational project and its relatively recent demise, it seems only reasonable to expect that this project would live on, for many of us, as an *unconscious* aspect of our education" (italics added) (p. 3). One challenge faced by those of us working within the English-teaching industry, then, is the task of shifting from unconscious to conscious planes our awareness of the role played by colonialism and Empire in ELT through teaching practice, teacher education, and institutional and national policies.

***Coloniality and Colonialism.*** What Willinsky (1998) refers to as "unconscious education" is related to Latin American globalization theorist Walter Mignolo's (1995) concept of "coloniality." The distinction between coloniality and colonialism is important because it helps us think about the difference between the actual historical moment of colonialism and the political, ideological, psychological, and epistemological effects of colonialism, which he refers to as coloniality. Nelson Maldonado-Torres (2007) notes that the end of colonialism does not necessarily mean the end of coloniality: "Coloniality survives colonialism. It is maintained alive in books, in the criteria for academic performance, in cultural patterns, in common sense, in the self-image of peoples, in aspirations of self, and so many other aspects of our modern experience. In a way, as modern subjects we breathe coloniality all the time and every day" (p. 243). Coloniality is woven throughout schooling procedures and language teaching. In Chapter 3 we will see detailed examples of ways in which school practices create or reinforce divisions between those from colonized nations and those from colonial nations and compel a hierarchy between the two groups.

***Postcolonialism.*** Pennycook (1998) traces some of the philosophies undergirding the English-teaching profession to historical colonial formations: "The colonial constructions of Self and Other, of the "TE" and the "SOL" of TESOL remain in many domains of ELT" (Pennycook, 1998, p. 2). The shift from what we conceptualize as European colonialism to postcolonialism took place largely after World War II as ex-colonial European nation-states were assuming formal governmental control of their own territories. The main line of thought within postcolonial studies was that although these nations were not under the direct rule of colonial powers, ways of maintaining subservience to them were being established (Young, 2001). The term *postcolonialism*, which has been problematized by scholars who ask what's "post" about it (Williams & Chrisman, 1994), refers not only to the historical era in question but also to the intellectual direction that accompanied it. I use the term *decolonization* primarily to describe the psychological shift to independence. Spivak (1990) has suggested that the word *postcolonial* should be replaced by *neocolonial*, in acknowledgment that rather than having moved past ideologies of colonialism, we are simply seeing them take on new forms. When Alexandra's Chinese student introduced in this chapter's opening and discussed in greater detail in Chapter 3 makes fun of his own language and accent, we must ask ourselves about his complicity in the context of not only Alexandra's classroom but also the history of colonized subjects consenting—often under threat of epistemic violence—to the devaluing of their languages.

Pennycook (1998), explaining clearly why the "post" of postcolonialism has never truly earned its place, has described the ways in which colonialism generated rich and lasting cultural production, propagating subjectivities and identities that were slanted in particular ways to produce hierarchy and inequalities. He illustrates the important role English has played in colonial processes and in reproducing discursive patterns of hegemony, and he emphasizes the importance of viewing colonialism not as a bounded historical era but rather as a set of epistemological legacies. His focus is therefore on these legacies within the teaching of English.

Ashcroft et al. (1989) suggest that a colonial residue operates not only through the teaching of ESOL (English to speakers of other languages) but through all English teaching:

> It can be argued that the study of English and the growth of Empire proceeded from a single ideological climate and that the development of one is intrinsically bound up with the development of the other, both at the level of simple utility (as propaganda for instance) and at the unconscious level, where it leads to the naturalizing of constructed values (e.g., civilization, humanity, etc.), which, conversely, established "savagery," "native," "primitive" as their antitheses and as the object of a reforming zeal. (Ashcroft et al., 1989, p. 3)

***Imperialism.*** Robert Phillipson's (1992) *Linguistic Imperialism*, which engaged with English's internationalism, and his 2009 *Linguistic Imperialism Continued* provided the field with an analysis of the complex hegemonic practices that become involved as English is transferred around the world, deftly situating these processes within economic and political terrain. In 1999, Suresh Canagarajah's related book, *Resisting Linguistic Imperialism*, took up the question of agency, pondering the degree to which learners can determine their own futures, and joined a growing body of work that framed periphery learners and teachers not as brainwashed victims uncritically appropriating, desiring, and transmitting the master's language but rather as analytical and discriminating consumers of English, making astute decisions about the role of English in their lives and the lives of their students.

**Empire.** How is imperialism related to Empire? The word *empire*, with a lowercase *e*, is essentially used synonymously with *imperialism* to describe one nation-state's historical, intentional control of and occupation of another. *Empire* (Hardt & Negri, 2000) with an uppercase *E*, on the other hand, represents a contemporary and more complicated power relationship, one that is less willfully intentional and more subject to economic rather than overt governmental forces. The concept of Empire is important because it helps us understand how in today's world cultural and economic control and inequity can be perpetuated unconsciously and inadvertently. Understanding the distinction between *empire* and *Empire* supports an understanding of the difference between, on one hand, the calculated historical expansion of the number of people speaking English in order to bring them more closely under administrative and cultural control of colonizers and, on the other hand, the inadvertent modern-day assimilatory and neo-colonial effects of the practices of a multiplicity of individuals, institutions, and media in "center" and "periphery" nations who participate, for the most part unconsciously and unintentionally, in constructing the desirability of "Western-ness" and English and in keeping legitimate ownership of English associated with Whiteness and "Western" identity.

The teaching of English follows in the footsteps of colonialism and imperialism. However, in their contentious and certainly debatable (as will be discussed in Chapter 5), yet nonetheless helpful, three books known as the "Empire trilogy"—*Empire* (2000), *Multitude* (2004), and *Commonwealth* (2009)—Hardt and Negri contend that there is something different about the ways in which ideologies circulate around the globe today, something that represents a departure from European imperialism as we have understood it to operate historically. As outlined in Chapter 1, faster communication and different modes and methods of interacting have not only altered the ways in which we interact but also led to changes in our economic, social, and political relationships. Individual bodies move around the globe more frequently and more rapidly than was common in the past, creating more literal contact between individuals who would never have met a century ago, and changing technologies permit previously unimaginable virtual contact between others. In these new contact zones, identities meet and the boundaries between them become blurred, creating a path to what Hardt and Negri view as "hybridity." I mentioned hybridity in Chapter 1 and will continue to return to the subject throughout the book. *Hybridity* is an important term when we're thinking about colonialism and Empire. Let's think about some examples of cultural hybridity. An Indonesian hip-hop artist now living in the Netherlands watches the online video of a performance group from Brazil and adopts some of their sounds. A Japanese chef moves to Belize and fuses the two cuisines. With more students than ever leaving their homeland—*home* itself being a loaded term (Brown & Silberstein,

2012)—to study in other countries, a Chilean and a Sudanese studying in Paris fall in love and have children.

Although hybridity has of course always existed, it becomes more accessible and more visible in the current context. Hardt and Negri perceive the models of sovereignty that are associated with modern European states, those that are connected to historical imperialism, as embracing purity of identities (for instance, through antimiscegenation laws), patterns that maintained fixity between the Self and Other (or colonizer and colonized, such as an insistence on categorizing biracial children as one race or the other), and rigidity of boundaries (for instance, strict controls over the use of social spaces that might be used by "natives" as opposed to "expatriates"). Hardt and Negri see contemporary workings of Empire as drawing rather on U.S. constitutionalism, influenced by concepts such as hybridity of identities and expansion of frontiers. Hybridity might indeed make itself present in the ELT context. It might translate to greater recognition of the potentially nebulous nature of linguistic and racial identities, for instance, through representations in teaching materials of biracial characters or characters who are competently bilingual, not merely language learners. Instruction could include respect for code-switching, or alternating the use of two languages within one conversation, as a sophisticated skill (Canagarajah, 2013) rather than as "broken English" or some sort of substandard "interlanguage" (Selinker, 1972). Another example of hybridity is code-meshing (Young, Martinez, & National Council of Teachers of English, 2011), which occurs when minoritized dialects are blended with Standardized forms of English. Yet another is the introduction of mixed-language pedagogies, using pedagogical strategies that draw on two languages simultaneously, not as a bridge or repair but rather as an end in itself (Bou Ayash, 2013a; Pandey, 2013; Young, 2013). Hybridity might translate to the promotion of creativity with language—the teaching of literature by writers who lean heavily on plurilingualism, such as Junot Díaz (in contrast to multilingual authors of the past who wrote primarily in one language at a time, such as Joseph Conrad or Vladimir Nabokov), or who include English that deviates markedly from forms that might be considered standard, such as Zadie Smith. Or hybridity might translate to acknowledgment of a broad range of language variation or of language practices that do not conform to the traditional, such as those used by hip-hop artists. Canagarajah and Silberstein (2012) propose a view of multilingualism as a strategic resource, one that helps speakers to negotiate the multilayeredness of their group identities while remaining mindful of the tensions and conflicts that multilingualism can foster.

Current patterns are no longer as straightforward as the governmental or military occupation of a country that once characterized colonialism, nor do they conform to the informal but intentional domination and subordination of a population that we associate with the word *empire* (or imperialism) as it has been used historically. Hardt and Negri, speaking not of English teaching but rather of the broader economics of globalization in general, use the word *Empire* to describe the new global political arrangement. Empire with a capital *E* is not the same thing as imperialism. Unlike imperialism, which is characterized by domination of one ideological center, Empire leaves us with no discernible center of power. There is no one nation-state exerting control over economic and political processes—one of these economic and political processes, I contend, being English language teaching. Throughout this book I make a distinction between *empire* with a lowercase *e*, a political structure of either formal or informal conquest and control of a population, and *Empire* with an uppercase *E*, referring to a new political order, the alternative organization of power that globalization theorists have written about more recently, in recognition of the more complicated and less overt intentional forces that need to be contended with in any social justice efforts.

Another significant difference between empire (or imperialism) and Empire relates to will and intentionality. Imperialism implies a deliberateness, a conscious and even calculated attempt toward domination in the footsteps of what Hardt and Negri characterize as European expansion. Empire, on the other hand, does not emerge from premeditation at one source, such as a monarch. Rather, power functions in a distributed network filtered through a variety of nodes. This is important because in Empire, patterns are already established to reproduce inequity and will default to repeating themselves unless they are actively resisted and rearranged. What Park (2009) terms "English frenzy" and Piller, Takahashi, and Watanabe (2010) refer to as the "overconsumption" of English and "the dark side of TESOL" is not manufactured and sustained by one individual sovereign. It emerges from countless sources that work in concert to feed and perpetuate each other. This philosophical transformation changes the ways in which we come to understand race and racism, identity, diaspora and migration, and control of the multitudes through communications industries. In this book I argue that one node through which all of these (and other) processes are being transformed is the English language. The spread of English, particularly throughout the 19th century and the first half of the 20th century, was a monarchical project, part of a deliberate and conscious effort to regulate and maintain ideological control over subjects. Even after the British Empire had ceded independence to most of its occupied territories and relinquished much of its official political domination, the United Kingdom remained the center of ideological control of subjects worldwide through the promotion and embracing of particular bodies of literature, accents, performing and visual arts, epistemologies, disciplinary conceptions, and pedagogies. This is not the same kind of influence we observe in the current context. The spread of English today is not controlled by one single power. The contemporary spread of English is driven at multiple levels: through media, educational institutions, practices of transnational corporations, commercial interests, language policies of various nation-states, and supranational entities—and through the English-teaching industry. However, these all function in a collaborative way within a common logic of power toward related goals. If we agree that there is no center-driven agenda, rearrangement of power relationships becomes more complicated because there is, essentially, no king to unseat, no palace to raze. For instance, the "illegitimate practices" described by Widin (2010) are part of a concerted—but not necessarily consciously intentional—effort driven by aid agencies, universities in English-dominant nations (in Widin's case Australia), teachers, students, and government officials in both Australia and the country receiving services to reinforce global inequality in the marketplace for English language teaching and teacher training by solidifying Australia's reputation as a provider of these services in, often, poor countries. In addition to the collusion of these institutions, organizations, and individuals, the buy-in would not be feasible without the seeds planted by media images linking English to wealth, success, and sophistication.

The theories advanced by Hardt and Negri (2000, 2004, 2009) and other globalization scholars are optimistic and potentially exciting. They leave us wondering about possibilities for a new world order, one that works to eliminate racism, language hierarchies, and global differences in wealth and poverty. One wonders whether the theories are, in fact, too optimistic, so hopeful as to border on blindness to the far-reaching and intense effects of racism and imperialism historically, perhaps overly eager to overlook the enduring effects of colonial injuries. English language classrooms continue to be saturated with imperialistic and colonial influences. However, the Empire trilogy provides a helpful framework for ELT professionals seeking to understand the changing arrangements of their classrooms, the shift from imperialist patterns to a new, deterritorialized distribution of power. Imperialism seems to inhabit a space so deeply embedded in and woven into the English language that the task of teasing it out remains a protracted and complicated process. For instance, while broader space for hybridity of identities in ESOL classrooms has opened up, borders between Self and Other, colonizer and colonized, legitimate English user and interloper all continue to work in complex ways—sometimes fluid, certainly; sometimes still rigidly present and observable; and sometimes deceptively invisible, promising a mobility between categories that is in actuality elusive. Indeed, in the introduction to their special issue on postcolonial approaches to TESOL in *Critical Inquiry in Language Studies*, Lin and Luke (2006) noted that the submissions they received primarily focused on coloniality, and that analyses of the "non-synchronous move from postcoloniality to new cosmopolitan, globalized capitalism" (p. 67) were more difficult to come by.

## Race and English Language Teaching

In the context of English language teaching (and, one could argue, in most contexts), it is nonsensical to talk about empire without talking about race, and vice versa. However, the relevance of race very easily becomes undetectable. In recent decades, new understandings from genetic research have led to the collapse of race as a biological category as we know it, discrediting my high school textbook, which authoritatively taught me that there were four separate races: Mongoloid, Australoid, Negroid, and Caucasoid. In later years, I learned to make a distinction between *race*, which was represented as a biological and unchanging category, and *ethnicity*, which was conceived of as a more cultural construct, taking into account national, religious, community, and linguistic nuances as opposed to mere biology. It was only in the early 2000s that I began to understand the artificial nature of the race-as-biology/ethnicity-as-culture dichotomy with the realization that biological theories of racial categorizing lack the validity I had previously imagined them to hold and that most genetic variation is within and not between races. Adelman (2003) goes as far as to label race an "illusion."

I should not have been surprised. Microinteractions in our everyday lives in and out of our classrooms highlight for us the idiosyncratic nature of racial categorizing. My awareness of this subjectivity has been particularly heightened through the experience of observing small children becoming socialized into a racialized world. During her preschool years, my oldest daughter, who could be described as being of Sri Lankan heritage, once characterized her Korean-born friend as "White" because she perceived his skin to be paler than that of her "White" friend. I heard her referring to herself as "Black" because her forearm, laid alongside that of her "Black" friend, was the same shade. We, her parents, couldn't decide whether to disrupt her ways of coding the world around her by teaching her the ever-shifting racial categorizations of that particular moment in history.

We know that ways of conceptualizing racial categories have changed radically over humanity's history, a possible clue to their arbitrary nature, and that, even contemporaneously, individuals are categorized differently depending on geography. For instance, the label *Black* includes a different group of people in Malawi than in the United States; someone of Black-White mixed-race heritage might be more likely to be categorized as *coloured* in South Africa but as *Black* in the United States. Historically, racial meanings have shifted internationally and within the United States. During the 1700s, Benjamin Franklin defined Italians, Russians, French, Swedes, and Germans as "swarthy" (Jacobson, 1998, p. 40), but it is difficult to imagine, in today's U.S. context, the word *swarthy* being applied to Swedes or Germans. The transition to Whiteness of Jewish Americans (Brodkin, 1998) and Irish Americans (Ignatiev, 1995) were complicated processes. During the early 20th century, Mexicans, Japanese, Syrians, and South Asians took legal action to appeal to be recognized as White (Hill, 2008). It has become clear that although race is an illusion biologically (Adelman, 2003), it is not an illusion socially and in fact has serious and material consequences. However, this new realization of the subjective existence of race makes it more difficult to talk about in a concrete way when we do not know what "it" is we are talking about.

In our eagerness to believe that a reversal of the historical patterns of domination and subjugation is possible, perhaps even afoot, it is important that we not discount the power and intensity of racism in imperialist projects, including in the project of teaching English. Schueller (2009) outlines the ways in which work on globalization has supported turning a blind eye to issues of race, perceiving "globalism-inspired forms of analyses as inadequate of dealing with U.S. narratives of race and gender" (p. 3). She asserts that "homogenized (too often purely linguistic) ideas of global diaspora, migration, and postcoloniality, all of which are being increasingly deployed as emancipatory paradigms, often beyond race, in fact meet their limits when we introduce the question of race" (p. 34). A superficial reflection might indicate that there is something different about today's more hybrid and fluid racial arrangements, that they offer hope for change and antiracist possibilities. One must ask, however, whether we are simply drinking old wine in new, better disguised bottles. The promises of hybridity, of a breaking down of racial categories, of the formation of more changeable and dynamic meanings associated with racial categories when deployed within school walls, appear empty and in fact more closely related to colorblind and postrace discourses, which assert that we have moved beyond a period in which race was a relevant category of analysis (Joseph, 2013).

The composition of ESOL classrooms highlights further the relevance of race in the teaching of English in public schools. According to the Center for Educational Statistics (2012), in 2009 in the United States, the number of children speaking a language other than English at home was 11.2 million, or 21% of the total school population. Of these, 94.3% were racial minorities (did not identify as White). Of the 5% of public schoolchildren in U.S. public K–12 schools who were reported to "speak English with difficulty," 98.9% were racial minorities. The increasing numbers of minority students in the nation's schools, referred to as "the Brown Paradox" by Contreras

(2011), is very much an English language learning issue. That race and racism are an inherent part of TESOL has been highlighted by *TESOL Quarterly*'s special issue on race in TESOL, guest edited by Kubota and Lin (2006), who are also the editors of the 2009 volume *Race, Culture, and Identities in Second Language Learning*. The chapters in this trailblazing collection explain the relevance of race in second language education in a number of different contexts. Many of those themes—racial silences, the invisibility of race, Whiteness, meanings of multiculturalism—are taken up and described in detail in the present book.

***Invisibility of Racism in ELT.*** The belief that the teaching of English is racially neutral is what Feagin and Vera (1995) term a "sincere fiction," or a myth with which individuals delude themselves. Feagin and Vera, Bonilla-Silva (2013), and Hill (2008) particularly charge Whites with embracing colorblind myths, but I suggest that racial-minority status offers little immunity from the pressure to embrace identities of colorblindness and that many people in contemporary America, whether perceived as White or not, collude to create a racial ideology that Bonilla-Silva terms *colorblind racism*. Racism has become so naturalized within the project of teaching English that its presence is no longer noticeable. Bonilla-Silva offers some examples of what he labels "now you see it, now you don't" racism unrelated to English teaching: overtly discriminatory real estate practices, such as steering minorities into certain neighborhoods or not showing all available units, have replaced the "Whites Only" signs of the past; people of color who have been denied voting rights historically now find that racial gerrymandering invalidates or waters down the effect of their votes today. Racism operates in a similarly concealed manner in English language teaching. Under the guise of correct grammar and intelligible pronunciation, naturalized ideologies about nativeness, and unquestioned language hierarchies, we have created an ideal climate for Bonilla-Silva's (2013) "racism without racists." For instance, in schools, what teachers intend as grammatical "corrections" are often actually a switch from racialized English varieties (such as Nigerian or Jamaican English) to forms that more closely approximate what is commonly defined as "Standard English," or varieties more frequently associated with Whiteness. Some items on the verbal section of the high-stakes Scholastic Aptitude Test (SAT) function differently for African American test-takers than White test-takers (Santelices & Wilson, 2010), resulting in a greater likelihood of African American students choosing an incorrect answer on several items. Although conscious and intentional racism are presumably not in play in the design of these test items, the maintenance of racial inequity is nonetheless the result. Teachers are for the most part not consciously trying to make students sound more "White" but are simply shepherding their language practices in the direction of varieties that are most richly rewarded. Although individuals might not have racist intentions, the terrain in which we operate has made practices that sustain racism a natural default so that even attempts at deliberately antiracist pedagogy are frequently and quietly thwarted.

**Whiteness.** A definition of Whiteness is elusive because it is first and foremost understood in terms of what it is not, that is, a category of racial identity that is "*not* racial minority" or "*not* person of color." It is further complicated by the subjective and arbitrary nature of all racial identity categories. Alfred López (2005) remarks that "Whiteness is not, yet we continue for many reasons to act as though it is" (p. 1). Whiteness, like other racial categories, has no biological basis, but it is a sociological fact with concrete consequences. The conceptualization and formation of Whiteness is fundamental to shaping the ways in which English is taught and learned, yet Whiteness appears superficially to be quite separate from the ELT industry, separate enough to awaken surprise when it appears in an ESL teaching methods textbook or syllabus. Whiteness is, of course, tautly connected to colonialism and particularly to the colonialism that propagated English—that is, the colonialism of the British Empire—because the British colonists who spread English were read primarily as White. López (2005) continues that "it would seem a simple enough assumption that the end of colonialism ushers in the end of Whiteness, or at least of its unrivaled ascendancy" (p. 1). This is a simple assumption, but a fallacious one because through the processes of colonialism Whiteness has become linked to ownership of English, throwing into question the claim to the language of those not perceived as or coded as White. The dynamic is all the more complicated because while Whiteness carries power, it is also understood to be neutral, leading to an invisibility of the privilege it carries. The past setting for the ELT profession has been one in which White English teachers with established ownership of English passed the language on to racial minority individuals, usually as part of a broader plan to save them from their savagery. In the context of ELT, therefore, Whiteness is associated with redemption, liberation, enlightenment, civilization, and modernity, and these associations with the English language follow. Whiteness then becomes a category for analysis, with White racial identity and dominant group membership becoming an important source of self-reflection for English teachers (Liggett, 2009).

**Multiculturalism and Race.** In the study referred to in this book, questions arose about the nature of multiculturalism in relation to race. What does multiculturalism mean? Is it simply an embracing of different cultures? Cheerleading for minorities? For James Banks (2013), two important ideas underpin multicultural education: access and recognition of inequality. Firstly, "all students—regardless of their ethnic, racial, cultural, or linguistic characteristics—should have an equal opportunity to learn in schools" (p. 3). Secondly, education that is truly multicultural must recognize and acknowledge school-based inequality: "Some students, because of their group characteristics, have a better chance to learn in schools as they are currently structured than do students who belong to other groups" (p. 3). Linguistic-minority students do indeed appear to experience inequitable schooling experiences, but the question of access is a complicated one. The educational configurations for ESOL students are so markedly different from the schooling of students who are not receiving ESOL services that comparisons are difficult to draw. What does multicultural education offer the ESOL classroom? How can teachers talk about culture or race without stereotyping specific groups? What are some potential routes for teachers who, for instance, pick up a book that is classified as multicultural literature but relies on stereotypes? In one example, Margaret encountered a negative reaction from a Korean student when she introduced a book with a Korean character. (This incident will be described in greater detail in Chapter 4).

Kubota (2004) makes a helpful distinction between liberal multiculturalism and critical multiculturalism. I return to this description frequently in my scholarly work and in my teaching. It is popular with students, often clarifying concretely for them a distinction that is difficult to articulate—that is, the ways in which some discourses that ostensibly encourage multiculturalism can actually support oppression. For Kubota, *liberal multiculturalism*, the fraternal twin of "benevolent multiculturalism" (Sleeter & Delgado Bernal, 2004), is an acknowledgment or even celebration of difference without a consciousness of the layers of power working around difference. Liberal multiculturalism is often characterized by colorblind and no-differential-treatment ideologies that use pro-equality discourses to support equal treatment for all individuals, regardless of differential needs or points of departure. Liberal multiculturalism ultimately obscures issues of power and privilege and consequently perpetuates racial and linguistic hierarchies. I once saw a cartoon that depicted a turtle, an eagle, and a bear all standing at the bottom of a tree. An assessment specialist bearing a clipboard and a stopwatch announced, "The test is to see who can get to the top of the tree first," illustrating that equal treatment does not always constitute equality. Similarly, teachers who seek to treat all students equally through colorblindness—"I don't care if he's black, white, yellow, purple, or green"—ignore an indispensable part of who students are, undermining rather than reinforcing equality. A more useful orientation is one of *critical multiculturalism*, which analyzes the ways in which power circulates in relation to "culture"—the construction of institutional, systemic racism, including the differential effects of testing, tracking, placement, school assignments, and resource distribution; our understandings of difference that avoid essentializing; and an acknowledgment of the ways in which culture as a discursive construct is connected to relationships of economics and power. The distinction between liberal and critical multiculturalism is helpful as we seek to understand the context of the study schools described in this book.

James Banks and Cherry McGee Banks (2004), with a similar goal of distinguishing among the differing ways in which multiculturalism might be perceived and deployed, have developed a multilayered perspective that considers five dimensions of multicultural education: (1) content integration, (2) the knowledge-construction process, (3) prejudice reduction, (4) an equity pedagogy, and (5) an empowering school culture and social structure. If teachers and schools are to implement truly multicultural education, they must genuinely engage with the meanings of each of these dimensions: incorporating content from a wide range of perspectives, including those from a variety of minority groups; attending to a diversity of epistemological lenses and supporting students' critical analyses of differential systems of knowledge valuing; helping adults and children in schools understand and combat racism and other forms of prejudice; analyzing and implementing practices that support equity; and committing to transforming institutional cultures.

Various obstacles stand in the way of teachers attempting to teach in multicultural and equitable ways. This exploration engages with questions about what types of racial differences and internationalization were acceptable within the schools of the study and which were sidelined or swept under the rug. In this study, despite the apparent connections between racial identity and linguistic identity, silences about race did not extend to silences about linguistic-minority status. In fact, talking about linguistic identity sometimes became a way to disguise racist discourses. Throughout the study, a tension emerged between drawing attention to difference and encouraging pride in national or cultural identity. Teachers also observed a parallel tension between underscoring stereotypes and drawing attention to difference in order to disarm stereotypes.

## Linguistic Variation and Language Hierarchies

Many of the challenges surrounding language variation and hierarchies involve the concept of *place* and the connectedness of place to *race*. The language we refer to as English, not so much a single language as a collection of varieties and variations that have been socially coded to belong under the same broad umbrella, is connected to places—be these nations, regions, cities, suburbs, islands—and also, less prominently, to other identity categories, such as gender, race, history, religion, or socio-economics, and attributed varying levels of social legitimacy accordingly. A helpful body of work for thinking about languages is found in movements toward "disinventing languages," the problematization of static notions of languages and language genealogies. Makoni & Pennycook (2007) start "with the premise that languages, conceptions of languageness and the metalanguages used to describe them are inventions" (p. 1). They note that languages were invented

> as part of the Christian/colonial and nationalistic projects in different parts of the globe. From Tsonga, Shona, Afrikaans, Runyakitara, Chinyanja in Africa (Harries, 1987; Chimhundu, 1992) or Fijian in the Pacific and Bahasa Malay in Indonesia (Heryanto, 1995) to Inkhain Latin America (Manheim, 1991) and Hebrew (Kusar, 2001) in Israel, the history of language inventions is long and well-documented. (p. 1)

The authors of the various chapters in the volume ask about how specific languages were named and developed, about the social and semiotic processes and contexts of language construction, and about ways of representing languages as separate. If languages are inventions, then what might it mean, ask Makoni and Pennycook, to disinvent and then reconstitute language?

As languages are invented, they are almost always attached to locations. Deleuze and Guattari (1986) use the term *deterritorialization* to refer to the detachment of cultural markers from the geographical place to which they (in theory, at least) belong, a process that is, in the contemporaneous context, often associated with globalizing forces. Suárez-Orozco and Qin-Hilliard (2004) explain that "globalization tends to detach social practices and cultural formations from localized territories" (p. 9). The attachment of new markers of culture taking on new meaning within their new space can then be referred to as *reterritorialization*. English was historically attached to England in the same way that Danish was to Denmark and Greek to Greece. As it has spread around the world, the "territory" of English has changed, broadened, become more multidimensional and complex. It is an official language in some contexts in which it remains largely constructed as an intruder; in other countries it is widely used as a lingua franca although it has no formal role and continues to be understood as "foreign." Within the U.S. context, some forms of U.S. English are accorded greater legitimacy than others. African American Vernacular English (AAVE), Spanish-influenced English, and other regional forms of English retain their identities because of their (socially constructed) attachment to particular places. In Chapter 5 we will ask what deterritorialization means for these forms of English. What role does deterritorialization play in challenging language hierarchies? As English travels around the world, what forces lead toward its deterritorialization, and which interfere with this process? Is a deterritorialized English achievable? Is it desirable?

**World Englishes.** The languages termed *World Englishes* rear their heads in placement decisions and teaching practices around the nation and indeed globally, raising questions about what constitutes a World English and about the culpability of race in sketching out that relationship. The journal *World Englishes* (previously *World English*) and numerous publications in recent years (cf. Jenkins, 2009; Kachru, 1992; Kirkpatrick, 2007; Melchers & Shaw, 2002) have lent an analytical lens to attempts to understand ways of categorizing various types of English. Kirkpatrick (2007) offers an unsatisfying although widely accepted definition: "By World Englishes I mean those indigenous, nativized varieties that have developed around the world and that reflect the cultural and pragmatic norms of their speakers" (p. 3). What is meant by *indigenous*? And *nativized*? Both terms imply a natural belonging of the language to the land. What is it that naturalizes a connection to a land? If we explore the everyday meanings of these words, we come to understand that they are so reliant on subjective judgments as to be almost meaningless. Let's look at some mainstream definitions. The *Merriam-Webster Dictionary* describes *indigenous* as "produced, growing, living, or occurring naturally in a particular region or environment," while the *Oxford English Dictionary* offers the definition "born or produced naturally in a land or region." These definitions do little to inform us about why the most widely spoken forms of English in Singapore are World Englishes, but the Englishes most commonly spoken in Cincinnati, Ohio, are not. The *Oxford English Dictionary* defines *nativised* as "to make native in character" and *native* as "inherent, innate, belonging to, or connected with something by nature or natural constitution." Natural constitution is, ironically, a social construction. Understandings of where languages belong are shaped by multiple social factors, in this case the most significant being race. The unproblematized use of the construct World Englishes throughout the study contexts contributed to a sustenance of inequality and discrimination. Parallel complicated questions remain unanswered relating to the differences among a language, a variety, a variation, a dialect, a creole, a pidgin. The lack of agreement around definitions of these terms contributed to the marginalization of the children in ESOL classrooms in the study.

**Nativeness.** Questions about nativeness and the supremacy of the native-speaker construct have increased in urgency in recent years. A series of provocative publications released beginning in the late 1990s (Braine, 1999; Cook, 1999) advanced awareness that the goal of nativeness or even native-like proficiency was not only untenable for language learners, it was of dubious utility and desirability. In 1999, Vivian Cook's influential article suggested that as a profession we should apply a second-language (L2) rather than native-speaker model and reconceptualize L2 users as legitimate speakers rather than as inadequate imitations of monolingual native speakers. In actual fact, "passing" as a native is crucial in a very narrow range of situations—when working undercover as a spy, for instance, or for a particular acting role. In most day-to-day interactions, nativeness (or the appearance thereof) is unimportant, with the exception of encounters with accent or linguistic discrimination. The ELT field's self-examination about its engagement with nativeness has led to greater attention to topics such as accent discrimination. Related to challenges of the importance of nativeness in language learning came parallel questions about nativeness in language learning. Is it always desirable to learn a language from a native-English-speaking teacher? Are there advantages to having had the experience of learning the language oneself? Do the numerous second language teachers and speakers of English as a lingua franca bring particular strengths to their pedagogies? Does preference for a native-English-speaking teacher constitute an unfair and discriminatory hiring practice? With race and English being as connected as they are, it becomes impossible to ask questions about nativeness and accent without interrogating race.

## WORKING IN CONCERT:
## EMPIRE, RACE, AND LANGUAGE IDEOLOGIES

In the schools of the study, the various institutional and social arrangements that sustained relations of empire inevitably also engaged racial and language ideologies. Similarly, in the context of ESOL, the production of racial inequalities was inextricable from empire and language discrimination. And linguicism was the progeny of, while simultaneously generating, both racial and colonial inequalities. For instance, the formation of the school category ESOL depended on the repeated social maintenance of colonial, racial, and language divisions. The ways language varieties are affirmed, discouraged, and erased depends on the colonial histories and racial meanings associated with the varieties. The sometimes extreme pursuit of "native-like" Standard English speech emerges from a belief in the superiority of a colonizing language, which in the case of English is associated with Whiteness. Given the interconnectedness of these three sets of ideologies, the project before us then is to understand how they work together within the teaching of English.

## Reflection Questions

1. How do I define myself racially? With how many of my students do I share a racial identification?
2. How often do I feel comfortable when I talk about race? What causes me discomfort in conversations about race? What is my greatest fear when I talk about race?

3. What is my historical colonial identity and how does it connect to those of my students? Am I perceived to be descended from a colonizing or colonizer nation, neither, or both?

4. What is my linguistic identity? What social legitimacy or prestige is accorded to the form of English I speak? How does it compare to the English spoken by my students?

5. What is the relationship between my national identity and those of my students?

6. What is my relationship to English? How has English served me? What images do I associate with English?

7. What do I believe English can do for my students? What do my students believe that English can do for them?

# CHAPTER 3

# Teaching Empire or Teaching English?

## DECOLONIZING ESOL

The relationship among empire, race, and language ideologies is shaped in significant ways by the structural arrangements of ESOL, which play a powerful role in modulating the subjectivities of not only learners in ESOL classrooms but, relationally, all individuals within school walls and even beyond. In this chapter, I connect a localized space, the K–12 ESOL classroom, to the positioning of English globally and argue that the practices of English teaching, other content teaching through English, English language teacher education, and English language education policy work are all part of an industry that is neither neutral nor innocent. It is no longer permissible for English-teaching professionals to feign ignorance of the role we can play in maintaining a connection between English acquisition and wealth production and accumulation. In this chapter, ESOL is examined as a site of struggle. The ESOL classrooms in the study were host to multiple practices that were simultaneously colonizing and decolonizing, constitutive and deconstructive of Empire. This chapter therefore moves beyond a critical analysis of how colonialist messages are produced and sustained through common, taken-for-granted, everyday school-based interactions in ESOL classrooms and seeks to develop richer understandings of how relations of power are collaboratively shaped by all participants in relation to individual and institutional desires (Motha & Lin, 2013), regimes of truth (Foucault, 1972), imagined communities (Carroll, Motha, & Price, 2008; Kanno & Norton, 2003), and imagined identities (Norton, 2000). Understanding the ways in which inequalities are maintained can support us in our pursuit of an alternative notion of what a globalization of counter-Empire can be, of a globalization that works to eliminate unjust differences in wealth and poverty.

The ways in which English organizes relations of empire in schools is the subject of this chapter. I examine four areas: the social and institutional formation of ESOL, the relationship between ESOL and the broader social imaginary, the tension between segregation and language support, and epistemologies of ESOL. I first explore how ESOL is constructed within the larger school culture, including the establishment and maintenance of boundaries relating to ESOL through scheduling decisions, structural organization, and social pressure such as teasing. I move on, in the second section, to challenge the commonsense nature of neocolonial disciplinary boundaries around ESOL, examining how English is represented and the relationship of these representations to the English-teaching industry, questioning promises of social inclusion, exploring ESOL students' buy-in to the marginality of their own subjectivities, and highlighting the gendered construction of ESOL identity. In the third section I grapple with the tension between language support and segregation, summarizing the history of school segregation and exploring the sustenance of racism through arrangements of ESOL. Finally, I consider epistemologies of ESOL, looking at the role of national standards, gifted and talented programs, and differential treatment in shaping what comes to count as knowledge in the lives of children receiving ESOL services.

## ENGLISH AS AN INSTRUMENT OF EMPIRE

At the front office, I sign the log of visitors on the bulky brown clipboard, wave to the receptionist, phone balanced dexterously against her ear as she scribbles on a notepad, and turn to make my way through the shadowy hallways, up the stale-smelling stairwell, to Alexandra's classroom. Although I have arrived during the middle of a class period, stray students wander through the hallways: man-sized boys, the downy uneven fur on their chins reminding me of a patchily covered newborn's scalp; short youngsters whose doors puberty seems to be bypassing; serious-faced girls in heavy eyeliner clutching mounds of books and folders. I feel a momentary rush of gratitude, as I often do when I walk through middle schools, that I have passed this age and need never revisit it, this age when it seems that one's entire future pivots on membership and belonging and affiliation, as randomly and heartlessly determined as these may be. I reach the slightly ajar ESOL classroom door and push it open. A short hallway leads from the classroom door to the room itself, so that if I stand quietly enough, I can remain hidden while I hear the quiet murmur of the class at work without their awareness of my presence. The light switch is next to me, near the door, and the lights are on, but the room is nonetheless dim, the blinds drawn securely to block out the radiance of the winter sun. I know from previous visits that the window looks out onto a pebbled courtyard and allows a glimpse into the other classrooms wrapped around the courtyard. This room has an aura of seclusion, of separateness from the world on the other side of the heavy blinds, on the other side of this door removed from the heart of the classroom by a hallway separating ESOL from the non-ESOL, in which I stand. Bhabha (1994) might have called this a *liminal* hallway. He used the term *liminal*, from the Latin word for "threshold," *limen*, to describe in-between places, metaphorical spaces that exist between the colonial and the colonized. For Bhabha, liminal spaces are spaces of hope and possibility because they can serve as sites of transition and ambiguity, sites in which individuals are permitted to be neither wholly one category or culture nor the other, sites in which hybridity is allowed and can therefore be formed and imagined, become visible and maybe even explored. Standing in this hallway, this in-between space, I think of the numerous times I have heard ESOL teachers describe their classrooms as a "haven," "refuge," or "sanctuary," a safe island cut off from the perils of the larger school community, and I wonder to myself whether these are the metaphors that this particular group of students would use.

To what degree does ESOL operate as a sanctuary, offering protection and support, and to what degree does the mere creation of the category ESOL (or any of its various appellations), both institutionally and socially, enforce separateness and isolation or even reinscribe societal divisions that exist outside school walls? What forces are working together to create a logic for the existence of the category ESOL, and how are these forces related to empire? Although the primary focus of English-teaching professionals has historically been language form, grammar, accuracy, skills development, and the accumulation of vocabulary, the work carried out by the profession actually has a much broader and less discernible goal. The processes of English teaching are a form of what Hardt and Negri (2000) call biopolitical production, the production of social life and specifically social order and hierarchy. The production of wealth is integrally connected to the teaching of English, and "in the postmodernization of the global economy, the creation of wealth tends ever more toward what we will call biopolitical production, the production of social life itself, in which the economic, the political, and the cultural increasingly overlap and invest one another" (p. xiii).

The first time I stood in that liminal hallway, before I had ever met any of Alexandra's students, I was able to imagine with reasonable accuracy what they would look like. When we consider the identities and demographics of ESOL students in public schools in the United States, we notice that the situatedness of the ESOL classroom within the rest of the school community mirrors, in an uncanny manner, broader social relations between White, "native" speakers of standard Englishes on one hand, and, on the other hand, the group of students represented in the ESOL classroom—that is, mostly racial minorities for whom English, defined narrowly in the sense of "mainstream," most-powerful, most-centralized varieties, is an additional language. Despite globalization discourses that optimistically wax poetic about the possibilities for new, hybridized identity options, an unmapping of racial status from cultural and economic capital is elusive, and the strangely outdated nature of the place occupied by ESOL institutionally not only mirrors broader, even global, relations but perpetuates these arrangements, which are often arrangements of racial and colonial inequality. It perpetuates them in invisible ways, creating sophisticated colorblind and power-evasive ideologies from mainstream globalization discourses, so that their persistence often escapes our notice. These lessons are implicitly and silently being taught within schools, and it could be argued that nowhere within school walls do empire and racism find more vociferous expression than in the location of ESOL.

Marcelo Suárez-Orozco and Carolyn Sattin have noted that a "glaring failure of formal education is happening at the very vital global link between the wealthy global cities in the Northern Hemisphere and the developing world. Schools are failing to properly educate and ease the transition and integration of large and growing numbers of immigrant youth arriving in Europe and North America" (p. 3). A closer examination of how these integrative and transitional processes play themselves out can illuminate for us the small, seemingly commonplace interactions that shape the broader positioning of ESOL and ultimately teach children and young adults about difference, hierarchy, and inequality and can further teach us about the role played by English language teaching in the United States in maintaining global economic inequalities. Accordingly, this chapter takes up themes of Empire and decolonization in relation to English, engaging specifically with the construction of the category "ESOL" as a school and institutional construct within the broader context of globalization. This chapter examines how the ESOL classrooms in the study and indeed the pedagogical discipline of TESOL frequently serve as a breeding ground for epistemologies and constructs that support unequal and often colonial-like relationships (Amin & Kubota, 2004; Kumaravadivelu, 2008; Lin, 1999; Lin & Luke, 2006; May, 2008; Motha, 2006b; Pennycook, 1998; Ramanathan, 2006; Vandrick, 2009). These constructs include a deep division between native- and nonnative-English-speaker identity (Braine, 1999; Brutt-Griffler & Samimy, 1999) and a reification of the English language and, consequently, its speakers. In this era of increasingly blurry boundaries, the ways in which the English language comes to be constructed and represented extend across national boundaries. In public schools in the United States, the cultural, economic, sociological, and psychological domination of immigrants, particularly immigrants who are linguistic and ethnic minorities, is a testament to the pervasiveness of subtle forces of empire. This chapter connects these forces and their accompanying ideologies to the classrooms of the study in order to situate them as integral to a concerted global tendency to preserve the legacy of centuries of colonial inequalities that pervades educational systems around the world (Edge, 2008; Motha, 2006b; Wong & Motha, 2007).

## Monolingual Habitus:
## Linguistic-Identity Positioning by Other Students

Not long after the school visit described above, at an afternoon tea, the teachers discussed the positioning of ESOL students within the broader school community, making explicit the interconnectedness of language identity and membership within various school categories including ESOL. Alexandra told us:

> There's a hallway between my classroom door and the classroom, so someone in the doorway can't be seen from the classroom. I leave the door open to ventilate the classroom. Students pass the door and shout "You can't speak English" into the classroom and play with the light switch at the door.
> ["How often does this happen?" I asked.]
> At least once or twice a week. (Alexandra, Afternoon Tea, April 10)

Jane, too, told us of high school students who had exited from ESOL who mocked current ESOL students for their supposed inability to speak English (Jane, Afternoon Tea, April 10).

Let us consider the role in the production of postcolonial subjectivities played by the taunt "You can't speak English," quite a commonplace taunt heard frequently around ESOL K–12 classrooms. First, it constructs ESOL students as deficient. Rather than highlighting the cultural and linguistic resources ESOL students have to draw on—most have transnational, transcultural experiences, access to a multiplicity of epistemological bases, and fluency in another language—insults such as this one represent an inability to speak English as the sole distinguishing characteristic of an ESOL student. Second, the taunt is almost always inaccurate. Most ESOL students arrive in their first classes speaking some amount of English, and most of the students in Alexandra's class had been living in the United States and attending English language schools since well before the beginning of the school year, 9 months earlier. In fact, more than half of all students defined as Limited English Proficient (LEP) by the U.S. Department of Education were actually born in the United States and have lived in the country all of their lives (Ruiz-de-Velasco & Fix, 2000). Students in ESOL classrooms typically speak quite a bit of English. The jeer refutes the vast, complex space between ESOL and non-ESOL and seeks to reinforce the dichotomy between the two categories. It constructs individuals who do speak English as an elite group, a club difficult to achieve membership in if, as is suggested by the jeer, all ESOL students are excluded. The jeer solidifies a boundary around this club of Empire and underscores "English speaker" status as a necessary prerequisite for admission to the club.

The blurring of boundaries associated with a new global arrangement by many globalization theorists is indeed visible in multiple ways in ESOL classrooms, and I will describe some in this chapter. However, reinforcing the rigidity of borders was a simultaneously persistent force throughout the year of the study. Postcolonial theorists have understood the repeated and insistent underscoring of binary oppositions to be a cornerstone of colonial discourse (Fanon, 1967; Said, 1978), and in this case it is evident that reinforcing the distinction between the two poles, ESOL and non-ESOL, serves to underscore their unequal status. Pattanayak (1996) in fact goes as far as to suggest that "binary opposites . . . are characteristic of First World thinking. . . . [In] the multilingual, pluricultural world . . . there is neither center nor periphery, core nor margin, but a network of relationships" (p. 47). If the ample terrain between ESOL and non-ESOL is ignored, it becomes possible to also deny the advanced level of English proficiency that some ESOL students have achieved and to consequently disregard the question of what distinguishes native-English-speaker (NES) English from fluent nonnative-English-speaker (NNES) speech and furthermore what makes the former superior to the latter. Ignoring the zone between ESOL and non-ESOL supports the viewing of English language learners in absolute terms, as either English speakers or not, without regard for the developmental nature of the process of language acquisition, nor for the diversity of linguistic identities that could potentially be attributed to an "English speaker" in the literal sense. This dichotomy between ESOL and non-ESOL is reflective of the mutual exclusivity of the larger social constructions of "native speaker" and "nonnative speaker," constructions that work tirelessly to exclude the possibility of bilingual minds (Pavlenko, 2006) or multicompetence, defined by Cook (1991) as knowledge of two languages in one mind, and to erase the fertile middle ground between the two categories.

Gogolin (2013) has applied Bourdieu's notion of *habitus* to the construction of national language identities, focusing on her context in Europe and charging that across that continent exists a "monolingual habitus," the persistent narrative that societies are irrevocably monolingual, despite ample evidence to the contrary. For the purposes of this discussion, I appropriate Gogolin's notion of monolingual habitus in order to apply it to the level of the individual and school, rather than to a society or nation as does Gogolin. While Blackledge and Creese (2010) have argued for schools to endorse multilingualism as a usual and normative resource for identity performance, I examine the ways in which the dominant culture of schooling in this study compelled students to gravitate instead toward a monolingual, monocultural

English identity, which appeared to be the only legitimate identity available within the prevailing ideology of the four schools.

Examples of monolingual habitus surround us. Recently, on one of the San Juan Islands off the coast of Washington State, I saw a bumper sticker that read, "Speak English. This is America." Shortly before I defended my PhD dissertation, I was walking along the canal near my then-home in the Washington, DC, suburbs and saw a sign asking the public not to litter. Underneath it was a Spanish translation: "POR FAVOR LLEVESE SU BASURA CUANDO SE MARCHE." Across the sign someone had scrawled, "Learn English." In another example, Julia Alvarez tells the story of her mother speaking Spanish to her and her siblings in a store. An elderly woman commented that if they wanted to be in the country, they should learn the language. "'I do know the language,' my mother said in her boarding school English, putting the woman in her place" (Alvarez as cited in Pavlenko, 2001, p. 330). In all of these examples is embedded a monolingual habitus, the assumption that use of a language other than English must signal an inability to use English, as though no one in their right mind would voluntarily choose to use any other language.

Monolingual habitus has an exclusionary effect: Blackledge (2002) notes that when a dominant ideology of monolingualism is constructed within multicultural societies, those who do not fit the "monoglot standard" (p. 68) become excluded. In many contexts globally, monolingual English carried a cachet historically, and English monolingualism became attached to class privilege. One way to affirm class privilege was to emulate colonizers by acquiring English and teaching the language exclusively to one's children, relinquishing one's heritage language. Monolingualism proves beyond a doubt that English is one's first language, allowing an individual to irrefutably claim NES legitimacy. The supremacy of a monolingual English identity went hand in hand with, and indeed was supportive of, the deficit construction of the category ESOL. All four teachers noticed that students in the upper elementary grades, the middle school, and the high school were ashamed of their ESOL student status. They cited numerous examples of students trying to hide their relationship with the ESOL department and perceiving the end of their need for ESOL services as a desirable victory because it freed them from the stigma of ESOL. In addition, many of the teachers, students, and parents the teachers interacted with revealed similar conceptualizations of the category of ESOL.

When Jane's high school students, themselves former ESOL students, were derisive of their more recently arrived peers, they were attempting to reinforce (with questionable success) the demarcation between the shameful category they had been assigned to previously and their current, supposedly respectable, status as separate from ESOL. Through their teasing, they establish distance from the deficient category of ESOL.

Like Alexandra and Jane, Margaret noticed that when she joined the school community some of her elementary-aged students were ashamed of their enrollment in ESOL classes. She told us about one 4th-grade student who ignored her when he was outside the classroom unless the hallway was empty: "If no one else is in the hall, he's very happy to see me. It's like something out of a movie. [If other students are present] he doesn't want anyone to see him!" When his ESOL class ended, he would furtively look through the doorway, and if he saw other students in the hall, he would hang back and wait in the classroom. Margaret would explicitly dispute his shame, telling him, "You know, you're bilingual and this is great. You're so talented!"

Alexandra perceived a relationship between the taunts and the shame that many of her students experienced about their ESOL standing, explaining her darkened classroom as she added:

> These are kids that *do* take it personally. . . . They pull the shades in the windows so that no one across the courtyard can see them because everyone knows [this classroom] is ESOL. (Afternoon Tea, April 10)

## So Alexandra Drew the Blinds: Responding to Postcolonial Shame

Teachers face difficult choices as they make decisions about how to react to the marginalized status of ESOL. A simple pull of the blinds . . . a student is embarrassed about being in ESOL and seeks to hide his presence in the classroom. Even if we do not consider the historical roots of his discomfort, his shame about being in ESOL does not seem surprising, nor irrational. It in fact seems natural, naturalized. The kindhearted ESOL teacher would prefer to let the sunlight in, but compassion compels her to acquiesce. In this unremarkable moment, relations of empire are being indiscernibly reinforced. As ESOL students internalize the voices of others and the shame associated with ESOL status, they come to accept their status as inferior.

Alexandra had to make a choice. In asking that the shades be drawn and their presence in the classroom hidden, her ESOL students were acknowledging the subordinate status of ESOL within the school, but were also affirming—even perpetuating—it. Agreeing to draw the shades could potentially reinforce to students the portrayal of her classroom as shameful, as though Alexandra is concurring that receiving ESOL services is a reasonable source of embarrassment and something students should conceal. This choice potentially interrupts the teacher's attempts to transform the image of ESOL within her students' minds and within the school. However, forcing students to open the blinds could disrupt her attempts to make the ESOL classroom a safe and comfortable space. Alexandra negotiated the terrain between her ethical responsibility toward her individual students and her desire for broader transformative practice. A facile choice between agreeing and refusing to draw the blinds was not available because she was operating in soil steeped in colonial ideologies. Her choice was made further multi-layered by, *inter alia*, the complexities of ethics and caring (Noddings, 1984; Valenzuela, 1999). She cared about her students' short-term needs—the desire to believe that they were saving face (regardless of how unjust that loss of face might be), the need for a space in which to focus on their English language development without feeling exposed to ridicule. So Alexandra drew the blinds. However, as she did so she, like her fellow tea-drinkers, turned her efforts to structural changes that she could enact in order to whittle away at the potency of the segregationist model offered to their students.

What did these changes look like? Some seemed small. For instance, all four teachers made an effort to refer to their students not only as "ESOL" students or LEP students, the official institutional label to be applied to students receiving ESOL services in both school districts of the study, but as "multilingual" and "bilingual"—during the teas, when they were talking to the students themselves, and in conversations with colleagues, administrators, and parents. I, too, adopted this terminology. This was an explicit strategy that the teachers had all been exposed to throughout their coursework, one promoted by their instructors (including me) and in their class readings (cf., Toohey, 1998). Butler (1997) uses the term *linguistic vulnerability* to highlight the power of language to shape who we become and who we believe ourselves to be. She asks, "Could language injure us if we were not, in some sense, linguistic beings, beings who require language in order to be? Is our vulnerability to language a consequence of our being constituted within its terms?" (pp. 1–2). The words *multilingual* and *bilingual* had been offered by the four teachers as more positively tinged descriptors than the terms they replaced because they highlight students' resources rather than their differences (English for speakers of *other* languages), what they are not (*non*native), or resources that they might not have (*Limited* English Proficient). More recent acceptance of terms that index hybridity of identity, such as *multilingual* and *bilingual*, could be read as indicative of a shift toward ideologies that eschew conceptual purity of identities (Hardt & Negri, 2000), but the use of these terms in lieu of *ESOL* or *nonnative* has been problematized recently. Matsuda and Duran (2013) caution against an uncritical use of the word *multilingual* in this context because (1) it is inaccurate, given that many Americans are multilingual or bilingual, and indeed multilingualism has always been a part of the American landscape; (2) it normalizes monolingualism as part of the American identity and therefore solidifies an ideology of national English monolingualism; and (3) as a consequence of a monolingual ideology, it restricts opportunities for global citizenship and limits support for foreign-language education nationally. Every time we use the word *multilingual* as a proxy for the term *nonnative*, we contribute to a social imaginary of monolingual American identity and support consequent policies and practices. For instance, the "English-only movement, policies that restrict the use of non-English languages in public spaces, and restriction of bilingual education are some well-cited examples of the manifestations of an English monolingual ideology" (Matsuda & Duran, 2013, p. 40). Furthermore, if English monolingualism becomes understood to be "American," then multilingualism, particularly multilingualism that is not anchored by nativeness in English, becomes un-American. Matsuda and Duran cite several recent examples of candidates in the 2012 Republican primary race who were cast as un-American after they publicly used a language that was not English. Because John Hunstman spoke Chinese during presidential campaign events, including a debate, he was referred to as "China Jon" and the "Manchurian candidate" and questions were raised about his commitment to "American values." Mitt Romney's fluency in French prompted Newt Gingrich to air an ad entitled "The French Connection," in which Romney was mocked for his ability to speak French (Summers as cited in Matsuda & Duran, 2013).

Certainly scholars and teachers who refer to English learners as multilingual (including myself and the four teachers over the year of the study) are seeking to challenge deficit constructions of ESOL students, and the colonizing consequences are unintended. However, what is accidental on an individual level is actually not so inadvertent on a broader social scale: We operate in terrain influenced by many centuries of colonial thinking, and without a conscious and strenuous struggle against these ideologies, reproducing the status quo is almost inevitable.

The mere question of how to talk about students remains unresolved because as a profession we don't have language that does not create a division between NES and NNES or ESOL and non-ESOL simply because we have yet to discover ways to think about language identity in terms that are not absolute. Pennycook (1998) has problematized the division engrained within the language of TESOL: "Some of the central ideologies of current English Language Teaching have their origins in the cultural constructions of colonialism. The colonial constructions of Self and Other, of the 'TE' and the 'SOL' of TESOL remain in many domains of ELT" (p. 2). The U.S. federal government and the school districts of the study use an unquestioningly deficit phrase, the term *Limited English Proficiency*, to describe children receiving ESOL services. The term *ELL*, or *English language learner*, ignores the fact that we all, regardless of nativeness, continue to be English language learners all our lives (when Margaret taught me the word *tintinnabulation*, I had been speaking English all my life). The term *English as an additional language* (EAL), while taking an additive rather than subtractive (Cummins & Swain, 1986) orientation and acknowledging that English is often a third, fourth, or fifth rather than second language, nonetheless applies new language to a bifurcating and limited conceptualization of language identity.

## Obscuring Fixity: The Bridge Class

As they refined their practice, the teachers began to tentatively question institutional patterns that had become so familiar as to appear commonsensical. They began to explore the dichotomy between ESOL and non-ESOL, related to the dichotomy between NES and NNES, in other, more far-reaching ways. For instance, Alexandra found a creative way to challenge what Bhabha (1994) calls the "fixity" of categories that affirm otherness. According to Bhabha, "An important feature of colonial discourse is its dependence on the concept of 'fixity' in the ideological construction of otherness. Fixity, as the sign of cultural/historical/racial difference in the discourse of colonialism, is a paradoxical mode of representation: it connotes rigidity and an unchanging order" (p. 66). Appadurai (1996) writes of the heavy dependence of colonial identity construction on "the fixity of the boundary between metropole and colony," the metropole, or colonial motherland, in this instance being represented by English and the colony, by the students learning the language of the metropole. Keeping boundaries solid ensures that individuals stay in their place. Bhabha refers to the stereotype as "the major discursive strategy" of fixity, insistently affirming categories, but he notes that the stability of stereotypes is not as lasting as we might imagine. On one hand, they are solid and permanent, "always 'in place,' already known," but at the same time they constitute "something that must be anxiously repeated" (p. 66) in order to endure and to remain recognizable. If they are not reaffirmed repeatedly they run the danger of disintegrating and disappearing.

Fixity is one concept often summoned as characteristic of colonial discourse that has more recently been problematized by globalization scholars who see its utility dissipating and its prevalence fading. For Hardt and Negri (2000), the decentering of power brought about in the shift from imperialism to Empire has diminished the importance of fixity:

> In contrast to imperialism Empire establishes no territorial center of power and does not rely on fixed boundaries or barriers. It is a decentered and deterritorializing apparatus of rule that progressively incorporates the entire global realm within its open, expanding frontiers. (p. xii)

For Hardt and Negri, weakening boundaries between categories means that an ever-increasing population is available for domination. Because colonial discourses provide the genesis for discourses of Empire, I argue that in the classrooms of this study, the role of fixity was neither consistently in play nor steadily absent. Rather, it is more fittingly described by the words of Amy Kaplan (2002): "I would argue that [imperialism and Empire] are not as distinct as Hardt and Negri contend, but that they both are at work in varied configurations throughout the history of U.S. imperialism. The American Empire has long followed a double impetus to construct boundaries and patrol all movement across them and to break down those borders through the desire for unfettered expansion" (pp. 15–16). Kaplan wrote these words about a historical situation, but this pattern of simultaneous fixity and blurring of boundaries is evident contemporaneously. Within public schools, boundaries around ESOL usually seemed fixed, with the ultimate apparent goal of ESOL being the grooming of students to move into the category "non-ESOL." However, the ways in which this crossing played itself out in this study was a testament to the simultaneous stability and nebulousness of the boundaries around the ESOL category.

One interesting example of the various ways in which fixity works is Alexandra's bridge class. The teacher critiqued the fixity achieved through discreteness of mainstream English classes and ESOL classes from each other. Throughout the schools of the study, classes in English were offered by one department and classes in English to speakers of *other* languages were offered by another. English was conceptualized as an academic subject, ESOL as a remedial class. This trend is echoed throughout neocolonial contexts. For instance, at universities and colleges nationwide, English classes are often offered by English departments, which are often largely separate from the ESOL classes offered by intensive English programs, which are conceptualized as corrective. The separation of ESOL and English classes achieves the effect of what Bhabha (1994) refers to as anxiously repeating a stereotype. Every time members of school communities see English and ESOL separated (for instance on class schedules, in discussions at faculty meetings, and at school assemblies), the separateness of the two categories is repeated and serves as a subconscious reminder, serves to "fix" the categories. Every time a teacher is identified as an ESOL rather than English teacher, the boundary is repeated. Every mention of ESOL is a reminder of its existence as a category, underscoring its fixity.

Alexandra developed what she termed a "bridge class," a transitional class between ESOL and English classes. She had noticed that her students typically clamored to take the ESOL exit test before they were prepared for it and to move to the English classes as soon as possible (or sooner) "because of the stigma" of ESOL (Alexandra, Afternoon Tea, April 10). Although the students continued to need the support of ESOL classes (and some even acknowledged this need), the embarrassment of receiving ESOL services was so great that it consistently superseded students' desires to fulfill their language learning needs. Foucault (1977) has written of disciplinary power, which works to attract individuals to certain identities and desires, in this case the identity of a non-ESOL student.

The bridge class played an important role in blurring the distinction between ESOL and non-ESOL, NES and NNES, chipping away at the fixity of those categories and threatening the established hierarchy between them, allowing space for inter- and intragroup membership. With the establishment of the bridge class, Alexandra noted that while leaving ESOL services had traditionally been a desirable goal, the students were now happy to stay in the bridge class:

> So it's getting to be a status symbol to be in the bridge class. . . .
> The kids wanted to be out of ESOL so badly, but now that there's a bridge class, they want to stay in it. It's like a cocoon, it's like a soft transition. (Alexandra, Afternoon Tea, April 10)

The "un-fixing" effect of the bridge class was fortuitous, since the class itself was, in fact, offered by the ESOL department. The success of the strategy seemed to be connected to the students' lack of awareness about which department was responsible for the bridge class and their apparent presumption that it was at least in part the responsibility of the English Department. Although Alexandra was the bridge class teacher, the students' (mis)impression that it was an English, rather than ESOL class, added to its desirability.

Alexandra made laudable efforts to create structural changes that would increase her ESOL students' comfort level with the idea of being registered in ESOL classes. However, the sociopolitical formation of schooling canceled the effect of this policy-level transformation. Although possibilities for new, hybrid identities seem within reach, these are often empty promises. Somewhat ironically, ESOL status—like NNES status—is not an identity that can be cast aside effortlessly. Just as many adults spend years in futile pursuit of unmarked, accentless proficiency in English, students who have been in ESOL, particularly those in middle and high school ESOL classes, will always be marked as associated with the ESOL community by mere virtue of their NNES status, the institutional memory of their previous association with ESOL services, their accent, and often their race. In many ways, the promise of an exit from ESOL is a scam, just like the dodgy promises of accent-reduction language schools to help students "get rid of their accents" or the pledges of "English Villages" to return participants to their homes "speaking English like a native." Students exit from ESOL on official paper only, but remain unable to shake the ignominy of ESOL. In this way, this border functions within patterns of both imperialism and Empire—first establishing an apparently stable and difficult-to-cross boundary between ESOL and non-ESOL, then rendering the demarcation more ambiguous (and possibly even nonexistent) once ESOL students cross it or raising the hurdle to be jumped over without any warning. Schools serve as an important ideological center, spawning effective reinforcement of the hierarchy between NNES and NES, engendering "fixity," falsely promising an exit from ESOL, and then spreading these ideologies within immigrant communities and larger society.

## THE PROMISE OF HAPPINESS: NO EXIT FROM ESOL

English, it seems to me, is what Sara Ahmed (2010) has termed a "happy object." We have been taught, through a network of nodes, to associate fluency in English, and particularly "native-like English," with happiness and to therefore develop deep-seated desires for the language and all that it represents. "If happiness creates its objects," says Ahmed, "then such objects are passed around accumulating positive affective value as social goods" (p. 21). The often-endless pursuit of an exit from ESOL, then, is the *promise of happiness.* In her book bearing this title, Ahmed writes, in a voice reminiscent of Alice in Wonderland's nonsensical yet sensical wisdom, that she is interested in "how happiness is imagined as being what follows a certain kind of being. The history of happiness can be thought of as a history of associations. In wishing for happiness, we wish to be associated with happiness, which means to be associated with its associations" (p. 2). Ahmed notes that happiness is highly associated with certain objects; it turns us toward some objects over others. She uses the term *objects* not in the literal physical sense, but rather conceives of them more broadly. For instance, family is a happy object. In the broader social imaginary, family is recognized as associative of happiness, and good feelings are expected to be directed toward family. This association, she notes, plays a regulatory function: "The happy family is both a myth of happiness, of where and how happiness takes place, and a powerful legislative device, a way of distributing time, energy, and resources" (p. 45). Marriage, too, is a happy object. Ahmed explores the representation of marriage as an object of desire, in particular tracking the figure of the happy housewife, which persists in the face of a divorce rate that belies the accuracy of the image and an increased understanding of the complexity of the emotional lives of housewives. She notes, *inter alia,* the importance of this association between marriage and happiness in perpetuating the role that wives play in ensuring her husband's (particularly White men's) access to professional life and concealing the labor of other (usually minority) women. We have been taught, says Ahmed, to associate family and marriage with happiness; they have become for us "happy objects."

Globally, the pursuit of English has become synonymous with the promise of happiness. Despite some evidence that English does not always deliver on its promises (Grin, 2001; Park, 2011), we have been taught to believe that English fluency is a passe-partout, and this helps English gain value as a commodity. Park (2011), locating his work in the Korean context, describes how adults developing their English language skills in order to be competitive in the job market are discovering that what counts as "good English skills" (p. 453) is being constantly revised. He could well be speaking about Alexandra's students when he writes:

English implies a promise of social inclusion in the sense that reaching a certain goal of measurable competence in the language is assumed to provide economic and social advancement; but with closer inspection, we can see that such a promise actually works to obscure the very relations of inequality that projects of social inclusion aim to address. (pp. 445–446)

According to Ahmed, "If we think of instrumental goods as objects of happiness, important consequences follow. Things become good, or acquire their value as goods, insofar as they point towards happiness. Objects become a 'happiness' means. Or we could say they become happiness pointers, as if to follow their point would be to find happiness. . . . When we follow things, we aim for happiness, as if happiness is what you get if you reach certain points" (p. 26). Objects become happy through a self-perpetuating constellation of social formations, media representations, commodification, and larger social imaginings. English has become a happy object through multiple influences, not the least among them being the capitalist efforts of the English-teaching industry (Widin, 2010). The more that English is held up as a golden key spoken by shiny, happy people, the more desirable it becomes. Worldwide, individuals make tremendous sacrifices to achieve not only English fluency but the appearance of English nativeness. In recent years, media coverage of "wild goose families" from Korea has highlighted cases of mothers who obtain student visas and take their children to the United States for schooling in English while the fathers remain in Korea, working and providing an income, with the hope that the children will achieve native-like English proficiency. Attention has also been drawn to the popularization of various controversial types of oral surgery designed to make "native-like" pronunciation of English easier to achieve. These and related trends are picked up by both popular press and academic writers. When I started receiving emails leading me to YouTube videos depicting stadiums filled with Chinese students learning "Crazy English," repeating roared-out lines such as "I don't want to let my country down," I was intrigued. However, there is a way in which these videos and articles objectify English and romanticize passion for the language, thereby sharpening its "happiness pointer" (Ahmed, 2010). The attention drawn to these extreme cases, the intrigue surrounding them, and the sometimes voyeuristic fascination of not only the English-teaching community but the general public with English language desire can have the effect of reinscribing English's global power. Race and national identity are implicated in predictable but also unexpected ways: Media attention is often particularly focused on trends within Asian contexts that deem the craze for English excessive, underscoring an image of Asians that Christine So (2008) has described as embodying the seduction of consumption, "as agents of capitalism gone awry" (p. 8), and as contributing to discourses that locate "the Oriental outside social and familial norms by casting him as the agent and object of excess desire and addiction" (p. 11). As we think about individuals' desires to "pass" for something they are not, we must consider the role of the English teaching industry in shaping these desires and in creating and perpetuating representations of these desires. The concept of linguistic passing is explored in greater depth in Chapter 4.

In Alexandra's class, the challenge that students faced was not so much the inescapability of ESOL, although they certainly appeared to experience it as such. Rather, the static nature of the division between ESOL and non-ESOL made border crossing a difficult, nearly insurmountable feat. The opportunity for them to linger on the middle ground between the two categories did not exist because this type of in-between space simply did not exist. Monolingual habitus contributed to the impermeability of the border. If broader possibilities for multilingual identities existed, if the limits around what constitutes "mainstream" or "ESOL" were less narrow, the category ESOL would likely be less imprisoning.

Margaret, too, intuitively sensed that she should seek a way to blur boundaries between ESOL and non-ESOL. The narrowly defined disciplinary limits that have evolved over centuries in school—keeping, for instance, math content limited to math classrooms and science to science classrooms—have also established norms around which faculty care for which students. In the study schools, ESOL teachers provided care to only ESOL students, and ESOL students were primarily the responsibility of ESOL faculty. Margaret presumed greater flexibility around disciplinary boundaries. Although she was charged with teaching only ESOL students, she positioned herself as a teacher to all students in the school, not only those in ESOL. She had been troubled by her students' various attempts to hide their connections to ESOL and noted that the trend became noticeable in her 3rd-grade class and carried through the higher grades at her school. She wanted to find ways to interrupt and challenge the trend with her 3rd-graders. As part of her teaching, she kept dialogue journals with the three ESOL students in one 3rd-grade class. On days that she picked students up for ESOL, she would stand silently at the classroom door until her students saw her, gathered their pencils and books, and moved quietly to the door to walk to the ESOL classroom with her. On Fridays, when she followed an inclusion (plug-in) format, coteaching with the students' classroom teacher in their regular classroom, she would collect the journals. She responded over the weekend and returned the journals the following week. As she collected journals one Friday, the students who were not in ESOL asked her:

> "What's the journal thing?"
>> "We write letters back and forth," she explained.
>> "Can I have one?" asked a native-English-speaking boy.

"Me too?" clamored another student.

"Me too?"

"Well, I'll have to see about that," replied Margaret. (Fieldnotes, December 3)

The following semester, she told me that the dialogue journals had become a tool in her quest to elevate the status of ESOL within the 3rd-grade class:

So I have three ESOL kids in that class but 15 dialogue journals. And it's really good because I'm always wondering, how do I explain ESOL, and I usually only have one sound bite to explain ESOL [when I'm picking them up from their classroom], but now kids are asking in the journals! (Afternoon Tea, April 10)

On one occasion, as she was collecting her three ESOL students from the classroom, a visible change had come over the class. Her presence evoked great interest among other class members, and the native-English-speaking students would ask to attend ESOL, calling out "Pick me!" and "Can I come?" On one occasion, a boy who was not in ESOL tried to persuade Margaret to take him instead of one of his nonnative-English-speaking peers, asking, "Why can't we go with you? Why? Why?" and then telling her, "Mrs. Chen, Juan speaks perfect English, why is *he* in your group?" (Afternoon Tea, April 10). Margaret had become engaged with and even formed relationships with students who were not in ESOL, and they had begun to see her as someone they were free to interact with. Margaret had thrown into question the representation of the ESOL teacher as someone who is responsible for ESOL students only. Using a simple and somewhat serendipitously discovered format, Margaret had posed a challenge to the shameful status of ESOL within the 3rd grade.

The entire communities of the four schools in the study contributed to meanings of ESOL, including not only staff, faculty, and students but also parents of ESOL and non-ESOL students. As part of Margaret's challenge to dominant conceptions of ESOL, she formed relationships with non-ESOL students. She spent spare periods and lunchtimes with students who were not in ESOL who had asked to spend time with her and even agreed to exchange homework assignments with some. She used these opportunities to share information about and demystify ESOL. However, one native-English-speaking student whom she befriended was the son of the PTA president:

His mother came up to me and said, "Is something wrong with Patrick? . . . He doesn't need special services." (Afternoon Tea, April 10)

The interpretation of ESOL as deficit was so engrained within the school culture that even the PTA president perceived students needing ESOL as having something "wrong" with them.

Reagan (2005) notes that a common theme in "non-Western educational traditions" is the tendency toward "community-based and communal" learning (p. 206). Not only is specialized knowledge, including discipline-based knowledge such as ESOL pedagogy, highly valued in "Western" nations, but the investment in delineating a distinction between those who are teachers and those who are not appears to Reagan to be a primarily Western construction. One ef´fect of Margaret's strategy is a departure from the epistemologies embraced within her context, which value discipline-based educational specialists, and a movement toward a redefinition of the teaching of all children, regardless of their linguistic heritage, as the social responsibility of all teachers. As a result, the boundaries between school-constructed student categories became slightly diffused. By being willing to widen her vision and look beyond the responsibilities outlined in her contract, Margaret re-envisioned not only her role but her students' place inside the school culture.

This strategy may not, however, be realistic for every overworked teacher—in fact, it was not even realistic for Margaret once the ardor and tendency to overcommit of first-year teaching lost its glow. However, the spirit of the strategy—that is, the blurring of disciplinary boundaries and the broadening of vision to include all students as part of a larger school community—is one that prompts us to contemplate possible alternatives as we consider the ways in which institutional arrangements, disciplinary limits, and interdisciplinarity come together to shape students' and teachers' identities inside school walls.

## AN NES GAZE: POSTCOLONIAL SHAME

One of my students who's Chinese started making fun of his own language. The Korean student was asking him how to pronounce something in Chinese, and he started mimicking some of the kids who make fun of his language. I said, "Why are you making fun of your language?" . . . He's picked on an awful lot. His accent is very heavy. (Alexandra, Interview, May 21)

One question that arises in discussions of the workings of Empire concerns consent, the degree to which those who are dominated collaborate in their domination. The quote above illustrates how students under pressure to conform can become complicit in their own marginalization because to do so is the most commonsensical position they can take. The propagation of colonial ideologies cannot take place without some amount of participation, some buy-in, from those who are dominated. The Chinese student James's strong accent becomes more disgraceful because James believes that it is worthy of mockery. Mbembe (2006) draws our attention to this issue of consent or agreement in postcolonial shame: "As Gandhi himself suggested, the universalization of imperialism cannot be explained by the violence of coercion alone: it was a consequence too of the fact that many colonized people agreed, for more or less valid reasons, to become consciously complicit in a fable which they found attractive in a number of respects" (p. 1).

Although the self-directed mockery reinforces the stigma of the student James's accent, it also creates a unity with those who mock his accent, and it helps James create distance between himself and the object of his ridicule, that is, his language. However, distancing himself from his language does not necessarily detach him from his language identity. W.E.B. DuBois (1903/1989) has written about double consciousness: "this sense of always looking at one's self through the eyes of others, of measuring one's soul by the tape of a world that looks on in amused contempt and pity" (p. 9). In a world in which White and NES are normative, it is to be expected that those who do not conform to the mainstream see themselves through eyes that borrow from a White and English-speaking perspective, an NES gaze.

James appears to be accepting the identification of someone who speaks a language worth mocking, and in this way his language becomes less valuable, less worthy of retention. Ellwood (2009), in a discussion of the ways in which teachers and students take up cultural stereotypes about passivity and participation in English classes, says that "we are both 'subject to' and 'subject of' discourses" (p. 113), meaning that not only are we continually positioned and repositioned by the discourses floating around us, but we are also actively aligning ourselves with them. James appears to be buying into a negative category, but his choices make more sense when we frame them, at Ellwood's (2009) suggestion, with Butler's notion of intelligibility. According to Butler (as cited in Ellwood, 2009), we draw on the discourses around us in order to become intelligible. If we cannot achieve intelligibility, we end up in what Butler calls "an uninhabitable identification," an identity that is unintelligible and therefore makes us seem less human. Ellwood explains the acceptance of a negative identification in this way: "There is thus a certain security and a certain safety in being positioned or constructed by others, even if one is positioned negatively. This security and certainty is sought in the name of intelligibility; we seek above all to be recognizable, knowable, and intelligible" (p. 113). Unintelligibility (as socially constructed by James's peers) is ironically the most intelligible (in Butler's terms) option open to James.

One consequence of shame about language identity is heritage language loss. Numerous studies have described immigrant families who professed a commitment to heritage language maintenance, who established family practices designed to subvert language loss, and who nonetheless saw their language slip out of their grasp (Alba, Logan, Lutz, & Stults, 2002; Bayley & Schecter, 2003; Canagarajah, 2008; Nesteruk, 2010; Park, Tsai, Liu, & Lau, 2012; Portes & Rumbaut, 2001). Willinsky (1998) tells us that "languages are not lost by accident or willingly forsaken. They give way to other desires, desires to join and be heard in other conversations, which left us happy enough to leave behind the accent and inflection of our former history and geography" (p. 190).

The incident might easily be framed as relating to identity and in particular accentedness, but ideologies about race and empire play an important role in positioning James within the social terrain of the school.

## ESOL AND EFFEMINISMS: "ESOL IS NOT MACHO"

Parents of ESOL students, too, revealed deficit understandings of ESOL. In the following example, students' parents associated ESOL with dependence and weakness. Alexandra described her twin students' understandings of ESOL as antithetical to "macho," an understanding constructed collaboratively with their parents:

> *Alexandra:* Their parents came to family night and asked why their sons were still in ESOL. . . . They're very into being the men. They just want to be macho . . . well, as macho as a 12-year-old can be. They want to be tough; they want to show that they can deal with all these hard-edged classes.
> *Suhanthie:* And ESOL is not macho? ESOL is hand-holding?
> *Alexandra:* Well, it can't be anything but when there are only 15 kids in the class, and in the regular English class there are 32 or 35. (Alexandra, Interview, October 7)

In yet another commonplace example of life in ESOL classrooms, colonial ideologies undergird the interaction, albeit in ways that might be fairly indiscernible. In this instance, understanding ESOL to be "hand-holding" contradicted the "macho" nature of the identity the twins wanted to embrace. For the two students, being "men" implied functioning without the support or scaffolding related to ESOL, being "tough," and being competent to attend "hard-edged classes," so that receiving ESOL services was constructed, for them, as in conflict with being "men." The quest for an identity of adult masculinity was reinforced by their parents, who wanted to see their boys exiting from ESOL. This exchange allows a glimpse into how meanings of ESOL can be created and maintained not only for ESOL students but also within their families. This construction of a desirable male identity as tough and rejecting of support has several ancillary effects. One result is the construction of female as dependent and weak; another is the construction of ESOL as appropriate for students who lack toughness and are incapable and dependent, which is a deficit representation. Even language such as "sheltered" instruction implies a need for protection. The characterization of ESOL as feminine reinforces and is reminiscent of a colonial construction of the colonized as feminine—in particular of the West as ordered, rational, and masculine and the East or Orient as chaotic, irrational, and feminine (JanMohammed, 1985; Said, 1978). In her book *Effeminisms: The Economy of Colonial Desire*, Revathi Krishnaswamy (1998) traces the association of weakness, softness, frailty, and cowardice to colonized male subjectivities and, indeed, understands the pervasive view of the English language to be "masculine" because it is presumed to be characterized by "precision" and "clarity." In locating the effeminate in the colonized Other and the masculine in the English language, we disrupt the possibility of ownership of English by the colonized.

## RACIAL SEGREGATION AND COLONIAL SEPARATION: LANGUAGE SUPPORT VERSUS SEGREGATION

In all four schools in this study, ESOL was repeatedly and insistently constructed as separate within the school culture through the formal structure of the program but also through smaller social interactions. The tendency both to enforce the segregation of ESOL students and to underscore the actual construct of ESOL as separate played a significant role in the conceptualization of ESOL as inferior and shameful. It is important to note that simply constructing ESOL as separate alone does not automatically cause ESOL to be understood as inferior. Other school categories are conceptualized as separate without becoming inferior, for instance, gifted and talented programs. ESOL is constructed as inferior because of the inferior status of nonnative-English speakers, and constructing it as separate merely reinforces its inferiority.

Decisions about the degree to which children of different language identities in the United States should be conceptualized pedagogically as a separate group and the extent to which segregation is desirable have been made for almost as long as there have been schools in the United States. It seems to many of us natural to place beginning English learners in a separate class so that a teacher can focus on their needs without holding back students who are capable of tackling more linguistically challenging material. However, this choice is not natural but rather has become naturalized because it is made according to a logic situated within a particular sociopolitical history.

Valdés (1996) perceives the division to be deep and to have a tremendous pedagogical effect. She refers to "two separate worlds: the world of ESL and the mainstream world in which 'real' American schooling takes place" (p. 139). Historically, in the two counties of this study (and in many schools across the English-speaking world), ESOL students were placed in separate "centers" and did not interact with their English-speaking peers until they had achieved a degree of English fluency and, parenthetically, of assimilation. Segregating ESOL students from their English-speaking peers can be detrimental to all students for many reasons. It reinforces the boundaries between mainstream and ESOL students and underscores the normativity of students who are not in ESOL. It underscores difference within a system that rewards conformity. It limits ESOL students' access to English language experience. It deprives dominant group students of interaction with the knowledge and experiences of ESOL students. And it is a poorly veiled form of tracking that keeps ESOL students isolated and then legitimates the resultant hierarchy.

Segregation is, however, a complex issue when applied to ESOL. The U.S. educational system has a long history of struggling with the relationship between segregation and social justice in the lives of language-minority children. The *Brown v. Board of Education* ruling in 1954 determined that the "separate but equal" doctrine has no place in public education. As commonsensical as this ruling might appear, it had the effect of giving school systems permission to ignore the language needs of linguistic-minority students. School administrators in San Francisco claimed that by providing the *identical* education (that is, instruction in English) to all students, they were providing *equal* education (Crawford, 2000), but parents of Chinese-speaking students disputed this logic and argued that children with different needs have a right to different instruction. The U.S. Supreme Court agreed, declaring in *Lau v. Nichols* in 1974 that public schools are required to provide language accommodations to language-minority students. In 1981, a federal court ruling, *Castañeda v. Pickard*, spoke more specifically about segregation, determining that the segregation of Limited English Proficiency students was permissible only when "the benefits which would accrue to [LEP] students by remedying language barriers which impede their ability to realize their academic potential in an English language educational institution may outweigh the adverse effects of such segregation" (U.S. Department of Education, 1991). The ruling acknowledged that segregation presented potentially "adverse" consequences and placed some limitations on the unnecessary exclusion of ESOL students from mainstream classrooms.

However, some degree of focused language support is necessary for children learning English (August & Shanahan, 2008), and ignoring language needs in the name of inclusion or integration serves to marginalize them further. The trend over the past handful of years toward Structured English

Immersion (SEI) represents a move back toward the days of *Brown v. Board of Education*. SEI, often implemented as a sink-or-swim model and adopted in a minimalist form by several states so far, including California, Arizona, and Massachusetts, provides school districts with an excuse to limit language support for ESOL students, making available minimal support, typically 1 year of instruction in English usually in a segregated classroom of only ESOL students. Students are then placed in mainstream classrooms with no further language support, despite ample evidence from the educational community that they will fall behind their peers academically without further support (Thomas & Collier, 2003). Early findings of recent research in Arizona suggest that children in SEI programs in that state are at risk of school failure, delayed graduation, and disenfranchisement from schooling (Gándara & Orfield, 2012; Rios-Aguilar & Gándara, 2012). The trend toward providing less language support has a tracking effect, leaving children learning English to fall behind their classmates academically and creating a social order in which the least successful students are those in ESOL or who were previously in ESOL.

Despite federal protections, segregation under the guise of ESOL continues. In 2006, the Mexican American Legal Defense and Educational Fund (MALDEF) filed suit against the Dallas Independent School District and won a case in which they charged that the principal of Preston Hollow Elementary School, a well-resourced public school in Dallas, Texas, segregated Latino and other minority children into ESOL classes on the basis of race, regardless of language proficiency, and discriminated against them in order to provide an exclusively White environment for the White students at the school. Students of color were segregated in all subjects, including art, music, and physical education, and were assigned to classrooms in separate hallways.

ESOL classrooms offer cover for overt and covert forms of segregation. Many of the interactions described by the teachers in the study revealed members of the school community to view ESOL students as peripheral, as not wholly belonging. Some examples were blatant, for instance in the case of Mr. Berwick, a veteran 5th-grade teacher at Katie's school who held exclusionary views about the participation of immigrants in U.S. society. On the day that Katie told us about the teacher, she was the first to arrive for afternoon tea. She reached my doorstep angry and distraught. I put the kettle on and sat down on the living room floor beside her, and she related a comment that Mr. Berwick had made during a conversation with a special education teacher:

And he said, "Well, [ESOL students] don't even belong [in the United States] anyway." (Afternoon Tea, November 1st).

Later that evening, she told us about another conversation between Mr. Berwick and a 6th-grade teacher:

They were talking about having sheltered classes to transition the children into the mainstream. And Mr. Berwick's like, "Well, I've been saying that for years. Just put these kids in their separate class. Have a separate program for them!" He didn't want them mainstreamed at all, just put them in a corner somewhere and keep them very segregated. (Katie, Afternoon Tea, November 1)

In addition to flagrant examples of segregationist ideologies such as Mr. Berwick's, many covert practices contributed to the situatedness of ESOL students on the margins of school culture. Margaret was surprised to hear some teachers openly express reluctance to work with ESOL students:

> *Margaret:* They had three teams for each grade level, and all the ESOL students were on one of those teams. And the staff were like, "Next year I don't want to be on the ESOL team." From teachers who I thought were pretty open-minded!
> *Suhanthie:* Like who?
> *Margaret:* Like one teacher who was a contributor to the [new district curriculum revised to better reflect diversity].
> *Suhanthie:* Why didn't she want to be on the ESOL team?
> *Margaret:* I think it stretched her too much to try to differentiate. (Afternoon Tea, November 1)

The practice of dividing the grade into three teams in a way that places all of the ESOL students on one team establishes a structural practice that contributes to a segregationist conceptualization of students. To place all of the Black students on one team would presumably be considered racist, and it would be reasonable to expect questions about sexism if all female students were placed on one team. What are the processes and ideologies that make this setting apart of ESOL students acceptable and even common-sensical? Does it serve their best interests? The implication of the teacher's reluctance to work with ESOL students was that ESOL students demand an unreasonable or unjustifiable level of effort. Implicit in the teachers' comments was the suggestion that ESOL students require but do not deserve special attention, which makes a deafening statement about who truly has a right to quality education, and whom the schools are for. This representation of schooling contributes to the construction of an underclass, in this case, one that includes ESOL students. Her comment also raises the issue of resources and preparation. If teacher education assumes a "typical" native-English-speaking student and prepares future teachers to engage with this type of student only, mainstream teachers will believe themselves underequipped to work intensively with ELLs. Beginning teachers typically feel that they have not been adequately prepared "and seldom choose to teach in multicultural schools, especially those with high rates of poverty" (Valli & Rennert-Ariev, 2000, p. 15). When teachers are inadequately prepared to meet the special needs of second language speakers, they are naturally reluctant to work with them.

## Epistemologies of ESOL: National Curricula

The school formation of ESOL shapes the processes through which knowledge is produced, defined, and valued. Part of being an ESOL teacher was being critically mindful of the periphery-center relationship that ESOL departments have with the larger school culture. This relationship reflects the periphery-center relationship between colonizing and imperializing countries, and an explicit awareness of the power of that hierarchy can forearm ESOL teachers to notice and even challenge inequitable institutional arrangements. For instance, the teachers made connections between their discomfort with the notion of a standardized national ESOL curriculum and the potential marginalization of students who do not represent the hypothetical center, in particular, ESOL students. Katie told us of a discussion with an ESOL colleague, Tracy, who believed that a national ESOL curriculum was essential to maintaining "high standards" for learning.

> *Katie:* Tracy was saying that ESOL students all need to know the same things around the country, I guess about the language. . . . She was saying she wanted every ESOL student to know what their goals were and have [the same] textbook.
> *Margaret:* Like a national curriculum?
> *Katie:* Like a national curriculum. (Afternoon Tea, June 19)

Alexandra perceived a national curriculum to stand in opposition to attending to the diverse needs of ESOL students:

> If you're talking about standards in which everyone comes out speaking the same language at the end, I think that's an impossible idea for ESOL. I know I couldn't teach under those circumstances. I don't think neighborhood schools are the same or have the same needs. (Afternoon Tea, June 19)

Alexandra believed that no one textbook could hold sufficient personal relevance for every student in every class in the country. The idea of a standardized curriculum or textbook is a complex one for ESOL students. Although it can cue teachers and students into the types of skills and knowledge that are most valued and help them to focus on these, a national curriculum that is aimed at all students has the potential to treat students monolithically and in doing so contributes to the construction of a norm, "the implicit referent, that is, the yardstick by which to encode and represent cultural Others" (Mohanty, 1991, p. 55). In order to include all students and in seeking to address the elements that the majority of students have in common, a national curriculum cannot help but have a centralizing effect on multiple levels. The standardizing, homogenizing effect of a national curriculum raises a number of concerns. First, it can establish differential valuing of the resources children bring to school and consequently place children's potential academic achievement on inequitable footing. Second, it is almost impossible to make content equally relevant for all individuals in the multiplicity of identities represented in school populations. Those who are left out are most frequently those not represented by the majority. Third, it can lead to the reproduction of epistemological norms in schools. For instance, some teachers have a tendency to place an emphasis on collaborative learning and others on more individualistic pedagogies. Some teachers tend to prepare English students for vocations and others for a broader humanities-based education. Some teachers focus on mastering traditional writing forms, while others focus on creativity. A national curriculum has the potential to coax all teachers in the same direction, resulting in less epistemological diversity and the potential loss of ways of thinking that are included less frequently in the national curriculum.

Apple (1999) has noted that curriculum functions to support what he terms a "selective tradition"—that is, the practice of only select knowledge becoming official knowledge. Sleeter (2005) uses the rather apt word *paradoxical* to describe the desire of educators to address an equity issue when the tools available to help us understand why the equity issue (the devaluing of knowledge associated with particular groups) exists in the first place are limited by the processes that created the inequity. Our capacity to understand why some knowledge is valued over other knowledge is shaped invisibly within the current-day context by the historical processes of colonization, which have taught us to value ways of thinking that were associated with colonizers. Wayne Au (2009), in his call to use multicultural education in the pursuit of decolonization of curricula, tells us that "multicultural education is rooted in an antiracist struggle over whose knowledge and experiences should be included in the curriculum" (p. 254). He himself was affected by the experience of having his childhood memories and his father's stories negated by his 9th-grade Honors World History teacher. He offered the following metaphor for the class he was a student in: "We were always on the outside looking in, and he and the textbooks were the sole authority" (p. 254). The teachers' engagement in this paradox is emblematic of a struggle that teachers all over the country face every day: Do we want all children to learn the same thing? If so, how do we decide what that same thing is? Is our task simply to determine what should be covered or is standardization itself not desirable? If we move away from standardization, how do we decide who learns what? How do we ensure that all children have equal access to legitimated knowledge without dispatching assimilatory and homogenizing forces?

Christine Sleeter (2005) has offered four central questions for educators to consider as they grapple with potentially homogenizing effects of curriculum:

1. What purposes should the curriculum serve?
2. How should student knowledge be selected, who decides what knowledge is most worth teaching and learning, and what is the relationship between those in the classroom and the knowledge selection process?"
3. What is the nature of students and the learning process and how does it suggest organizing learning experiences and relationships?
4. How should curriculum be evaluated? How should learning be evaluated? To whom is curriculum evaluation accountable? (p. 8)

These guidelines can support teachers and curriculum developers as they consider the processes of knowledge valuation.

In another example of the devaluing of ESOL student knowledge, Alexandra was outraged at school administrators' implication that ESOL students did not have valuable knowledge to share:

> This general call went out asking teachers for names of students they felt could tutor. I sent a list of ESOL kids. And they were like, what can *they* tutor? I was like, they can tutor ESOL and they can tutor their native language. (Alexandra, Conversation, January 24)

Although students were not deliberately being left out, through each of these interactions, their knowledge and participation in the school culture was becoming constructed as valueless.

Margaret noted that ESOL students were assumed to be ineligible for gifted and talented programs. She sought to challenge institutional structures that did not serve her students well:

> We were given a list identifying the GT (gifted and talented) kids. . . . This one teacher was saying, "Can you believe Esmeralda [an ESOL student] is GT? She can't even read and write." So I went down to the chairperson of the committee and asked her to explain all of this data to me. And I thought, "Hmmm. I wonder how you get on the GT committee. This sounds like a committee I should be on." And I asked the chairperson, "Can I be on this committee?" and she said, "Yes." (Margaret, Afternoon Tea, March 21)

Through a structural analysis of access, Margaret was able to challenge the assumed mutual exclusivity of the school categories ESOL and GT. The underrepresentation of ESOL students in magnet and GT programs is no revelation—a well-worn groove runs from ESOL classrooms to those of the less "academic" subjects (Valdés, 1996; Valenzuela, 1999), but Margaret's sociological scrutiny of systemic barriers to the GT program is, for her, a way to make a difference for not only one child but on a policy level.

## Marginalizing Practices: Grading, Representing, Participating

Grading policies, too, are connected to the participation of ESOL students in the broader school culture, to inclusion and exclusion. Alexandra noted that classroom teachers' popular practice of withholding a grade for ESOL students inhibited their motivation. Furthermore, because it establishes separate expectations and requirements for the ESOL students, it sets them apart from the other students and can amount to a subtle policy of exclusion:

> A lot of teachers there have a habit of giving the ESOL kids no grade. I think that undercuts their desire to progress, their self-esteem in the classroom, their feeling of "why should I bother?" (Phone conversation, January 26)

Similarly, teachers sometimes made fewer or no comments on ESOL students' work compared with that of other students':

> They get things back with no comments because the teacher thinks, "If I write something they're not going to understand it." (Phone conversation, January 26)

Neglecting to assign a grade to ESOL students' work can be interpreted as a reasonable accommodation, an attempt at social justice, because teachers may hesitate to measure ESOL students by the same standards as their peers. However, the practice might also appear as dismissive and as signaling to students that their work doesn't matter. Furthermore, the stark disparity between expectations for ESOL students and for the rest of the school population contributes to the construction of ESOL identity as Other. Alexandra also noticed that some ESOL students were receiving high grades for sitting silently in class. Her classroom teachers would tell Alexandra, "Oh, she's very good; she just sits there and does her work" (Phone conversation, January 26). Alexandra was dubious: "Is she really doing her work, is my question, or is she just not being a problem in class?" Rewarding ESOL students for being silent in class discourages their participation (which frequently influences their language development) and encourages them to remain on the margins of the class, constructing an outsider identity and diminishing the degree to which they belong to the classroom community. Furthermore, it reinforces colonial subjectivities by contributing to the construction of an identity similar to the identity often attributed to NNES adults: quiet, compliant, obedient, and childlike. It is the image of the colonized, the obedient servant ready to take orders, lacking in leadership qualities. Without realizing it, participants in school culture were adopting practices that underscored the "colonial shadow" (Vandrick, 2002) of ESOL. Teachers of linguistic-minority students face a tension. It might be unfair to grade them in the same way as their English-speaking peers, but it is simultaneously unfair to keep them separate. The tension points to the problematic nature of the traditional grading systems revered in public schools. The most popular grading systems establish one global standard, are embedded in a competitive hierarchy, assume uniformity of experience, and encourage homogeneity in learning. They discourage teachers from leaving room for complexity of experience instead of always trying to simplify it so that such experience can be represented on a grade scale or by a percentile score. However, the issue is even more complex: While Alexandra argued against uniform pedagogy as seen in a national curriculum and high-stakes testing, she would still like to see her students held to the same high standards as their NES peers. Parallel standards might compel classroom teachers to recognize their responsibility to teach their students rather than having them sit separately in a corner of the classroom playing on the computer or completing worksheets.

## Participation in Class

Another way in which racial and colonial segregation made itself present was in patterns of classroom participation. Katie noted the attempts of some classroom teachers to bar ESOL students from entering into the classroom conversation until their rate of speech was sufficiently fluent to ensure that their participation would not slow down the pace of instruction:

> Some teachers will put them in a corner and say, "Okay I'm not going to let you participate until you can learn enough English to participate." (Afternoon Tea, January 24)

She cited teachers who assigned new ESOL students worksheets to complete alone, who deliberately seated them with students they could not speak with, and who directed them to play alone on computers during class. The irony of these tactics is that it is almost impossible to acquire a language if one is prevented from using it in authentic, meaningful interaction. These strategies keep ESOL students isolated and their focus diverted from their classroom peers. It closes them off from the language learning that could result from their interaction with other speakers of English, and it similarly deprives the other students in the class from ESOL students' perspectives and their ability to influence the shape of the class's learning.

Linguicide is understood to be the deliberate killing of a language (Hassanpour, 2000). However, a distinction should be made between, on one hand, formal and intentional state control of language and, on the other, governmentality (Foucault as cited in Pennycook, 2002), or the production of discursive regimes through linguistic, cultural, and educational practices. Although U.S. public schools are not intentional actors seeking to extinguish minority languages, some practices and procedures that have been naturalized within the schools of the study keep ESOL students out of the conversation. Van Dijk (2000) offers a definition of linguicism that helps us to see the trajectory from linguicism to linguicide: "Linguicism not only involves being barred from using your own language, but also being excluded from or marginalized in communicative events" (p. 73). Schooling practices that ensure that ESOL students' talk does not count exclude them from access to public discourse and ensure that NNESs are not heard.

## Invisibility of ESOL Students in School Metanarrative

The teachers were particularly in tune to the susceptibility of their students to the ways they were represented in the larger social imaginary. Alexandra noted that one of the textbooks she was required to use was so outdated that some of the students' countries of origin did not appear in it. She had multiple reasons to clamor for newer teaching materials, one being the importance of students being able to see their countries on a map:

> I have a Ukrainian student now. We couldn't even find the outline of his country on the map! So I asked the [appropriate staff member] for a new map. I mean, I have students whose relatives have died over the establishment of these countries! This man said, "The countries change every day, just change it on the map with a marker." . . . I wanted to say, "Don't you see how important it is to see your own country? Are you crazy? You're really stupid." I wanted him to understand why I need a new map. . . . I said, "That's a really interesting response" and I ducked into the bathroom to get a hold of myself. (Alexandra, Interview, January 26)

Alexandra's solution was to find an up-to-date map in a *Newsweek* magazine and provide photocopies to all of her students in an attempt to underscore the legitimacy of their national identities.

In another example of subtractive schooling (Valenzuela, 1999), the administrators at Alexandra's school encouraged her to provide her students with only a cursory sweep of the material that native-English-speaking students would be covering and to privilege material that would be included on standardized tests:

> They were like, "You don't even need to bother with the [state] curriculum, just teach them map skills." . . . I was like, why do I have to teach them map skills, why can't I teach them the higher-order skills? (Alexandria, Interview, January 24)

Although the intention was, presumably, not to disadvantage ESOL students by making only a perfunctory education available to them, to teach them only what they knew would be included on the standardized test, the effect of this unofficial policy would have been to underscore the message that ESOL students either do not deserve or are incapable of benefiting from the same quality and depth of education as their native-English-speaking peers.

The concept of "dependency theory" put forth by Wallerstein et al. (1982) can help us to connect the classroom to a broader concept. Dependency theory explains that the world economy is based on a division of labor between a technologically developed center and a poorer periphery, which has ensured the dependence of poorer countries on imperialist countries. Wallerstein extends this theory beyond economics to ideology. Norms are dependent on non-norms because without something to compare a norm to, a norm has lost its centrality and ceases to be. One way to ensure the continued division between non-ESOL as normative and ESOL as peripheral is to minimize the level of education that ESOL students receive (in this case, with ostensibly commonsense arguments that underscore ESOL students' supposed deficiencies), preparing them for the lowest rungs of the socio-economic structure and thus ensuring that immigrant children, especially ethnic and linguistic-minority children, remain on the margins of the U.S. educational system and, eventually, U.S. society.

## CONCLUSION: ESOL AS A SITE OF EMPIRE

In this chapter, I critically examined the relationship between modern-day institutional practices embedded within the teaching of English in K–12 schools and the broader historical project of empire, including its contemporary manifestations. This examination drew attention to a number of questions that remain unresolved for ESOL practitioners. First, what role can educational professionals play in guiding the ways in which ESOL as a school category is shaped by broader colonial, racial, and language ideologies, particularly those surrounding nativeness, multilingualism, and monolingualism? Second, what disciplinary arrangements and rearrangements might contribute to a transformation of the meanings of English and English-speaker identity within school walls and within the broader social imaginary? A third question relates to the tension between providing language-specific support and reifying the category of ESOL and the possibilities offered by a movement away from segregation. And a final question that has surfaced through our discussion is about the epistemologies of ESOL, the ways in which knowledge is conceptualized within ESOL classrooms.

In Chapter 6, "Toward a Provincialized English," I discuss these questions alongside, and necessarily intertwined with, those raised in Chapter 4 and Chapter 5. In Chapter 4, I extend the exploration of empire by examining the ways in which it shapes and is shaped by race.

## Reflection Questions

1. What language do I use to describe my students? ESOL? English as a Second Language (ESL)? English as an Additional Language (EAL)? English Language Learner (ELL)? Limited English Proficient (LEP)? Multilingual? Nonnative-English Speaker (NNES)? What are the advantages of and problems with each of these terms?
2. What structural arrangements of ESOL have I observed or participated in? At my institution, what is the relationship between English education for ESOL students and English education for students who are not receiving ESOL services? Are English and ESOL administered as separate departments? Do structural arrangements underscore a division? When does separating students allow for specialized language support and when does it constitute unnecessary segregation?
3. Do the ESOL students I have encountered demonstrate pride, shame, or another emotion about their association with ESOL?
4. What examples or models do I provide for my students in ESOL? Is sounding "native-like" a goal? Under what circumstances do I use the terms *native* and *nonnative* with my students?
5. Do I have a policy surrounding the use of students' first languages in the classroom?
6. Is there a consistent body of knowledge that all ESOL students across a country (such as the United States) should be taught?
7. How should teachers grade students in ESOL? Should the same grading practices be applied to ESOL students as to their non-ESOL peers?

# CHAPTER 4

# English,
# Antiracist Pedagogies,
# and Multiculturalism

## ESOL AS RACIALLY NEUTRAL

Within the United States, most ESOL teachers identify as White, while most ESOL students are coded as racial minorities and are situated within a history in which English has most often been transmitted from Whites to minorities within an inequitable power dynamic. In the modern context, the dialectic is reproduced, with English most typically taking up the role of a more valuable language being passed on to a speaker of a less powerful language. The social and educational practices that have evolved within this history have therefore shaped the school category of ESOL into a deeply ideological category that is far from race-neutral. This book makes the case that the mere act of teaching ESOL reproduces racism. This is, of course, not to say that English should not be taught as an additional language, but rather that it should be neither taught nor learned without a consciousness of the racialized effects of its acquisition.

In this chapter, I first discuss the intricate and intriguing ways in which silences around race and its connectedness to linguistic identity are sustained within school discourses, curricula, texts, and pedagogical practices, including what I term *palliated difference*. This chapter also discusses the relationships between silences around race and silences around linguistic-minority status. I go on to connect this work to broader social discourses and representations that connect ESOL and race, including negotiations of stereotypes and expectations. In the third section, at the suggestion of Todd Ruecker (2011), I draw on the literature on race passing to shed light on the processes of linguistic passing and in particular on ways in which the mere possibility of passing destabilizes categories that were previously unquestioned. I conclude this chapter by focusing on the centrality of teachers' identities within ESOL classrooms.

As I show in this chapter, school and classroom practices provide the terrain in which meanings of identities are dynamically and continuously constructed and negotiated. Neither race nor linguistic-minority status are clear-cut or absolutely defined categories. These categories, like all dimensions of difference, evolve in relationship to other categories, and their meanings are both subjective and negotiable. As such, ESOL practitioners cannot afford to pretend that the school category *ESOL* is a racially neutral site of language learning. In recent years, and particularly with the election of the country's first racial minority president, the subject of race—one that has historically been difficult to talk about in direct terms—has become more widely discussed in ELT classrooms and within broader public discourses, but these exchanges have been difficult to engage in without falling into the trap of power-evasion. Dominant discourses surrounding race, which Bonilla-Silva (2013) calls *colorblind racism* and Kubota (2004) calls *liberal multicultural discourses*, represent ESOL as race-neutral and discourage open discussions about issues of race and inequality.

Many of the recent conversations about global flows (Pennycook, 2007), translanguaging (Blackledge & Creese, 2010), hybrid and translinguistic practices, fluidity, transnationalism, multiplicity of identities, and related critical language theories of globalization have highlighted the exciting new possibilities offered by a new, rapidly changing global order, by increased interconnectedness among nations and people. The deservedly optimistic tone of these conversations, however, can sometimes overshadow the foundational role played by racism in the construction of the TESOL profession and a need for a deep critical analysis of race within ELT. Schueller (2009) has in fact drawn our attention to ways in which recent work on globalization can sometimes serve to cloak the relevance of race and racism in understandings of inequitable distribution of capital.

Many changing language practices offer hope for a more racially equitable future. Some theorists explore the spread of hip-hop, a racialized performance genre; Pennycook and Mitchell (2009) write about hip-hop's ability to draw local traditions into and thus reinvent global cultural forms, while Alim (2009) has associated hip-hop culture, including its language practices, with decentralized authority and the privileging of local epistemologies. Other theorists have written about porous boundaries between languages. Rampton (1999) sees the language-crossing practices of high schoolers as representative of a loosening of boundaries of inclusion and exclusion, helping to redefine notions of belonging in racial categories and beyond. Ibrahim (2009) writes of *métissage*, which he describes as "the transmutation between two or more cultural components with the unconscious goal of creating a third cultural entity" (Glissant as cited in Ibrahim, 2009, p. 232). However, particular attention needs to be paid to the ways in which different contexts implicate differential power dynamics within these practices of hybridity and fluidity. Ibrahim, for instance, notes that "métissage assumes two or more cultural entities that are equally valorized; hence it is an egalitarian hybridity, where ambiguity, multiplicity, fragmentation, and plurality become the new landscape" (p. 233). While a wider range of racialized language practices and identities are becoming more available in informal contexts, such as community gathering places, homes, shopping malls, and even school playgrounds, this is less true for more-formal contexts such as classrooms, many work environments, government sites, and other localities that allow particular access to power. May (2012) has noted that in many diglossic situations, in which two languages or varieties are broadly used—such as, in the schools of the study, "Standard" English and African American English, or "Standard English" and "World Englishes"—minority languages tend to be confined to low-status situations, their use and scope being therefore limited. He emphasizes the "recursive" influence of differential recognition of languages, which publicly and repeatedly underscores the hierarchy between the two languages (or varieties) every time they are used. Because minority languages are often associated with racial minority speakers and dominant languages with White speakers, the ultimate effect of this hierarchy is the shaping of "ethnicity's complex and ambiguous relationship to modernity" (May, 2012, p. 12)—the juxtaposition of ethnicity (represented by the minority language or variety) and the nation-state (represented by the legitimated dominant language or variety), with ethnic minority groups being identified with primitivism and particularism and the nation-state with modernity and universalism. Ethnic minority groups, asserts May, then become constructed as atavistic and regressive and their incorporation into the nation-state as incomplete. Because all languages, but especially English, carry racialized meanings, attitudes toward languages are usually representative of racial attitudes. May in fact notes that contempt toward languages spoken by racial minorities has "more to do with the (minority) ethnicities with which they are historically associated than with the languages themselves" (p. 20).

Optimism about new hybrid-language practices therefore needs to be tempered by a consciousness of the role being played by race in our constructions. There is a delicate balance to be achieved between highlighting exciting cultural developments and shrouding or discounting the racism embedded in our everyday discursive and school-based practices. How do evolving language practices change English? How does the global spread of English shape the language's racial identity? If it is used and even owned by a more racially diverse population, does it somehow become more racially neutral, and if not, why not? What forces serve to thwart a more widespread global ownership of English?

In this chapter, I focus on the racialization of the English language in general and English language teaching specifically, exploring the ways in which school and classroom practices shape meanings of racial formations and provide terrain for the dynamic and continuous construction and renegotiation of racialized identities. This chapter also takes a hard look at the significance of the four teachers' own racial identities in their process of negotiating the inherent racialization of ESOL in their language teaching contexts, as they examined the implications of their own privileged status as native speakers of Standard English, a raced category (Motha, 2006c), within an institutional culture that underscored the supremacy of both Whiteness (Howard, 1999) and native-speaker status (Motha, 2006a).

## RACIAL SILENCES

For all four teachers of the study, the dominant discourses surrounding race in their teaching contexts supported silences about racial identity, which posed a challenge to their attempts to craft antiracist pedagogy. Beyond an examination of the racialization of TESOL practice, this chapter will focus in on the ways in which issues of race become invisible in the terrain of ELT and will take up questions about the role of colorblind and postracial ideologies and liberal multiculturalism in unwittingly creating a smoke screen for inequality.

In many teacher preparation and professional development contexts, race is considered to be of only incidental relevance to second language learning (Kubota, 2004), with the topic of race often being overshadowed or even concealed by other dimensions of difference with which race intersects in complex ways, most notably culture, economics, ability, class, and linguistic-minority status. Race is further camouflaged by widespread liberal multiculturalist discourses (Kubota, 2004) that embrace a colorblind perspective, thus obscuring racial inequities and hierarchies (Bonilla-Silva, 2013) and silencing attempts at discussions of race (Dei et al., 2004; Hill, 2008).

The following example illustrates the difficulties of engagement in open conversations about race. It illustrates ways in which race can remain peripheral in a conversation that is largely about race, the ease with which a speaker can unintentionally leave him or herself open to charges of racism, and the pressure to remain silent about issues of race. Margaret told us about a professional development workshop in which a discussion about race came up:

> The whole theme was in 4th grade there are boys who happen to be Black, with a few Latino boys, and they're misbehaving. . . . It's very interesting. One teacher stood up . . . it is true that these boys are having a hard time in school . . . there is this group of boys . . . who have a lot of anger in them and who are in the principal's office a lot . . . and people were trying to dance around it, they kept trying to qualify it, "They happen to be African American," and then people kept saying, "Don't forget that there's also Julio and there's also . . ."

and then they kept bringing in this one boy who has red hair to make it sound like it wasn't, you know, a racial definition of this whole thing . . . and then this one teacher, she stood up and she said, "Why is this happening? I want tools to reach these kids" and this one teacher, she's been teaching about 5 years, she stood up, a young woman, and . . . she said, "I've been teaching a lot of African American kids and what I think you need to realize is a lot these kids, at home, the kind of discipline that's used is yelling; they're yelled at and they often don't have a dad or any male figure in their life" and she did a long list of things. And then this older African American woman, you could see that she just couldn't take it anymore, she just stood up and she said:

"Well, I can tell you, when I grew up, I only had to hear 'no' once. I don't know what's going on in these classrooms, but I only had to hear 'no' once and that was it."

And then other teachers, other African American teachers, said, "Yes, me too, we knew what to do in our house, the confusion came in school." It was very interesting, she said, "Something's happening in school."

But that couldn't be the focus, people were like, "Well, anyway, these boys, what can we do about these boys?" (Afternoon Tea, March 21)

This is another example of an everyday conversation in schools. If you've spent much time within school walls, in professional development settings, or in teacher education classes, you may have heard some version of it. Much can be made of the complicated racial dynamics being constructed within Margaret's story, but for now I focus on only one facet, the embedded understanding within this story that there is reason to either avoid mentioning race or, if it is permitted to enter the conversation, to assert that race is irrelevant.

Silences around race are not new. James Banks (2006) tells of the day that the U.S. Supreme Court rendered a decision in *Brown v. Board of Education*, deeming separate-but-equal segregated schooling unconstitutional. Banks was a 7th-grade student in Arkansas on that day, May 17, 1954. He uses the term *conspiracy of silence* to describe his observations: "My most powerful memory of the Brown decision is that I have no memory of it being rendered or mentioned by my parents, teachers, or preachers" (p. 37). There is something a little different about contemporary silences around race. An unspoken ban on mentioning race, or at least on recognizing its salience, compelled the teachers within the conversation above to seek out ways of discounting race when they spoke about a group of mostly racial minority boys. This was achieved with the disclaimer that the boys "happen to be" Black and some of them Latinos, as if to say that they are indeed Black and Latino, but only incidentally so—that is, that their race was irrelevant. Of course, their race was not irrelevant, but the embeddedness of the conversation within colorblind discursive conventions compelled the teachers to find ways of downplaying race. In the current climate of a new recognition that race has a limited biological-scientific basis (Adelman, 2003), it becomes difficult to talk about race if we consider race to be nonexistent. However, the flaw in this logic is that race is not nonexistent and is in fact very real with material consequences. That race is a social rather than biological reality does not mean that it is not, nonetheless, a reality.

Hardt and Negri (2000) touch upon the ways in which this pressure to minimize or ignore differences supports the workings of Empire. "Setting aside differences means, in effect, taking away the potential of the various constituent subjectivities," they tell us, which creates a "public space of power neutrality" (p. 198). Ignoring differences allows us to construct a narrative of power neutrality, in which everyone is assumed to have received equal treatment and opportunity. They describe the "magnanimous, liberal face of Empire":

> All are welcome within its boundaries, regardless of race, creed, color, gender, sexual orientation, and so forth. In its inclusionary moment Empire is blind to differences; it is absolutely indifferent in its acceptance. It achieves universal inclusion by setting aside differences that are inflexible or unmanageable and thus might give rise to social conflict. Setting aside differences requires us to regard differences as inessential or relative and imagine a situation not in which they do not exist but rather in which we are ignorant of them. (p. 198)

The example related by Margaret reveals a reluctance to talk explicitly about race in the inservice context without inserting small repudiations throughout in order to avoid creating the impression of grouping individuals according to race—for instance, grouping the minority boys together because of their race. Rather, we want to be taken to be grouping them according to their similar behavior, regardless of race, perhaps even implying that their race has no bearing on their behavior. The mention of the red-haired, presumably White, boy seemed to Margaret to be offered as further evidence of not singling out the Black and Latino boys, as substantiation of colorblindness.

These discourses, referred to by Eduardo Bonilla-Silva (2013) as "colorblind" discourses and by Melanie Bush (2011) as "post-racial discourses" are seductive to everyone involved. For those in dominant groups who might be grappling with the guilt of unearned (and often unacknowledged) privilege, colorblind and postrace discourses provide an avenue for denial. Dei, Karumanchery, and Karumanchery-Luik (2004) offer this explanation: "For the privileged to accept the scope and stature of oppression, they would have to accept their complicity in that condition. As a defense mechanism, it becomes necessary not simply to deny the reality of oppression, but to see that reality from a perspective that is less personally injurious" (pp. 14–15). How does one proceed through life with an awareness that one is living alongside a people who were enslaved, robbed, raped, conquered, or murdered by members of the group you identify with and belong to? One way is to seek erasure of the relevance of these group identities and to claim that racial categories no longer carry meaning nor produce material consequences, as they did in the past. This point was most firmly brought home for me by a White female teacher candidate in my Embracing Diversity in Classroom Communities class a decade ago, whose words still return to me regularly to echo in my ears: "Slavery was 150 years ago. How many years go by before you drop it?" Her words exemplify for me the widespread social belief that the legacy of U.S. slavery has now been overcome. However, the words of Gavin Stevens, a lawyer in Faulkner's *Requiem for a Nun*, warn us, "The past isn't dead. It isn't even past." Bush (2011) notes that "most Whites believe we have achieved racial equality in the United States, while social and economic measures indicate otherwise" (p. 4). The consequences of centuries of historical domination, violence, and global economic exploitation continue to be experienced today, and furthermore, modern-day racism and neocolonialism pervade contemporary life, most pressingly in schools. But the desire to deny these consequences is persistent. Postracial and colorblind ideologies are closely related (Joseph, 2013). Bonilla-Silva (2013) notes that racism is perpetuated by an ideology in which individuals claim that they "don't see any color, just people" (p. 1) despite the fact that "racial considerations shade almost everything in America. Blacks and dark-skinned racial minorities lag well behind whites in virtually every area of social life" (pp. 1–2). Furthermore, although both Bush and Bonilla-Silva discuss ways in which colorblind and postrace discourses are appealing to Whites, I maintain that they can be infinitely alluring for individuals from minority groups, too, and therefore serve as a powerful tool in indoctrinating minorities into self-condemnation. As a person of color, I want to believe that if I work hard I will be rewarded regardless of my skin color, that any failures I experience result from my own absence of effort. Myths of meritocracy are difficult to relinquish because they offer a sense of agency and control over one's destiny, artificial though it might be.

The young woman teacher in Margaret's story, whom Margaret later told me was White—let's call her Julie—was seeking a solution and making an attempt to talk openly about the root of the problem. She recognized on some level that race was not irrelevant and offered a cultural mismatch explanation, seemingly trying to apply some sort of framework of culturally responsive pedagogy (Gay, 2010), which relies on the assumption that children will learn more effectively if teaching is filtered through the lens of their own cultural experiences. Unfortunately, what she ultimately offered could be characterized as a cultural-deficiency explanation. As ELT professionals, we might all benefit from support in making sense of the competing representations of various racial categories we encounter throughout our professional and personal lives, but this support is elusive when the pressure to avoid talking about the effects of race is so intense. The cultural-mismatch narratives Julie evoked emanate directly from colonial narratives, from a long tradition of talking about racial minorities in terms of deficit group identities, of attempting to solidify the borders between "us" and "them." As Julie is articulating meanings of the Black family in America (as ruptured and incomplete) and of particular types of discipline (yelling), she is also producing through contrast what is not-Black and therefore normative, which is a type of discipline that is not-yelling (read as more civilized) and a nuclear family structure that meets heteronormative expectations. Julie did not invent from nowhere these images of Black male children; she was appropriating representations and stereotypes that surround us all, through media, our textbooks, subtly inserted into class materials, and surfacing often invisibly in professional and informal conversations, and she is offering an explanation that makes sense to her within the frames and discourses to which she has had access. These discourses follow a well-traveled trail that leads to what Bonilla-Silva (2013) calls "racism without racists," the production or perpetuation of harmful racial stereotypes in spite of intentions that are not racist.

The temptation to label Julie or her comments racist has the effect of deflecting the attention of participants in racially charged conversations from deconstructing patterns of racism to avoiding the label "racist," often by simply remaining silent. Wildman and Davis (1996) have remarked that "calling someone racist individualizes the behavior, ignoring the larger system within which the person is situated. To label an individual a racist conceals that racism can only occur where it is culturally, socially, and legally supported. It lays the blame on the individual rather than the forces that have shaped that individual and the society that the individual inhabits. For white people this means that they know they do not want to be labeled racist. They become concerned with how to avoid that label, rather than worrying about systematic racism and how to change it" (p. 573).

The older African American woman's response to Julie's comments seems to imply that the blame ought not to be placed solely on Black children, but rather that educators should look to what is happening in schools to produce the reactions and behaviors in question. Many minority children experience a sense of disenfranchisement from schools (Hughes, Newkirk, & Stenhjem, 2010). Adults in schools often perceive minority boys' conduct in a more seriously negative light; perceive them to be unsalvageable, expendable, or inevitably bound for incarceration; and punish them more severely than when the same patterns are evident in, say, girls or White boys (Ferguson, 2000). However, Margaret seems to perceive the other teachers in the conversation as unwilling or unable to permit their focus to be turned toward the school's role in creating the misbehavior, so that the responsibility for the problem remained with the boys and their families.

The two White characters in the story, Julie and the red-haired boy, are not identified racially, part of a prevalent practice of unconsciously constructing Whiteness as neutral, so widespread as to be almost universal in mainstream conversations across the United States, including those conversations among us tea-drinkers. Indeed, it occurred to me only after the tea-drinkers had left my family room, making their separate ways into the darkness later that night, to ask Margaret about Julie's race. I had assumed her to be White, but it was only upon reviewing the recording that I realized that her race hadn't been mentioned. In his book *White*, Richard Dyer (1997) tells us that "to apply the color white to white people is to ascribe a visible property to a group that thrives on invisibility " (p. 42).

## Palliated Difference: Another Form of Racial Silence

We similarly see colorblind and postrace discourses present within the construction of multicultural literature surrounding students. In spite of the complex diversity that characterized their ESOL students, the ESOL teachers in this study found that oversimplified stereotypes of ESOL students played an influential role in their teaching lives. For instance, Katie questioned whether some of the materials that the district touted as multicultural were masking abstruse messages about racial and ethnic norms:

> I really want to make [my classroom library] a true multicultural
> library, but a lot of the multicultural books are not about their culture.
> It's about a person who looks different in American culture. Some
> books, the people in it may be from another culture or may have
> the appearance of another culture, but the lesson or the storyline or
> whatever is American culture. Like that book, *Jamaica's Find*, they
> classify that as multicultural. It's about this little girl who comes to
> a new school. She makes a friend, she does some things, it's about
> an American child. Her name is Jamaica and she's Black. It's nothing
> about Black culture, but it's classified as multicultural. I mean, they're
> stories about American people, but they're basically just painting
> them. (Afternoon Tea, November 1)

Producers of children's literature walk an uncomfortable line between cultural essentializing and whitewashing. It is difficult to create materials that offer a representation of a particular culture—for instance, in the example above "Black culture"—without defining the culture and in doing so essentializing, universalizing, or fabricating trite stereotypes or drawing on superficial cultural symbols such as foods, articles of clothing, or holidays. Without an explicit focus on power, educators and producers of children's literature inevitably swing between denial of race and assertion of race, between ignoring and advertising difference.

The book Katie describes belongs to a category of multicultural literature that is ostensibly representing and embracing a wide range of racial identities but that unintentionally functions on two levels: The first creates the impression of expansive racial welcoming, and the second operates as an assimilationist mechanism. Students pick up a book with the expectation of encountering a racial minority character, but instead they learn how dark-skinned faces should fit into a White world. This is one example of what I might term *palliated difference*, or difference permitted to an extent that is limited, a situation which arose frequently throughout the study: Students received the message that certain types of multiculturalism and difference are permissible to a certain point, but not at the long-term expense of assimilation.

Another example of palliated difference was International Night at Alexandra's school. Within the school culture, the ESOL department had been so isolated from the larger school community that Alexandra wasn't informed about a schoolwide International Night.

> At my school, they had an International Night. I didn't even know about it. . . . Why wouldn't you include ESOL? Hello?!!! (Interview, January 24)

At the International Night, students displayed costumes, performed dances, and served food that was associated with the national identities of their parents and grandparents. In short, International Night communicated a broad and universal acceptance of internationalism, of a diversity of races, ethnicities, and languages. Failing to inform the ESOL department was, of course, not a deliberate attempt to disenfranchise ESOL students but was merely an oversight. However, the fact that such a lapse could occur makes a statement about the invisibility of the ESOL community within the school. The incident raises questions about the types and degrees of internationalism considered acceptable. Was the form of internationalism represented by ESOL students too raw, too closely associated with poverty, insufficiently assimilated, not prestigious enough? Was it *too* international?

## Silences and Linguistic-Minority Status

Strangely enough, these silences around race do not extend to include silences around linguistic-minority status, which is itself a racialized category.

In fact, sometimes it appeared that speaking about ESOL students in terms of language identity provided a shroud for discourses that might otherwise be read as racist. As outlined in the previous chapter, throughout the year of the study the four teachers told numerous stories about parents not wanting their children to be in contact with ESOL departments and students, about teachers wanting to minimize their contact with ESOL students. This disparagement was not invented in the school but rather extended from beyond it, including the broader communities and neighborhoods in which ESOL students lived. Margaret told us about a neighborhood publication that included transcriptions of voicemails called in on a phone line in a "Letter to the Editor" format. One voicemail was about Margaret's local public school, complaining that "I do not want my child going to Green Leaf Elementary School. The education there is horrible because there are so many non-English speakers." Margaret also related a story about a colleague:

> I was having tea with an old friend, she's also a teacher, she's a 2nd-grade teacher at [a neighboring] elementary school. She was saying how one of her students had moved to California last year . . . and then they just moved back, and she said, "Yes, I was talking with [the student's] mother, they were in San Francisco, and she said the education in California is horrible," and I said, "Really? What was she not pleased with?" and she said . . .

Here, Margaret dropped her voice to a whisper and we all leaned in toward her to catch her words:

> *Margaret:* She said, "It was all non-English speakers in the classes."
> *Suhanthie:* Does she know that you're an ESOL teacher?
> *Margaret:* Yes!
> *Alexandra:* So she's stupid on top of everything.
> *Margaret:* But I don't think she even thought of that as something I would react to. Like, in my mind, the opposite is a given; in her mind, that's a given that you would not want your child to be in that environment. (Afternoon Tea, March 28)

Margaret refers to the unquestioned assumption that the quality of schooling is diminished by the presence of children she terms "non-English speakers," who were not considered to be a natural or legitimate part of the school population. The conceptualization of the children as outsiders is connected to broader social ideologies about the illegitimacy of immigrants. Margaret defended her friend as not having entertained the possibility of any objectionable element in her comments because the undesirability of English learners in schools was such a given. It could be argued that the friend is not

actually "stupid" after all, but rather that she is simply reflecting in an unquestioned way established discourses. It should be noted that the teacher was not
unequivocally oblivious to the problematic nature of her comments—she must
have had some reservations about speaking them because she whispered them.
She was, however, not sufficiently aware to examine them more critically.

## REPRESENTATIONS OF ESOL STUDENT IDENTITY IN THE SOCIAL IMAGINARY

The ways in which ESOL students are represented and learn to understand
their identities has been explored at different levels by various researchers.
Bannerji's (2001) concept of "inventing subjects" can help us understand
how images of ESOL can shape the ways in which ESOL students as "cultural and ideological objects" come to understand and assume their identities,
partly as the subjects of others' invention, partly as agents in the invention of
their own subjectivity, always as a mediation of the two. All who participate
in the making and shaping of the social construct of ESOL both invent and
are invented by meanings of race in interaction with meanings of ESOL.

Harklau (2000) has applied the notion of *representation* to ESOL
learners. She describes representations as "archetypal images of learner
identity" and argues that "representation is an inevitable part of human
meaning making and identity formation" (p. 35). In the context of her study
of U.S. immigrants coming of age within the U.S. educational system, she
described the prevailing images of ESOL that surrounded students—for
instance, images of outsiders or cultural Others or images of hardship and
perseverance consistent with "Ellis Island" mythology. The teachers and
students in her study sometimes adopted, sometimes resisted, and sometimes embraced select elements of these images. Toohey's (1998) detailed
descriptions of the shaping of ESOL identity in a 1st-grade classroom illustrate the ways in which the dominating images in her study site depicted
ESOL students as having deficit identities that required "normalization"
(p. 78). To a degree, the children in that study began to live out those
identities. Similarly, the continental African youths in Ibrahim's (1999)
study joined a Euro-Canadian public school community that had already
constructed them in a social imaginary in which all Black students were
represented monolithically, regardless of national origin. Roles and identities had already been assigned to them, and they, like Toohey's 1st-graders,
assumed these identities to varying degrees in relation to the "disciplinary
social conditions" (p. 353) under which they lived. Other researchers have
shown how ESOL students are socialized into certain identities within
school walls, and consequently into certain roles within society (Olsen,
2008; Valdés, 2001; Valenzuela, 1999). These representations develop into

stereotypes, a form of hegemony that contributes to metanarratives that sustain the existing social order. Participants in the making of school culture contribute to the reinscription of representations and stereotypes, and ESOL teachers are no exception. Ellwood (2009) and Kumaravadivelu (2003) have illustrated the tendency of TESOL professionals to fall into the trap of stereotyping Asian ESOL students, despite evidence that Asian students do not actually fit neatly into the available, presumably intelligible categories (Zheng, 2010).

Representations and stereotypes are powerful ingredients in a colonial enterprise that reinforces inequitable relations of power. Gramsci (1972) described "hegemony" as the dominance of ideological norms of the ruling class over the subordinate class (in this case, immigrants and racial minorities) through intellectual persuasion. JanMohammed (1985) views static portrayals of racial Others in literature as a mechanism to denigrate and fetishize ethnic minorities. Bhabha (1994) has referred to the stereotype as a cornerstone of colonial discourse and claims that the stereotype is a form of knowledge that relies on being "anxiously repeated" (1994, p. 370) for its fixity and consequent perpetuation. The dominating images that surround ESOL students play a crucial role in coercing them toward or away from given racial identities by feeding what Foucault (1977) terms *disciplinary power*, an alluring and potent form of social control. Disciplinary power derives its effectiveness by attracting humans to certain desires, norms, and identities. As such, examining the ways in which representations, images, and stereotypes of ESOL identity are offered to language-minority students can illuminate our understandings of how students construct their racial identities in language classrooms and the consequences of these identities for their lives beyond school walls.

## DRAWING ATTENTION TO DIFFERENCE

Another element of colorblind discourse was the tension that surfaced for the teachers between, on one hand, ensuring that students were surrounded by cultural or racial representations that they could connect with and, on the other hand, drawing unwanted attention to difference. Part of what makes colorblind discourses effective is the shame associated with difference, a shame frequently internalized by minority children in schools. Teachers are under pressure to ignore difference for several reasons: to spare their students embarrassment but also because they are obliged to present the appearance of colorblindness. They are expected to assume the identity of someone who embraces all students regardless of color, and acknowledging an awareness of racial difference might be interpreted as noticing race and therefore not viewing all children equally.

At one afternoon tea, Margaret told us about her efforts to use materials that would allow students to see representations of characters who physically resembled themselves. She had been unnerved by her student Kang-Dae's unexpected reaction to her materials:

> *Margaret:* So I got the book *Counting in Korea*. . . . On the cover, there's a picture of a [boy wearing a] traditional Korean outfit. All the kids looked at it and said [to Kang-Dae], "He looks like you." So he looked at it and said, "He's stinky! Stinky boy." And he pushed it away. So I just said, "Oh no, he's handsome, look at him" . . .
>
> *Katie:* I wonder if he wants to fit in. That would be my most immediate guess; he wants to fit in, he doesn't want to be singled out for anything. (Afternoon Tea, November 1)

I asked Margaret later, by email, why her response was to describe the boy on the book cover as "handsome." She explained:

> I told my student the boy was handsome because I assumed that he was noticing and regretting his difference from his peers. He and his brother are the only Asian boys in the kindergarten/1st grades. My young charges are so quick (as are their elders) to see and fear (?) the different. (Margaret, Email, April 25)

She then connected the boy's reaction to the experiences of a childhood friend:

> A dear friend of mine from Cambodia moved here [to the United States] when she was 7. There was a time when she colored her face with a white crayon, stretched her face before the mirror, wanting to look differently. To not like what you inherently and beautifully are is dangerous, scary to me. I assumed the beginnings (incorrectly?) of this in my student. (Margaret, Email, April 25)

As teachers make decisions about whether and how to make difference visible, they navigate a complicated landscape. On one hand, teachers recognize the importance of students seeing themselves in curriculum materials, of children learning about and feeling pride in their ancestries, of exposing their students to alternative epistemologies such as other ways of counting, of the difficulties of maintaining a heritage language that a child might be ashamed of, of the importance of a child liking and feeling comfortable with the image in the mirror. On the other hand, students are not impermeable to broader historical societal discourses. In pushing away the counting book,

Kang-Dae was responding to ideas that he had received long before he ever walked into Margaret's classroom. Students in ESOL classes, and indeed people of color the world over, have been taught to be ashamed of their racial subjectivities repeatedly and consistently, but usually through interactions so minute and ephemeral as to be almost unidentifiable. Stephen May (2010) notes the near-inseparability of multiculturalism and essentialism, asking, "How can multiculturalism, based as it is on a notion of group-based identities and related rights, avoid lapsing into reification and essentialism? In effect, how can it codify without solidifying ethnic group identities, thus accounting for postmodernist understandings of voice, agency, and the multiple and malleable aspects of identity formation?" (p. 37)

Adult language learners are hard-pressed to discover ways to carve out a middle ground between these competing ideologies or to accept them only in mediated ways, as did the learners in Canagarajah's (1999) study of Tamil speakers in Jaffna, Sri Lanka. However, such nuanced critique is a tall order for a child. When I had heard the story, I too had understood Kang-Dae to be unhappy about his difference, probably also influenced by my own childhood experiences. As Margaret told this story, I felt myself whisked back in time to the memories of my own early years in Canberra, Australia. My Sri Lankan parents had moved with me to Canberra when I was a preschooler from the San Francisco Bay Area, where they had been living for several years, and I grew up for a while thereafter knowing almost no people of color. I lived in Canberra, on and off, until I was 17. The city was small, and Australia was emerging from many decades under a racist immigration policy, the White Australia Policy, which sought to keep "Australia for the Australians" and had been in effect until the early 1970s. I remember a childhood of trying desperately to ignore the fact that I was not White, as if by denying it I was somehow going to convince everyone around me that I had another heritage, a White heritage. While I was in elementary school, when I was asked where I was from, I would stubbornly reply, "Australia, Australia," in order to refute any association with a nation of origin in which most people were Brown. I remember being called derogatory names that were typically used against the aboriginal population in Australia and desperately wanting to distance myself from any population with any significant amount of melanin in their skin. Although this internalized self-colonization is widespread and a reasonable, logical reaction, it raises questions for educators about what to do with it in our teaching practice, teacher education, and educational policy. In the context of my childhood, the image of the boy on the book cover seems almost brazen in its unequivocal Koreanness, and as Margaret related Kang-Dae's reaction, I squirmed uncomfortably on his behalf.

Just as colonial shame is steeped in racism, racial shame has colonial roots. Shame is constructed in the context of small, fleeting moments, many of which take place in classrooms. I see my childhood reflection clearly in the words of Aimée Césaire. For Césaire (1972), fear lies at the root of colonization, fear instilled in the colonized to ensure that they feel inferior and thus incapable of defending themselves. He says, "I am talking about millions of men whom they have knowingly instilled with fear and a complex of inferiority, whom they have infused with despair and trained to tremble, to kneel and behave like flunkeys" (p. 20). And Frantz Fanon (1967) writes about the psychological destruction that colonialism has produced. He sees the colonized striving to emulate the colonizer, to become White, telling us that "the total result looked for by colonial domination was indeed to convince the natives that colonialism came to lighten their darkness" (pp. 210–211). Desires to emulate colonizers, to find ways to become more intimate with Whiteness and nativeness in English (whatever these might mean), while sometimes ambivalent or unconscious or inconsistent, are present in our English language classrooms. However, change, too, takes place in transitory instants of pedagogy. It is difficult for ESL teachers to have conversations with children about emulating colonizers, but TESOL teacher educators can encourage teacher candidates to consider how that legacy of harm and psychological damage makes itself present in TESOL practice.

Talking about difference was a complicated line for Alexandra to negotiate, too. She expressed a reluctance to assign a specific cultural association to an individual student, giving the example of a girl from India, Amara. In particular, she disapproved of the practice of singling out students as representatives of a particular culture:

> We were talking about mendi the other day. The kids draw on their hands, so I suggested, "Why don't you use mendi? Can anyone tell us about mendi?" And the Indian girl raised her hand and said, "I can tell you about mendi." And she was very happy to tell everyone about it. She was able to contribute, but *I* didn't ask her specifically to contribute. (Alexandra, Afternoon Tea, January 24)

Alexandra sought to create a space in which students could share information specific to their individual cultural history, but she hoped to do so without attracting attention to ethnic difference. The sheer might of normative power is illustrated clearly in this example. The social stigma associated with cultures that are different from the dominant culture, and particularly cultures in which the majority of the population is not White, is so potent that to even single out an Indian student as more likely to know about mendi is to risk shaming her. This places teachers such as Alexandra in an awkward position. To ignore difference, pretending that students' races and national identities are homogeneous, may make students more comfortable in the short term but does nothing to challenge the stigma of difference and in fact underscores dominant constructions of identity. However, Alexandra's responsibility was not only to a global desire for transformation but also toward her individual student, Amara. As a caring teacher, she was unwilling to risk betraying and stigmatizing her pupils. Her strategy of asking the class in general about culturally specific information provided Alexandra with a way to integrate her desire to create space for students' culturally specific knowledge and her reluctance to betray Amara by pointing out her difference.

Katie noted a complicated identity dynamic in the case of a boy who identified with his language, French, but not with his home country, Cameroon:

> Frank likes things in French, he associates with his language, but not with his culture. He's from Cameroon. A lot of my students will say, "In my country, blah, blah, blah," but he never does (Afternoon Tea, March 21).

One possible interpretation of Frank's choices is that he perceives his Cameroonian heritage as affording him limited status or privilege, while he understands a prestige to be associated with his French linguistic identity. Although he was only in 5th grade, Frank may have already come to understand French to be a language associated with White colonization, supremacy, and civilization—as represented by the prestige associated with that country's wines, cuisine, fashion industry, and perfumes—but his Cameroonian heritage to be disconnected from social power within the American context.

## PURLOINED IDENTITIES: PASSING AS A NATIVE SPEAKER

There are multiple ways of narrativizing the desire to "pass" as native or non-ESOL, and the issue raises interesting questions about shame, identity, and judgment. In the schools of the study, passing took various forms. As described in Chapter 3, some students were eager to exit ESOL so that they could "pass" as non-ESOL, and some asked to have the blinds drawn in order to conceal their presence in the classroom and thus their enrollment in ESOL. One student habitually pretended not to know the ESOL teacher in order to publicly repudiate any relationship with ESOL services. In the context of the study, passing seemed to be related to performativity. The desire to "sound like a native" is an assumed goal in most English language teaching, despite Vivian Cook's (1991) call many years ago to reframe our goals for English teaching toward a language user rather than native-speaker model. Over the years I have taught numerous students who struggled to sound like native-English speakers, and for years I unwittingly encouraged their desires for all that is represented by native-English-speaker status. Just as individuals have sought out, for instance, skin-lightening treatments to pass as White (or Whiter); have used prosthetics, wigs, makeup, clothing, and other appearance-altering products to pass as the opposite sex; and have acquired opposite sex spouses to pass as straight, passing is a driving force in the shaping of linguistic identity. Ruecker (2011) has called on ELT scholars to draw on work on racial passing to inform research on linguistic passing, and indeed the body of work on racial passing offers us useful ways of illuminating our understandings of linguistic identity. Within the American tradition of African American racial passing, passing for the dominant group (White) has been associated with a lack of loyalty, self-hatred, and an abdication of Black identity (Pfeiffer, 2003), all undergirded by an assumption that Blackness and Whiteness are mutually exclusive. Similarly, attempts to pass as a native-English speaker might superficially be construed as a hatred of the part of oneself that is not a "native-English speaker," the self-hatred of the colonized. The wish to pass or necessity (or perceived necessity) of passing can be connected to the meanings and degree of undesirability associated with the category "nonnative" and, in K–12 settings, parallel school categories such as ESOL.

The idea that nativeness in English is more desirable than fluent, comprehensible NNES speech and an unquestioned belief in the necessity of passing in order to be truly successful are rooted in both racism and colonialism. However, these understandings of passing rely on limited interpretations of identity, race, and language. Pfeiffer (2003) notes that the association of race passing with deception and betrayal are dependent on a "racially correct" (p. 2) manner of reading a situation, one in which Black and White have static and widely agreed-upon meanings, and she calls on us to consider a more complex reading of passing. Similarly, while linguistic passing can be read as denial or even loathing of one's own linguistic identity, intertwined as it is with one's racial and colonial identity, processes of passing simultaneously represent a challenge to linguistic essentialism and ideologies surrounding meanings of English and nativeness. Just as the concept of racial passing is reliant on Black and White being conceived of as completely distinguishable, fixed, and concretely defined, linguistic passing requires a separability and fixity of the categories "native" and "nonnative." The mere possibility of students passing demonstrates the frailty of the category in the same way that the possibility of a Black individual passing as White demonstrates the nebulousness of the line between Black and White. The feasibility of passing stands as evidence that the conditions of legitimacy and privilege are subject to disordering (Wald, 2000), opening up opportunities for ELT professionals.

Passing suggests theft, implying that the identity being donned is illegitimately obtained, purloined. In order to pass as something, logic demands as a point of departure that one is unequivocally not that thing. If one is considered to be "passing" as a man, it must be assumed that underneath it all, one is not in fact a man. If one is considered to be "passing" as White, it must be assumed that one is in actuality not White. Such ideologies exclude the possibility of gradation in these identities. One cannot, within this ideology, be "a little bit a man." Either one is or one isn't. However, the reality is that nativeness is not a concrete category. Numerous examples exist of individuals who are in fact "a little bit native." Immigrants who move to English-dominant contexts as children often experience language loss and as adults function more effectively in English than in the language that one might deem their native tongue. Numerous individuals around the world are simultaneous bilinguals and are no more fluent in one language than another. Even more common in today's globalizing world, individuals may develop varying rates of fluency depending on where they live at a given period of time and, for instance, lose a little of their facility in German while they are living in England, only to regain proficiency after returning home to live 20 years later. Many speakers are more proficient in one language in one domain but another language in another domain, in one language in technical or academic contexts but another in familial or social settings. The possibility of passing therefore calls into question the tenacity of these linguistic categories.

In a case that is interesting because of the way it calls into question racial boundaries, Belluscio (2006) explores what he terms the "passing" as White of European immigrants who were not Anglo-Saxon during the late 19th and early 20th centuries. During this time, the United States saw a larger influx of Jewish and Italian immigrants than immigrants of any other origin, and their Whiteness was contested. Jewish and Italian immigrants "found themselves in racially in-between subject positions from which they could escape only by adopting the social, religious, economic, and intellectual mores of the better-established white dominant culture. One might say, then, that many first- and second-generation ethnics, in an attempt to achieve occupational security and social acceptance, passed for white" (p. 2). This "passing" pushed against the boundaries of racial categories and ultimately reshaped them to a degree, creating spaces for potential transformation of fixed understandings of race. Successful White "passing" in this case softened a boundary and broadened the category so that Jews and Italians could enter Whiteness. Today, to speak of an Italian or Jew "passing" as White creates a potential lapse in logic. Conversely, Hispanics in much of the rest of the world are considered White, but in the U.S. context a separate category has been developed and is repeated and reinforced in multiple ways—for instance, on census forms and in educational institutions—which on some level creates and reinforces a border, a demarcation between an "us" and a "them."

The dichotomies between ESOL/non-ESOL and NNES/NES are related but do not always map directly onto each other. ESOL students need to learn several skills: how to perform native-speakerness, how to repudiate nonnative-speakerness, and how to negotiate the terrain between ESOL status and nonnativeness, which are not exactly the same thing. When former ESOL students at Jane's school pass the door and shout, "You can't speak English" into the door of the room, they are performing non-ESOLness by solidifying the boundary around the category "ESOL," making it less permeable and reiterating their position outside of that border. They are, however, not touching the borders around the category "native speaker." Their ability to pass as native in the near future is a possibility, their young age of immigration meaning that many of them will eventually develop accents that pass for standard American accents. It serves to their advantage for the boundary between native and nonnative to remain undefined. Their position on the desirable side of the line around ESOL, however, means that they have a (presumably unconscious) interest in the permanence of that line. Margaret's young student pretends not to know her when he encounters her in school hallways away from her classroom. Because his accent and language proficiency might mark him as a nonnative speaker, his ability to perform nativeness is limited. However, the possibility still exists for him to perform non-ESOLness by maneuvering other signifiers of ESOL status, such as familiarity with the teacher known to be associated with ESOL. Alexandra's intermediate students long to exit ESOL or to be in her transitional bridge class because it signals to them the end of their servitude in ESOL and the beginning of their admittance to a context that is unmarked and associated with nativeness—that is, mainstream schooling. Once they have left ESOL, they are one step closer to passing as native speakers. Sitting in an ESOL classroom is unquestionably a form of performing ESOL, which runs counter to the performance of native-speaker identity (although ironically the point of being in ESOL classrooms is arguably frequently framed as the pursuit of a closer approximation of native-speaker identity). They cannot avoid sitting in the ESOL classroom, so they ask Alexandra to draw the blinds in order to conceal this performance of ESOLness.

When we engage with the phenomenon of passing, we most frequently consider minority individuals who pass for the dominant group in order to access some sort of privilege. One such example is Jazz musician Billy Tipton, who lived not only his professional but also his personal life as a man, most likely in order to gain access to his profession (Kroeger, 2005). It was discovered only upon his death in 1989 that he was biologically a woman. Clare Kendry, the light-skinned African American main character of Nella Larsen's (1929/1997) novel *Passing*, married a White man in order to access a life lived in the context of a White middle class and allowed her husband to believe that she, too, was White. In terms of linguistic passing, my own great-grandparents on both sides of the family chose to start speaking only English in their homes in Colombo, Sri Lanka, because it was a more instrumental language than their minority languages, Tamil and, less prominently, Singhalese. The desire to perform nativeness meant that my family's heritage languages were lost within a generation, with their children (my grandparents) and then parents becoming native-English speakers. Losing a heritage language provides an undeniable confirmation of nativeness. However, passing does not always involve minority group individuals seeking to belong to a dominant category. Angie, a third-generation Puerto Rican American teacher in a graduate-level second language acquisition class I taught many years ago wrote a class paper that she titled "The Secret." In the paper, she didn't use the term *passing*, but she described her shame of her limited proficiency in Spanish despite her mixed Latina heritage. Her family had instituted English-only policies in their home after being told that using Spanish would impede their children's English development, so she learned Spanish only when she determinedly undertook to learn it during her high school years. The secret referred to in her paper's title was her lifelong habit of feigning fluency in Spanish when interacting with individuals who were not sufficiently Spanish-proficient to detect her ruse. On one hand, Angie could be represented as succumbing to the shame of not having acquired Spanish more proficiently and resisting the identities she may have associated (or feared that others associated) with a Latina who didn't speak Spanish fluently—of being inauthentically Puerto Rican perhaps, of selling out for White privilege, or of self-hatred. Her choice could be read as an uncritical acceptance of ideologies that wed race and linguistic identity and of an unquestioning acceptance of Puerto Rican authenticity being reliant on Spanish fluency. Alternatively—and setting aside Angie's own intentionality and framing of her positioning—one might consider her choice not only in terms of the individual Angie but rather in the light of its broader social effects, reading her decision to pass as the taking up of opportunities to confound static identity categories and as posing a creative challenge to ideologies that insist that Puerto Rican authenticity include native-speaker fluency in Spanish.

As I was developing an awareness of and discomfort with the meanings associated with my lack of proficiency in Tamil and Singhalese, particularly when I found myself interacting with others of Sri Lankan heritage, Angie's story highlighted for me some of the identities frequently associated with language loss—identities of self-loathing, opportunism, inauthenticity, abandonment of heritage—and opened my eyes to the ambivalence and conflict that frequently accompany language identity choices. Signithia Fordham (2010) has coined the term *disremembering* to describe the "deliberate, always incomplete effort to expunge . . . cultural DNA" (p. 26). Passing as a native-English speaker can be characterized as requiring an impossible degree of disremembering because it demands the speaker to suspend, at least temporarily, the depth of her or his connection to other languages. When the participants in Piller's (2002) study "passed" as native speakers, they did so with a deliberateness and consciousness of the fleeting nature of their performances, which Piller described as "temporary, context-, audience- and medium-specific" (p. 179). Passing can indeed imply an abdication of personal history and can be construed as "painful, deceit-ridden contortions" (Kroeger, 2005, p. 9). However, an alternate reading of passing might suggest that provisional and transitory suspensions and appropriations of linguistic identities represent ingenuity, resourcefulness, and experimentation; allow us to call into question the permeability and instability of language classifications; and ultimately lead toward the crumbling of the inadequate category "native speaker" itself. I am not suggesting, of course, that linguistic passing is a solution to linguistic discrimination but rather that it becomes an opportunity to challenge the logics on which restrictive linguistic categories depend when it is accompanied by an explicit consciousness of the language ideologies that make passing appealing or even necessary and a concrete long-term plan for transforming inequitable language practices.

## TEACHERS' IDENTITIES

In 2013, the recipient of TESOL's *National Geographic* Teacher of the Year Award, Anne Marie Foerster Luu (2013), opened her talk with the line, "Who you are is just as important as who you teach." Teacher education programs have encouraged teachers to focus on students and to lead student-centered classrooms and curricula, which has sometimes led to teachers' own identities, including their colonial and racial identities, taking a backseat. Foerster Luu reminds us that every facet of our identities is present as we teach.

Because the meanings of all identities are both situated and coconstructed, the racial, colonial, and linguistic identities of ESOL teachers are as significant to school processes as are the identities of ESOL students. The four teachers grappled with the significance of their own identities in the process of negotiating the inherent racialization of ESOL in their language-teaching contexts. The majority of ESOL teachers in the two counties of this study were White, and most ESOL students were of color. Educators must ask to what degree to teach English in this context is "to repeat the colonial history embedded in the classroom between White teachers and students of color" (Ibrahim, 1999, p. 349). Any discussion of the connections between ESOL students' identity and their linguistic-minority status consequently needs to include attention to their teachers' identities. George Dei et al. (2004) highlight the importance of recognizing the different vantage points that come with different racial identities:

> If racism and oppression constitute the experience and lived reality of both the oppressed and the oppressor, if both feel its effects, then why do racism and oppression continue to flourish? The answer is simply this: . . . They both feel, live, experience, and know [the reality of oppression] differently. (p. 14)

What does it mean to teach English as an additional language when teachers' racial identities are assumed to be inextricable from the process? In this section I focus on the ways that race is significant in the teachers' pedagogy, language, and identities, seeking to extend understandings of (1) the ways in which identities acquire racial meanings within school walls, (2) teachers' negotiations of dominating images surrounding ESOL, and (3) the implications of the teachers' privileged linguistic identities for their pedagogical practice. As I speak of teachers' racial identities, I inevitably speak of their linguistic identities; the inextricability of Whiteness from the construct of "mainstream" or "Standard" English renders unachievable the disentanglement of race and language in English language teaching.

During the year of the study, I watched four teachers struggling with what it means to be a teacher in an endeavor that they recognized could promote inequities. The three White women (Alexandra, Jane, and Margaret) constructed themselves as working against layers of colonialism and racism embedded in the ELT enterprise, and they were conscious of the potential hegemony to which they could contribute as White women. The Korean-born woman (Katie) sensed that her authority was in question because of her racial identity, and she was influenced by her own history of shame about her race. All four teachers in the study were native-English speakers, and they therefore needed to make thoughtful decisions about how to position themselves within an institutional culture whose dominant ideology underscored the supremacy of both Whiteness (Fine, 2004) and of native-speaker status (Cook, 1999).

Nieto (2002) has noted that it is often difficult for idealistic teachers to accept the existence of institutional racism within school systems. Over the years, I have seen time and time again graduate students entering teacher education programs and trying desperately to identify alternative explanations for racial disparities in educational achievement. In fact, I sometimes catch myself wishfully searching for other reasons myself. It is disquieting to consider that the prevailing American philosophy of meritocracy is a falsehood, to entertain the idea that hard work may not always be rewarded and that not all privilege is earned. Van Ausdale and Feagin (2001) contend that adults, particularly White adults, in U.S. schools are in denial about the seriousness of racial prejudices in the society around them.

In recent years, theorists have been paying greater attention recently to the ways in which race interacts with teaching identity in the lives of TESOL practitioners (Haque & Morgan, 2009). For professionals of color, establishing a teaching identity is often complicated by an unspoken assumption that White English teachers are more legitimate than those of color (Amin, 1997; Curtis & Romney, 2006; Lin et al., 2004). Race is salient not only in the teaching lives of professionals of color, but also in the professional lives of White teachers. The construct of Whiteness has been examined in Whiteness studies

(Frankenberg, 1993; McIntosh, 1997) and has specifically been explored in relation to teaching (Howard, 1999; Paley, 2000). Important but scant work examining Whiteness in relation to ESOL teaching has begun to emerge (Appleby, 2013, Liggett, 2009, Michael-Luna, 2008), but more is needed. If English can be viewed as an imperialist language (Canagarajah, 1999; Phillipson, 2008), and English language teaching can be viewed as a colonial endeavor (Pennycook, 2001), then the practice of White English language teachers not only echoes colonial patterns of domination but also affirms Eurocentric values and epistemologies in students who are not White. Mackie (2003) seeks to "dislodge" (p. 24) the colonized identities of ESOL teaching by questioning the nature of racial identity, including her own White identity. Vandrick (2002) has similarly discussed the importance of White ESOL teachers' reflection on their colonial privilege, asking them to be thoughtful of the "colonial shadow" (p. 411) cast over ESL teaching by the powerful positioning of the English language, both historically and contemporarily.

As Alexandra, Jane, Katie, and Margaret shared stories of their complex struggles, fascinating images emerged of teachers striving to come to terms with their role in an enterprise that they clearly understood to be problematic, asking questions about the implications of their racialized identities for their teaching practice, and wondering how to help their young charges negotiate a world in which race is unquestionably present yet heavily shrouded. I begin by providing three examples to illustrate the ways in which difficult and complicated issues of race are often embedded in short, fleeting moments of classroom life. All four of the teachers in the study had antiracist agendas. However, antiracist agendas are enacted in tricky ways because racism is not confronted solely through a large-scale agenda, but rather in very situated ways that are sometimes clear-cut but sometimes not so straightforward at all. In the two examples that follow, the teachers are striving for antiracist teaching. In each example, I explain how the teacher's racial identities, although less overtly visible than their students', quietly come into play.

Alexandra sensed that the representations within her school context of her Black and Latino male students were negative, and she, like other teachers who wrestle with stereotypes in the lives of students, had to make decisions about whether and how to acknowledge these controlling images. She sought to preemptively equip her students to confront the stereotypes that they would eventually encounter. She discussed three of her students: two Black students, Gamma and Rafe, and one Latino, William. Gamma in particular posed classroom management challenges:

> *Alexandra:* But every now and again I try to get him to see how
> intelligent he is but he has to show that, and unfortunately he has
> to show that more than others because he's battling this thing in
> the United States where Black boys are not seen as intelligent.

*Suhanthie:* That was actually addressed aloud? That a Black student has to work harder because of racism?

*Alexandra:* He has to know what he's doing. Like if he wants to show how intelligent he is, he has to show it. . . . William was saying that everybody's unfair to Hispanic boys too, and I said, I recognize that, and that's why I want you to show how intelligent you are. (Interview, January 26)

This exchange is an important one, but it makes me deeply uncomfortable. I once presented it at a conference and sensed that the audience was judging Alexandra, who was committed to supporting her students in the best possible way. Alexandra's primary concern was for her students to enact as much agency as they could in the mediation of their own racialized identities. She used a strategy in which she presented the stereotype, assuming that the boys would absorb it elsewhere if not through her. In retrospect, I believe that a large part of my strong visceral reaction against her naming of the stereotype stemmed from my unconscious but questionably accurate belief that speaking the stereotype aloud sets it into circulation and solidifies it. Such a flagrant naming of a stereotype is a type of transgression in the context of socially sanctioned silences around race, and a small part of me believes that if the stereotypes are not named aloud, they will wither away and disappear. A larger part of me recognizes that silences around race play an important role in allowing inequalities to flourish. Alexandra seemed to believe that if the boys were not aware of the stereotypes, they would not be equipped to work explicitly against them. In articulating the stereotypes, she was positioning the boys, indeed defying them, to challenge the stereotypes. She urged her students to own their own identities as Black and Latino men, but she simultaneously hoped that they would define these identities for themselves rather than assuming the dominant representations surrounding them. However, this dynamic was complicated by her positioning as a White woman. When White teachers draw attention to and explicitly name racial stereotypes, do they risk propagating the stereotypes and concretizing the established social order? Conversely, to what extent do silences around race sustain inequality by failing to challenge it?

Jane, too, found her own positionality as a White woman playing into her support of her students. For Jorge, a young Latino in Jane's class, "Hispanic kids" were invisible in the social imaginary of life at his American high school. Jane told us:

The school newspaper came out last week. This one kid flipped through it and said, "Ms. Fitzpatrick, this paper is racist!" I said, "Okay, why?" and he said, "Forget it" like he thought I was going to yell at him. I said, "No, no, no, I pretty much agree with you, but

I want to hear why you think that." And he said, "It doesn't reflect anything about the Hispanic kids; it's all about the American Black kids and their music." I said, "Okay, I agree; now what are you going to do about it?" You have to find these small pieces and let them be able to do something with it. I said, "Who are the kids who write for the paper? Do you [and] your friends write for the paper?" He said, "No. I should complain." I said, "Do you want to write a letter to the editor? . . . If you want to write a letter, I'll edit it; I'll help you with the grammar changes." And I said, "You and your friends need to be represented on that paper. You can't sit back and complain about it. That's the first step, realizing there's a problem . . . but you can't stop there." (Afternoon Tea, March 21)

This exchange appears to be about Jorge's racial identification and its connection to representations within the school culture. However, this snippet allows us to see how salient teachers' identities can be while seeming to be irrelevant (Morgan, 2004). Both Jane and Jorge were negotiating their racial identities. Jane was encouraging her student's critical analysis of his own representation (or lack thereof) in his larger school culture. She draws his attention to one of the reasons that Latino kids are underrepresented in the paper, that is, that the contributors to the papers are not Jorge and his presumably Latino friends.

Jane's own position as a teacher is given further authority by her White identity, and Jane exercises her authority in a way that represented integrity for her, moving quickly to support his reticently expressed observation, then encouraging his transformative action to challenge the invisibility of Hispanic racial identity. However, race and empire are inseparable, and dynamics such as this discussion therefore take place in the shadow of colonialism, with Jane advocating from her position of teacher-authority as a White native-English speaker guiding the actions and reactions of a racial minority nonnative-English speaker. The hierarchy was present, and it was apparent that Jorge was quite conscious of it, as evidenced by his apparent fear that Jane would "yell at him." Furthermore, it could be argued that Jane's confidence in the power of proactive behavior (such as letter writing) to provoke change is shaped by her positionality as a White, middle-class woman (Payne, 2005) who is accustomed to being heard and responded to.

Teachers' identities figured prominently and in complicated ways within questions about what counts as multiculturalism and multicultural education throughout the year of the study. These questions sometimes helped us think about power and privilege and sometimes became entangled with and obscured issues of empire and especially race.

Alexandra struggled to challenge the processes that privileged Whiteness. She was concerned that her students were reading literature that was insufficiently diverse—that is, literature that bore little connection to their own lives. She suggested that her school offer a class in multicultural literature. Her situation was fraught with complexities. She was operating in a context that was characterized by what Kubota (2004) has referred to as liberal multiculturalism. One feature of this ideology was the use of words such as *multicultural* and *diverse* to mean *minority*, a substitution that muddies the definition of the word *multicultural* by positioning it in contrast to *White*. If a multicultural literature class is marked as multicultural, then a literature class that is not marked as multicultural can somehow come to be understood as not multicultural. This tendency sets mainstream and multicultural classes in opposition to each other, thereby potentially excusing literature classes that are not multicultural from including diverse voices. Using the terms *minority voices* and *multicultural voices* as synonymous underscores the construction of Whiteness as normative by juxtaposing it against multiculturalism. Similarly, when the phrase *teaching diverse students* is taken to mean *teaching minority students* or *teaching students of color*, it sets students of color apart from an unnamed norm. Alexandra saw herself as an inappropriate choice to teach the multicultural literature class because she was White and therefore "not multicultural." She told us about a conversation she had had with an African American administrator:

> I said to her, "Who am I to teach this course?" and my ideal would be just to coordinate parents coming and discussing a piece of literature with the kids. (Interview, January 26)

She considered the strategy of including parents, part of her ongoing efforts to draw on community resources and increase parent involvement at the school, to potentially downplay her presence within the lesson. I asked her why she thought that she lacked the qualifications to teach the class, and she responded with a reference to her Whiteness:

> I might do the reading strategies, I might do the work around it, but the actual discussion is not coming out of a White face. I feel really inadequate saying to people, think of it in terms of this, when that's not my experience with my very narrow view of the world. (Interview, January 26)

There is no simple answer to this dilemma, but Alexandra's strategy was to integrate both sides of the tension into an uneasy solution: She participated in the course development but agreed to teach only material such as reading strategies, leaving the actual discussion to someone whose face was not White. The situation raises numerous questions about identity-based credibility and professional authority (Brenner, 2006). For instance, if Alexandra had taught the class, would "multicultural literature" have had more legitimacy in the eyes of the school community? Does the bifurcation of "White" and "multicultural" dig a greater socially constructed trench between those two groups? If Whites are not acknowledged as legitimate participants in antiracist movements, does it then follow that responsibility for antiracism rests solely with racial minorities? Is it only racial minorities who benefit when institutional patterns of racial exclusion are challenged?

The position Alexandra ultimately took embraced humility and acknowledged that her own experiences as a middle-class White woman had not equipped her to relate to subaltern experiences, but it underscored the division between White and non-White. As a testament to silencing discourses, throughout this discussion, although we spoke of Whiteness, we failed to notice that we were conceptualizing Whiteness as neutral.

## WHITENESS BENEATH SKIN'S SURFACE

One practice that sustains the normalization of dominant culture is to color White characters to resemble racial minorities and to then name them multicultural, supporting the fallacy that racial difference relates simply and superficially to nothing more than skin color. This practice pays lip service to multiculturalism without any concern for the meanings of race as they relate to social power and, furthermore, sends messages about how people of color should *be* by contributing to a culturally homogeneous metanarrative. Sarup (1991) in fact suggests that liberal multicultural practices such as these are the instrument of capitalist government and have been introduced to diffuse minority resistance.

The dominance of Whiteness in ESOL students' lives becomes even more complicated with the addition of the English language and its historical, colonial association with Whiteness. Katie expressed concerns about mainstream American ideologies being infused under the guise of bilingual literature:

> Sometimes in the catalog, they'll say this is bilingual, but it's just American stories translated into Spanish but it doesn't really speak to the culture of the students who are learning. It's American stories written by an American author translated into Spanish. So a child with American background knowledge will understand these books more readily than a child who doesn't. Because I think they're saying it's bilingual and therefore it's bicultural. (Afternoon Tea, November 1)

The literary practice Katie described is a form of linguistic tokenism, purporting to support the development of multilingualism and multiculturalism, when in actuality it surreptitiously suppresses a variety of Spanish-speaking cultures by falsely implying that they are represented. The teacher also expressed concern about the practice of translating American books into Spanish and presenting them as multicultural because this disregards the actual experience and knowledge of native-Spanish-speaking children. It contributes to the loss of their cultural resources and results in their exclusion from the discourse if they are not able to connect with the material:

> *Katie:* And I know that with the readers, some readers are totally irrelevant to a Spanish-speaking child's experience. I'll read it, but it'll have no meaning to them. For example, there's a little reader about Halloween, or Halloween costumes, and if the child doesn't celebrate Halloween, it has no relevance.
> *Suhanthie:* Or what if the child celebrates Halloween, but not in the American context? Like going trick-or-treating as opposed to going to the cemetery?
> *Katie:* Yeah, the experiences are different, and translating doesn't mean that it's going to speak to the child's experience. As we know, the readers all try to draw on the child's background knowledge, but that's an American child's background knowledge. (Afternoon Tea, November 1)

Presenting as "bilingual" or "multicultural" material that was actually generated by and is representative of only White, NES Americans has the effect of reinforcing normative constructs of all culture as White and NES and is dismissive of the presence of immigrant students within American culture. Stacy Lee (2005) has described first- and second-generation immigrant Hmong students as being positioned "up against Whiteness" in her study of youth in a well-resourced public school in Wisconsin. These students experienced their surroundings to reproduce White privilege, and success was a possibility for them only if they were willing to mimic Whiteness. The ESOL programs in the school provided a contrast that supported a reification of White normativity and an excuse for teachers to abdicate on their responsibility to include Hmong students in their classrooms. Constructions of Whiteness are integrated subtly into the lives of ESOL students through multiple avenues.

Another way in which Alexandra sought to decenter Whiteness was by disentangling *White* and *American* in her teaching. When her students were selecting folktales to read, she said:

> I gave them a couple of choices, but I really encouraged the Native American perspectives because I think that unfortunately the American folktales are very me, rather than what America really is, they're very White America and they're not representative of America at all. (Afternoon Tea, January 24)

Through many of Alexandra's stories, we see her struggling with constructions of *American*. According to her categorizations, "Native American perspectives" are more legitimately American than "White American perspectives." Alexandra was aware of the weight of White privilege and eager to discount its authority, and she did this by assigning validity to Native American cultures, whose members came to the United States long before European immigrants did. However, this line of logic raises a new quandary: Suggesting that legitimacy correlates to length of time in the country calls into question the Americanness of first-generation immigrants, including many of her students. At the same time, in saying that White Americans (the majority of the American population) are not representative of America but that Native Americans (a small minority) are, she made an important statement: She rejected the notion that larger groups carry greater representative power and affirmed the value of minority perspectives. Margaret struggled to find a way to challenge an invisible norm of Whiteness by drawing on the tool of specificity. Although she didn't address issues of power and justice, she did seek to disengage the terms *Anglo* and *neutral* from one another: "It's hard for me to realize that although I am Anglo, my family and their heritage is *specific* and *meaningful*." She then described the ways in which being Anglo does not, for her, mean being cultureless:

> For me, culture is my mom making popovers in cold weather as her mother did. It's my grandmother's childhood diaries at the bottom of the Chinese cherrywood trunk. And it's the poems my grandfather still remembers. It's the piano études my father has played all my life. And the soft blanket forts my sister and I would make on rainy days. . . . And now *my* culture also includes things and ways Chinese that my husband has shown me. (Margaret, Email, April 21)

As Margaret considered her ethnic identity, she constructed Anglo identity as not neutral because her experience of being Anglo included multiple cultural experiences that were not neutral.

Katie was the one teacher of color in the study. Over the course of the year, she made several references to the undermining of her professional capabilities in relation to her racial or gender identity.

For instance, she said of another faculty member with whom she experienced significant ideological distance, 5th-grade teacher Mr. Berwick:

> I want to come to an understanding with Mr. Berwick, but it's hard because I don't know what approach to take. He doesn't see me as a credible teacher, as a credible equal peer. Because . . . I'm a woman and I'm a minority. . . . How am I going to be able to advocate for my students? I'm not Caucasian, I'm not male, and I'm not a mainstream

classroom teacher. It's a tough thing to negotiate. I just have to do what I can for my students. (Katie, Afternoon Tea, November 1)

Like many other women educators of color (Amin, 1997; Lin et al., 2004; Ng, 1993), Katie experienced her gender and racial identity to contribute to a subtext of inequality in some interactions within her professional context. Katie's personal experiences of racism heightened her consciousness of the relevance of race in the lives of schoolchildren:

> I was teased . . . in kindergarten. I remember it. . . . I came home from school and I was really upset because this other kid was making fun of my eyes. . . . You know how little kids do that thing [pulling at outside corners of eyes] and they say "Chinese, Japanese." . . . I think I just didn't want to be Korean because it was cool to be something else . . . something White. (Katie, Afternoon Tea, October 11)

Katie's story shows us how her classmates' teasing about difference led her directly to construct Korean features as somehow inferior. She later wrote, "These events gave me firsthand experiences of racial and ethnic issues and help me to understand the difficulties and experiences that many of my students face, even today" (Email message, June 25).

## CONCLUSION: RACIALIZING ENGLISH

In this chapter, I have extended the discussion of empire and colonialism within English language teaching to examine the inseparability of empire from racial formation. The complicated ways of talking about race that have evolved over decades and even centuries have resulted in socially sanctioned silences around race, which are related to but often do not extend to silences around linguistic identity. I next connected discourses about race to broader discourses and representations of English learners and the teaching of English within schools. Third, I turned to a theoretical discussion of the notion of passing, taking a lens that is usually applied to race and gender and considering its relevance for discussions of linguistic-minority status. Finally, I focused on the coconstructed nature of identity, examining the imprudence of attempting to disengage teachers' identities from ESOL classrooms (Motha, Jain, & Tecle, 2011). More-specific implications of the interconnectedness of race and empire for the practice of teaching ESOL will be taken up in Chapter 6. In the next chapter, I discuss the rootedness of language ideologies within frameworks of race and empire.

## Reflection Questions

1. Think of a time when you avoided talking about race. Think of a time when you addressed an issue of race head-on. What were the consequences of your silence or engagement?
2. What principles guide me as I decide whether it is wise to treat all students similarly, regardless of race, or to explicitly name race?
3. What are texts and materials that are, in my opinion, adequately "multicultural"? What makes them adequate?
4. What principles guide me as I make decisions about whether and how to draw attention to student differences, particularly differences in racial, linguistic, and national identity? Would I ever name a stereotype aloud? Why or why not?
5. How is my racial identity relevant in my classroom?
6. Are some Americans more "real" or authentic than others? What is a "real American"? What characteristics increase American authenticity?

# CHAPTER 5

# Producing Place and Race: Language Varieties and Nativeness

## PROVINCIALIZING ESOL

In English classrooms across the United States and indeed the world, ideas about what constitutes English remain surprisingly static despite the language's transnational reach and the multiplicity of forms under which it appears. What is English? What counts as English in English classrooms and within the broader social imaginary? As Alexandra, Jane, Katie, and Margaret engaged with the concept of English, exploring the range of ways in which English is defined, the tension between heterogeneity and homogeneity of language varieties, the connectedness of language varieties to geographical places through racial meanings, and the ways in which language hierarchies were constructed and reinforced, it became clear that all forms of English were not equal. The teachers struggled to negotiate spaces in which they could challenge the silent privilege accorded to Standard American English (Nero, 2005, 2006) by problematizing school policies and discourses. All four of the teachers might be constructed as speakers of mainstream and "native" varieties of English, leaving us with questions about the racialized nature of the teachers' linguistic identities and demonstrating the ways in which race is implicated in the constructs of native English, Standard English, World Englishes (Kachru, 1990), and African American Vernacular English (AAVE) (Lippi-Green, 2011). I concur with Reagan (2002), who replaces the term *Standard English* with *mainstream English* to avoid "an implicit and unarticulated assumption that a standard variety is in some way 'better' than a nonstandard one" (p. 5). However, I sometimes use the term *Standard English* in this discussion to more closely reflect the language used by the teachers in the study. What varieties of English were the four teachers teaching? What Englishes did they speak and consequently legitimate in the course of their teaching? Nero (2005) has noted that "while the ESL class might celebrate cultural diversity in theory, it requires linguistic uniformity in practice"

(p. 198). In the context of school systems that legitimated only varieties of English constructed as mainstream or standard, how might main-
stream-English-speaking teachers position themselves in relation to quietly
racialized school policies surrounding language variation?

In this chapter, I first examine the ways in which languages and language varieties are territorialized, that is, attached to specific places, and
then question the desirability and feasibility of rupturing that connection. I
go on to argue that Standard English is a construction, or what Makoni and
Pennycook (2007) term an *invention*, one that contributes unwittingly to
inequitable relations of power among former empires and colonized nations
and that continues to play an important role in the persistence of a particular international racial status quo. Although language hierarchies are not
constructed deliberately, they do not occur randomly either. Rather, they
evolve because the meanings given to the range of English language varieties
develop within particular racial and colonial patterns that are often unquestioned. Third, I demonstrate the ways in which "World Englishes" have
been unintentionally put into the service of racism. In the fourth section, I
explore teachers' negotiations of a language variety that is not associated
with recent immigrants, African American Vernacular English, concluding
with questions about what it means to disrupt the connection between place
and race, to deterritorialize English.

## THE PRODUCTION OF LOCALITY

Central to the functioning of the notion of language variation is the concept
of *place*, not only place as a static fact but on a deeper level the "production
of locality" (Hardt & Negri, 2000, pp. 44–45). The ways in which language
varieties, accents, and nativeness are positioned and conceptualized in English teaching contexts play a significant but unconscious role in producing
place. What do I mean by "producing place"? On one hand, a place is
concrete and indisputable. No one can claim with any credibility that Mo-
rocco is Mongolia or that Lagos is Rio de Janeiro. At the same time, place
is something beyond geographic coordinates. The ways in which a place is
understood and takes on meanings, the constructions of authenticity related
to a place, the circulation of power and ideas associated with a place, the
patchwork of images and adjectives that spring to mind at a mention of a
place, all of these are shaped by broader social processes. These processes
are what I mean by "producing place."

As an example, let us consider the ways in which Jeffrey Eugenides
(2011) conceives of Kolkata in a short passage from *The Marriage Plot*,
which is set in the 1980s (when the city was still named Calcutta), through
one of his characters who travels there and muses:

Some cities have fallen into ruin and some are built upon ruins, but others contain their own ruins while growing. . . . Calcutta was a shell, the shell of empire, and from inside this shell nine million Indians spilled out. Beneath the city's colonial surface lay the real India, the ancient country of Rajputs, nawabs, and Mughals, and this country erupted too from the baghs and alleyways. And, at some moments, especially in the evening when the music vendors played their instruments in the streets, it was as though the British had never been here at all. (p. 315)

In this way, Eugenides constructs a sense of place as having an inherently authentic nature, a primordial identity: "the real India," with solid lines between Indian and British and assumed national boundaries. What is produced, through this passage, as the real India is a construct frozen in time sometime in the early 1700s, before British influence has trickled its way across the land. But if an identity becomes less authentically part of a place because it is imported, how real then is the "real India"? Some of the groups mentioned by Eugenides—the Mughals and the Rajputs, for instance—are believed by some historians to have themselves been invaders at some point in history, which begs questions about how realness is defined. What is the relationship between mobility and authenticity? As we think about what constitutes proper English, or the idea of a real America, the social and discursive formation of place is an important notion to keep foregrounded.

In the context of this study, the production of locality was a deeply, although certainly invisibly, racialized process. "Place" and "race" worked together in complicated ways, shaping identities and subjectivities and ultimately reinforcing inequalities in race and postcolonial status within the schools of the study. As ESOL teachers negotiate linguistic variation in their classrooms, they make choices, either consciously or unconsciously, about how to connect language, race, and place. Because the relationships among these three have been established quietly over centuries of language evolution and social history, they often operate on an unconscious level. In this chapter, I argue that when teachers develop an explicit consciousness about the effects of their choices, they are better equipped to teach in a way that reflects their pedagogical goals surrounding language variation. In contrast, teaching without a consciousness of the interrelationships among race, place, and language will, given the racialized and colonial nature of the terrain in which they practice, lead individual teachers to simply reproduce existing power arrangements.

In recent decades, globalization theorists have observed the shrinking significance of location in social and cultural arrangements (Appadurai, 1996; Giddens, 1990; Scholte, 2000), and many have expressed their approval. In their description of the new world order they label *Empire*, Hardt and Negri (2000) describe the bright-eyed promise offered by contemporary formulations of placelessness. During these days of fast travel, instantaneous communication over vast distances, and greater connectedness among far-flung points around the globe, place has become less important, they tell us, the boundaries that define a given place less stable, and the distinction between the global and the local increasingly contrived. They explain that social movements toward place-based forms of resistance, which emphasize local identities, activities, ethnicities, and histories, are misguided because they rely on a manufactured naturalization of local differences to preserve heterogeneity and difference. These fresh ideas, which initially arouse energy and optimism for an equitable future in which a wide range of variously hybridized identities are not only permitted but embraced, are echoed in complex and exciting ways in the work of many second language education scholars who frame their work within critical globalization studies, including Pennycook's (2007) writings on Global Englishes and transcultural flows, Canagarajah's (2011) work on code-meshing, Blackledge and Creese's (2010) exploration of translanguaging practices, the ideas about metrolanguaging put forward by Otsuji and Pennycook (2010), and Mario Saraceni's analysis of the location of English (2010). All of these lenses (and others) seemed to abound with potential for the analysis of my study. However, as I considered the ways in which placelessness and the deterritorialization of English worked within the schools of this study, I found myself repeatedly running up against solid walls that interfered with the flows of cultural and linguistic hybridity, walls erected by racial formation and racism. The relationships between language and place seemed particularly significant in these interactions.

## THE INVENTION OF STANDARD ENGLISH

How does the local get produced? Mignolo (2011) has connected the construction of colonial location to modernity, noting that coloniality is constructed in contrast to the modern and in this way helps to distinguish what is modern from what is not: "Coloniality . . . is constitutive of modernity . . . there is no modernity without coloniality" (p. 3). Hardt and Negri (2000) ask about "the social machines that create and recreate the identities and differences that are understood as the local" (p. 48). One of these social machines, I argue, is the shaping of the English language. In the context of English language varieties and accents, the local is produced in relation to not the global—because there is no form of English that could be accurately categorized as global—but rather the metropole language, or motherland language (a gender-neutral term being lacking). However, although no global form of English exists in practice, one does operate in a theoretical sense— that is, "Standard English." And although the notion of Standard English occurs only in the hypothetical, it is understood and constructed as an objective fact in everyday interactions, the popular media, academia, and schools. For instance, Standard English is presented as a fact by both a major British newspaper and an examination board in an article in the *Daily Telegraph* that bore the headline, "Standard English in Decline Among Teenagers," which went on to report that "Cambridge Assessment, one of the country's biggest examination boards, surveyed more than 2,000 teenagers in 26 English secondary schools. They were presented with various phrases—and asked to mark out those employing non-standard English. Half of teenagers fail to spot the difference between standard English grammar and colloquial language" (Paton, 2008). The article's author assumes universally accepted boundaries around what counts as standard and what is colloquial. Rather than highlighting the widespread permeability and arbitrariness of language boundaries, the fact that half of teenagers do not perceive these boundaries seems to be presented by the author as fodder for the argument that teenagers are ignorant. Even academic linguistics texts sometimes define Standard English in unquestioned ways. In *From Old English to Standard English: A Coursebook in Language Variations Across Time*, Dennis Freeborn (2006) defines Standard English as "a common system of writing . . . also the dialect of what is called 'educated speech'" (p. 1).

The term *Standard English* tends to summon definitions that rely primarily within popular discourse on place or geographical classifications— British English, American English, Australian or Canadian or New Zealand English—although none of these "Englishes" exists as a unitary and homogeneous variety. Standard English is an invention. English is English because of its connection to a place, England, but also to other places that have moved in and become representative of the English-speaking "West," what Kachru calls "inner circle" countries or what Holliday (2005) refers to as BANA (Britain, Australasia, and North America). These languages, too, are inventions. Makoni and Pennycook (2007) in fact assert convincingly that all languages are inventions, that the boundaries among them are so porous as to be nonexistent, and that rather than struggling to preserve the fiction of linguistic rigidity, our efforts would be better directed toward acknowledging and embracing language hybridity. The connectedness of language to place is then also an invention. Our engagement with the notion of place sets into motion processes of identification and differentiation, producing locality by positioning varieties in relation to geographic origins and in the process inventing the metropole, which is as dependent on its produced periphery for its existence as the colonies are dependent on the motherland for theirs (Mohanty, 1991). The notion of a "Standard English" collapses without "nonstandard Englishes" or "World Englishes" to set it apart, to serve as an Other to its standardness. As we invent Standard English, we are in fact inventing the metropole by producing the local to serve as a contrast.

Pennycook's (2007) ideas about Global Englishes "locate the spread and use of English within critical theories of globalization" (p. 5). Pennycook suggests that we shift our attention from a focus on *place* to one on *flows*. Using global hip-hop as a heuristic, he explores the production of new forms of localization and global subjectivities, proposing that "we need to move beyond arguments about homogeneity or heterogeneity, or imperialism and nation-states, and instead focus on translocal and transcultural flows" (pp. 5–6). He uses the term *transcultural flows* "to address the ways in which cultural forms move, change, and are reused to fashion new identities in diverse contexts" (p. 6). As I first read these ideas, they struck me as inventive and potentially enormously constructive in the context of the present study, in which multiple forms of English found their way into ESOL classrooms, from Ghana and Jamaica but also from across the street, from fellow playmates in the neighborhoods ESOL students lived in, from the hallways of school, from the media children were consuming. Ideas about a diminished focus on place also surface within Canagarajah's (2006) work on code-meshing. The author notes the effects of changing demographics of English users, which now include a greater proportion of multilingual speakers globally. This shift "compel[s] us to think of English as a plural language that embodies multiple norms and standards. English should be treated as a multinational language, one that belongs to diverse communities and not owned only by the metropolitan communities" (p. 589). Similarly, Blackledge and Creese's (2010) work on multilingualism explores flexible bilingualism and translanguaging (García & Wei, 2014) practices in a context in which multilingualism is legitimated—that is, complementary (or heritage language) schools in the United Kingdom. The practices they describe indicate that "we are moving towards a conception of linguistic practices as multiple, plural, shifting, and eclectic, by drawing on features of what we might call 'languages', but calling into play linguistic features and means from diverse sources" (p. 25). In writing about metrolingualism, Otsuji and Pennycook (2010) observed that "current cultural, social, geopolitical, and linguistic thinking is predominated by a celebration of multiplicity, hybridity and diversity. Within this trend, terminology such as multiculturalism, multilingualism, and cosmopolitanism are taken as a focus and a desirable norm in various fields including academia, policy-making and education" (p. 243). The authors express concerns related to potential take-up of static identity categories alongside the appropriation of local forms of cosmopolitanism and about the potential for "happy hybridity"—that is, hybridity conceptualized as fixed and unproblematic. These new, fluid representations of language highlight the potential for new, more equitable conceptualizations of language use, particularly English use, within school walls.

    In contrast to these optimistic discourses, in this study the potential for new forms of localization and global subjectivity were largely unfulfilled, and in this chapter I explore why. I describe the ways in which linguistic hybridity and fluidity were impeded by racial constructions that were impervious to change. As you read these examples, I ask you to consider the importance of an understanding of the construction of the local and of the relationships among race, place, and language.

## Standard English and Whiteness

In Chapter 4, I discussed teachers' identities, focusing in particular on racial formations. In a discussion of English language teaching, it would be inadequate to attend to teachers' racial identities without addressing their linguistic identities. On a superficial level, these two may appear to be distinct, if loosely related, dimensions of difference, but a careful deconstruction of Whiteness helps us to see that they are actually inextricable, one from the other. Just as a certain degree of unquestioned legitimacy is attributed to White teachers, teachers who speak mainstream English—a variety that is silently but enduringly coupled with Whiteness—are perceived to be more legitimate than speakers of English that is not mainstream, including English spoken by nonnative-English speakers.

The identities of English language teachers are multilayered and cannot be examined without an eye toward race and language. Race and place have a complicated relationship with one another. For example, my own heritage is Sri Lankan, and as a TESOL professional of color, I have grappled with a (perhaps imagined, perhaps founded) sense that my ownership over the English language is sometimes perceived as less than rightful, particularly by my ESOL students. However, the form of English I speak is privileged, taking its cues primarily from my childhood in Australia, my undergraduate years in Canada, and my graduate schooling and current academic life in the United States. That is to say, like Katie, I speak a form of English associated with Whiteness, although I am not White. Race and place have not mapped onto each other in prescribed ways within our lives, although the acceptability of my disconnecting privileged English from Sri Lankan or Korean ethnicity might certainly be disputed, and legitimately so. Our identities, like the identities of all humans, including the other three teachers, Jane, Margaret, and Alexandra, are multiple and fluid and fluctuate according to context, and the degrees of authority associated with each facet of identity are not constant. Those of us who speak legitimated forms of English have a responsibility to consider the implications of privileged-speaker status for the pursuit of social justice in our practice.

## Language Legitimacy and Race

Questions about how race shapes the perceived legitimacy of languages and language variations are of pressing concern to TESOL practitioners. Grant and Wong's (2008) analysis of the implications of Bourdieu's work for the teaching of English language variations is helpful for understanding the arbitrary ways in which mainstream or standard varieties of speech are socially and educationally sanctioned, while those that do not represent the majority can be "categorized, manipulated, even demonized" (p. 21). Language can achieve legitimacy when it is racialized in certain ways. Discrimination on the basis of language variety and accent has received attention from researchers looking at language attitudes. Hudley and Mallinson (2010) tell us that "listeners (of many diverse social backgrounds) consistently rank speakers of standardized English as being smarter and of a higher status than speakers of non-standardized English dialects" (p. 2). If we break this quote down further and think about actual incidents, it doesn't take too long to realize that not all nonstandardized dialects are equal. My British-accented friend Sharon jokes that on the phone, she gains 10 gratis points on her IQ assessment by virtue of her accent, which is not standard within her American context. (She says that she then loses another 50 points when she turns up in the flesh as a Black woman.) Responses to accentedness and language variety are deeply racialized and related to coloniality. At the individual level, numerous studies have shown participants to accord a higher degree of competence, authority, and even comprehensibility to speakers they believe are White than those they believe are of color. Stephanie Lindemann found that U.S. undergraduates typically rated nonnative speakers with a category of stigmatized or "broken" English (2005), with the exception of nonnative speakers from Western European countries. Rubin (1992) played audio excerpts of a native-English speaker to participants, presenting a picture of either an Asian or a White teacher whom the researchers claimed was the speaker. The students who saw an Asian speaker rated the speech "more foreign" than the the speech that was presented as spoken by a White person. The "Asian" speakers were also evaluated to be lower-quality teachers on the basis of the speech sample. These individual-level responses are shaped by and contribute to discrimination at the global level—creoles, pidgins, and indigenized varieties of English are termed as such not because they are grammatically or structurally inferior to "native" varieties of English but because they are spoken by people of color (Mufwene, 2001).

## Deterritorialization and Race

If place, race, and language variety are intimately enmeshed with each other, what might it mean to challenge these connections, to tease them apart? What role does deterritorialization play in this endeavor? It has been argued that English is already deterritorialized. It has spread around the globe to become an official language in about 60 countries worldwide, but it does not have official status in some of the countries with which it is most tightly associated, including the United States, the United Kingdom, and Australia.

In his book titled *The Relocation of English*, Mario Saraceni (2010) describes shifts that might promise a deterritorializing effect, which he sees currently (but as yet insufficiently) in process: a shift from English conceptualized as the language of England to English as the language of many countries; from an emphasis on the importance of nativeness in English to the use of English as a second language or lingua franca; from English as owned by native speakers to English owned by those who use it; from English as a monochrome standard to a recognition of a multiplicity of valid Englishes; and from English as vehicle for Anglo-Saxon culture to English as capable of expressing any culture.

Hardt and Negri (2000), too, argue that placelessness is desirable, that localist positions and the celebration of local identities reinforce global economic disparities. They suggest that producing, maintaining, and encouraging local differences ultimately serves to falsely naturalize differences of the local in a way that is nostalgically misleading, and that it is impossible to establish local identities that exist outside global flows. One key to deterritorialization that they propose is mobility of labor, which in abundance can alter the meanings of locality. For instance, it is because of mobility that race and place have mapped onto each other as they have in Katie's life—her parents adopted her from Korea when she was 4 months old. So her labor as a teacher in the United States results from mobility and adds to the confounding of the meanings of race and place. Another example of mobility of labor is in the outsourcing of telecommunications labor to workers in India. When a U.S. inhabitant calls a U.S. company and hears an Indian accent once, the exchange is unremarkable, but when it happens with frequency, Indian accents move more centrally into U.S. life. This is where deterritorialization arguments start to come apart at the seams.

Racially tinged forces rally volubly against placelessness. Customers who are uncritical of discourses about U.S. job displacement resist Indian customer service representatives, complaining about poor service and unintelligibility, the latter itself being a social construct. Underlying such complaints is resistance to the type of mobility that places the voice of an Indian customer service representative into the living room of a U.S. household. Often mobility—moving from one country to another, international adoption—requires some capital, be it cultural, economic, or symbolic (Bourdieu, 1984). Katie struggles to establish legitimacy with an older White male colleague, knowing that her interactions with him are racialized and gendered. Her mobility contributes to placelessness, but it is resisted because of her race. Because of racism, English teachers are less mobile than Hardt and Negri (2000) might hope. These authors presume that the mobility of capital (in this case, the English language and labor, that is, English teachers) creates a "place" that is a "non-place" (p. 208). English language teachers are indeed mobile, but differentially so according to race, with teachers who are constructed as White being most mobile. The permanence of place is intensified by race. Despite the advocacy efforts of organizations such as TESOL and the American Association for Applied Linguistics (AAAL), students who come to the United States to complete graduate degrees in TESOL frequently encounter trouble securing jobs in the United States upon graduation, often because of linguistic discrimination on the basis of nativeness or accent (Moussu & Llurda, 2008). While the importation of White, native-speaking English teachers into postcolonial and other international contexts is so routine as to be institutionalized by numerous governments, the importation of a racial minority, "World English"–speaking English teacher from an expanding or outer circle country to provide labor in an "inner circle" country (Kachru, 1990) is rare. Even in their home countries, English teachers are discriminated against, tripping over job advertisements for "native-English speakers," or even "White native-English teachers only." Even when nativeness is no longer in question, as with second-generation immigrants, the legitimacy of teachers of color is called into question (Curtis & Romney, 2006; Tinker Sachs, 2006). For these reasons, a "place" cannot become a "non-place." Is a deterritorialized English even a feasible concept? What would English look like with all traces of locality erased? Is it possible for places to keep their (mutable, negotiated, subjective) meanings but for us to haul up the anchors linking English to particular places? Beyond feasibility, do we even want a deterritorialized English?

Dipesh Chakrabarty (2000) offers us an alternative to the elusive notion of deterritorialization. In *Provincializing Europe*, Chakrabarty acknowledges that European colonization has occurred and cannot be undone and that the effects of this process have become such a significant part of human history that to imagine a reversal of colonization is almost absurd. Rather than seeking deterritorialization, Chakrabarty writes about the project of provincializing or decentering the intellectual footprint left by Europe across the globe—that is not to say rejecting European thought wholesale but rather understanding the ways in which European thought is woven throughout everyday life. He argues not against universals but rather describes the inherent instability of universals, shaped as they always are by particular histories. He notes the relationship between thought and place.

The ways in which we think are shaped by the language we use. MacPherson (2003) provides a clear example, telling us about how forestry discourses introduced by an international development agency to an Indian Himalayan village might rely on utilitarian terms such as *wood* and *lumber* and *harvest*—language more appropriate to a commercial forestry model and language that naturalizes the cutting down and taking of the trees—rather than terms closer to *tree* and *forest*, which better represent the elaborate ecosystem involved and its complex relationship with and spiritual value to the village. The English language has been territorialized by its centuries of history, and it, too, carries particular epistemologies. Yet, the project of teaching English rarely includes as part of its mission the provincializing of Europe, a critical scrutiny of the ways in which epistemologies are changed as English is learned. Might the provincialization of English be a better alternative to its deterritorialization or, perhaps, a necessary accompaniment? Let us examine the ways in which deterritorialization and provincialization functioned within the study.

## "IT'S A BIT OF A DIFFERENT ENGLISH": WORLD ENGLISHES

One significant factor in shaping the relationship between racial and linguistic identities, although invisible, was the school systems' policies surrounding what they labeled "World English." During my master's program, I was moved by the energy and commitment of a guest speaker in my methods of teaching ESOL class, Jessica Schneider. Jessica was an administrator for ESOL in a local school district, and as she spoke, it became clear that she cared deeply about social justice, about improving the lot of the children in the ESOL program that she helped direct, and furthermore that she was knowledgeable about the ways in which power circulated within the schools under her supervision. A few years later, when Alexandra, Jane, Katie, and Margaret were in the same master's program, Jessica gave the same presentation as a guest speaker in their class. Jessica provided the first exposure I recall having to the term *World English* (WE). She began her presentation by asking us to hazard a guess at the most commonly spoken language in her district's ESOL program. I had expected it to be Spanish—the schools I knew had large Mexican and Salvadoran populations—and I was surprised by her answer: "World English." Have you encountered "World English" speakers in schooling contexts you know? What are the defining characteristics of WE and WE speakers? What makes WE different from other Englishes you know? Close your eyes and picture a WE speaker. How are WE speakers different from other English speakers you know? What sets WE speakers apart? During that guest lecture, the term *World English* was not defined, although I know that I came away from the class with a notion of a fairly static and monolithic language variety, and certainly one that did not count as "English," as evidenced by the placement of its speakers into ESOL classes. The term *World English* was at one point used synonymously with *pidgin*, another term that lacks a clear definition. Jessica explained some of the needs particular to World English speakers. As an audience, we managed to accumulate through this conversation a series of images to associate with the term through the stories that Jessica told. She spoke about the needs of students from various Caribbean and African countries whose schooling had been interrupted, who experienced miscommunication in their new school contexts, and who needed special support in socialization into U.S. public schooling, two examples provided being holding a pencil and remaining seated in a chair in the classroom. Although I didn't process the images consciously, the children I imagined were racial minorities, well behind their peers academically, frustrated and disruptive.

At the beginning of the school year in both counties of the study, each ESOL teacher received a roster of their ESOL students that listed each student's name, age, class, country of origin, and native language. Placement decisions were made at the district ESOL office using an informal, picture-based assessment. In both counties, many of the students were listed as speaking "World English" as a first language. The term *World English* has come to refer to any of the varieties of English that have emerged in postcolonial (Bhatt, 2005; Kachru, 1990) and other international (Brutt-Griffler, 2002; Llurda, 2004) contexts. Through the lens of this study, I perceived that World English became constructed as marked and devalued and that furthermore, the factor that relegated a language to World English status was not degree of language variation, but race. Through the schools' institutional structures, World Englishes were constructed as socially illegitimate rather than as "an additional resource for linguistic, sociolinguistic, and literary creativity" (Bhatt, 2005, p. 25). This construction contributes to a devaluing of people of color globally and to assimilationist pressure to coax into Anglicization the varieties of English spoken by people of color. Other than the talk by Jessica Schneider, Katie, Margaret, Alexandra, and Jane (and I) had received little instruction about World Englishes throughout their graduate coursework and in their schools. Language hierarchies had been supported to some degree in some of their classes but specifically deconstructed in historical context in other classes.

One day, watching a young boy who I read as White speaking to a teacher in an elementary school hallway, I became keenly aware that a blurry area existed between the district's definition of World Englishes and other varieties of English that also differ structurally and prosodically from the governing American standard. It took me a moment to recognize the boy's accent as Scottish, and the brief conversation had ended and the child departed before I realized that although I'd been within easy earshot, I didn't know what he had said. My ear had not had time to adjust to the rhythm and flow of his speech, and his words were therefore unintelligible to me. The child was not, however, in ESOL. The students who were referred to as World English–speaking students in the context of this study were all racial minority students, almost all Black, and came from African, Caribbean, or Asian countries. At a superficial glance it would appear that students were defined as World English speakers if their first language was a variety of English that differed significantly from Standard U.S. English. However, upon deeper scrutiny it became apparent that beyond speakers' first languages, their racial identities were relevant to how their languages were described.

As we consider the construction of place, the ways in which the local is constructed in relation to the global, the category and categorization of "World English" become important. Typically, layers of the local are particularized—by city, region, nation, perhaps even continent. When we think of the local, we might refer to microfinance practices of rural women from Ghana, English spoken by Americans of Puerto Rican descent in New York, or silk weaving by artisans in Chiang Mai, Thailand. So what is "local" in relation to "world"? To catalog under the broad label *world* is unusual. One might wonder where Englishes not classified as "World English" come from, if not from the world. Outer space, perhaps? It would appear that the term *world* stands as a proxy for something else. The term *world music* codes music in a similarly sweeping manner, as if to convey that "world music" is from the world but that music that does not fall under the label *world music* must be unworldly or otherworldly. Both the Merriam-Webster dictionary and the more modish Bing dictionary shed light on usage of the word *world* defining *world music* as "non-Western." This definition could apply, in a rudimentary way, to the use of the term *world* in *World English*, leaving aside the impossibility of clearly defining *Western*.

The use of the term in its singular form—*English* rather than *Englishes*—belies the multiplicity of varieties represented within this category. Boundaries among languages (and indeed languages themselves) are a social formation, so that the placement of languages or varieties under one label presupposes some uniformity and assumes that they share important, even defining characteristics. "World English"–speaking students in the public schools in this study do not all speak one monolithic, consistent form of English. What, then, is the unifying factor? What causes these varieties from all over the world to be grouped together? Examining the context of this study, it becomes apparent that the unifying factors are race and colonial status. The terms *world music* and *World English* function as racial and colonial categories.

Arguably, the most widely cited model of World Englishes within TESOL is the one developed by Braj Kachru (1990), who has made a distinction among *outer circle* countries, in which varieties of English that are locally established and standardized are not typically the first languages of the citizens and are not legitimated globally (examples include Ghana, Liberia, Nigeria, Sierra Leone, Kenya, Tanzania, Zambia, Bangladesh, India, Malaysia, Philippines, Pakistan, Singapore, and Sri Lanka); *inner circle* countries, which dictate dominant standards in outer circle countries and around the world (including the United Kingdom, the United States, Australia, Canada, and New Zealand); and *expanding circle* countries, in which English has no governmental or official historical status but functions widely as a lingua franca or is studied widely (for example, China, France, Brazil, Saudi Arabia, Japan, Korea, Russia, and Sweden). The majority of the populations in inner circle countries are White. Native-English speakers from Jamaica (which is not included in Kachru's 1988 model) were classified as World English speakers in this study's public schools, but Jamaica does not fit smoothly into any of Kachru's categories because most Jamaican citizens speak a form of English as their first language. I propose that race is the most significant factor keeping many language variations, including Jamaican English, from amassing the same linguistic power as, for instance, British, American, and Canadian English. I contend that Jamaican English was categorized as a World English simply because that country's population is predominantly of color. Katie, Margaret, Alexandra, and Jane's World English–speaking students spoke varieties of English that were not validated by their school system, and they had been placed in ESOL classes to encourage their English to quickly approximate American English. Brutt-Griffler (2002) notes that "the center-driven narrative of English language spread writes people residing outside the West out of their central role in the spread of English and their place in making the language we call English" (p. viii). I believe that the scope of the "center-driven narrative" extends far beyond "people residing outside the West" to reach people living in Western countries—if they are not White.

The placement of World English speakers into ESOL in the first place presented a fundamental social challenge to the teachers. Within the cultures of all four schools, ESOL was socially constructed as deficit, with ESOL students perceived as unable to speak English rather than in a more positive framing of *bicultural/lingual* or *multicultural/lingual*. Jane, who taught students from Jamaica, Ghana, and Sierra Leone (coded by the main ESOL office as L1 speakers of World English), wanted to legitimate multiple varieties of English, including World Englishes. However, her efforts were hampered by the mere placement of World English speakers into ESOL classes, because the policy communicated to the school community that these students were not native speakers of English and could consequently lay no rightful claim to English. Hill (2008) has written of practices that have the effect of publicly producing racism even where overt racist discussion is not permitted. This positioning is an example of one such practice, unobtrusively refracting a history of colonialism and contemporary persistent racism. One interesting aspect of this thread was the invisibility of race within processes that were intensely racialized. The teachers and I had numerous conversations that we only later conceptualized as deeply race-related.

New teachers receiving directives from a central district office, while they are attempting to acclimatize to new procedures and policies in an unfamiliar professional context, are less likely to question the logic of the reporting of their students' linguistic identities. Jane's students questioned the presence of native-English-speaking peers in their ESOL classes. The teacher tried to offer her students an explanation without openly criticizing the racism and linguicism undergirding the placement policy: "World English is tough, and it's tough for a couple of reasons," she told me. Of one student in particular, Terrell, Jane said, "So it's almost like they're putting him down, like 'Why are you in this class?'" She went on to explain:

So I say, "Well, it's an English; it's a bit of a different English, and we're working on the writing skills." Some of the kids really don't understand why they're in the class. It's almost like, "What are you, dumb? Why are you in here?" I know why he's there, I know the writing structures are different, and what needs to be focused on is the reading and writing. (Jane, Interview, June 25)

Jane did not want to contribute to the stigmatization of World Englishes, so she framed the difference between World Englishes and mainstream English as a gap between speaking proficiency and reading and writing skills. She perceived spoken World Englishes to pose no complication within the school context but believed that writing structures in, for instance, Granadian and Jamaican vernacular English were sufficiently different to necessitate support to World English–speaking students:

*Jane:* Some of the words he uses I have to have him clarify because I don't know what he means. Yeah, it would probably be an issue of standard versus nonstandard English. Trying to help him communicate more. Sometimes I understand what he means, but . . . structure, too. I'm thinking that some of my kids are from Sierra Leone, and the structure is so different. And organization, too.
*Suhanthie:* Is that because they're speaking a different form of English?
*Jane:* You mean, could it just be their education? Could be. It could be where they're coming from and what they've worked on and what they haven't. (Interview, June 25)

The school's placement of World English speakers in ESOL supported linguistic hierarchies that Bhatt (2005) has referred to as "English-linguistic apartheid" (p. 27) and made it impossible for Jane to present World Englishes as anything other than varieties of English that were unsanctioned by the school without openly criticizing the school's policy. However, by implying that students were in ESOL in order to acquire written, academic varieties only, she legitimated at least the spoken varieties of World Englishes. A further complication was presented by the indistinct lines among interrupted education, World English, and ESOL. Students whose education had been interrupted were often placed in ESOL regardless of their first language and were labeled *World English speakers*. Using this term to refer to students whose education had been interrupted reinforced the false construction of World English speakers as students without formal schooling, with both categories consequently acquiring a deficit meaning. In this instance, it is difficult to avoid slipping into a discussion of deficit in terms of a lack of literacy or education because in some cases, real conditions of poverty accompany the interruption of education.

## "THEY'RE LEARNING THREE LANGUAGES AND THEY ALL SOUND LIKE ENGLISH": AFRICAN AMERICAN VERNACULAR ENGLISH (AAVE)

A second way in which race was made invisible in the schools of the study was in the silences surrounding AAVE. Despite the fact that all four schools had large numbers of AAVE speakers, there was no formal discussion or even acknowledgment of AAVE within the schools. In Jane's and Alexandra's schools, almost all of the native-English-speaking students spoke African American language varieties colloquially. However, every ESOL teacher practicing within all four schools of the study spoke mainstream English. The teachers understood that they were to teach mainstream English and that school-based and standardized testing would assess students' facility in mainstream English. However, no guidance was provided about how to address AAVE.

The term *Standard English* is heavily—albeit for the most part invisibly—racialized. The term *AAVE* is usually juxtaposed with the apparently neutral Standard English. *Standard English* often serves as a code for *White English*, with its ostensible neutrality suppressing the racialized nature of language discrimination. The tacit assumption that Standard English is racially neutral is related to the social, and particularly discursive, construction of White as neutral (Frankenberg, 1993). When Whiteness is equated with neutrality and transparency, it becomes normative, "the implicit referent, i.e., the yardstick by which to encode and represent cultural Others" (Mohanty, 1991 , p. 55). Similarly, when the standardness of Standard English is reinforced, varieties of English that are not typically associated with Whiteness, including AAVE and World Englishes, can become pathologized (Grant & Wong, 2008).

Alexandra understood that she was charged with two tasks that were frequently in conflict with each other: to teach her immigrant middle school students to communicate with their peers as part of their quest to belong and to teach them the language of power so that they might achieve academic success. Within their school lives, her students were surrounded primarily by AAVE: "So you're picking Black vernacular up quicker than you are Mrs. Lau's English" (Afternoon Tea, June 19). Alexandra experienced her task as daunting because she taught in the context of a culture that devalued African American students' culture and language. She objected to the teaching of only Standard English in school primarily because it was disconnected from the lives of her students: "If one of the outcomes is to speak standard American English, then that's a different language than we speak around here" (Afternoon Tea, June 19). Alexandra appreciated the value of recognizing multiple language varieties and advocated unambiguously teaching students to navigate among them. She would ask her students to consider, "What does this mean, why do you say it differently?" and commented to me, "You have to teach them that there's different settings that you're going to use Black vernacular and you're not going to use it" (Afternoon Tea, June 19). She recognized that students were receiving mixed messages about the nature of English and sympathized with them: "I feel sorry for these kids [ESOL students] because they're learning three different languages and they all sound like English." Part of her antiracist agenda included challenging the supremacy of Standard English. In order to decenter the unjustified authority carried by Standard English, she chose to downplay it and focused instead on teaching colloquially used language: "What's most important is speaking with your peers and being 'part of'" (Afternoon Tea, June 19).

Alexandra's choice is situated on complicated terrain. As they choose how to navigate among language varieties, teachers negotiate the conflict between what Bakhtin (1981) characterized as *centripetal forces* and *centrifugal forces*. Centripetal forces (literally center-seeking forces, from the Latin roots *centrum*, "center," and *petere*, "to seek") are the social forces that pull students toward the center, encouraging them to assimilate, to conform, to use standard, prescribed varieties of English. A normalizing energy, centripetal forces cast a wide net in an effort to capture and then standardize the varieties spoken by all and to exclude those who do not or cannot conform. Centrifugal forces (center-fleeing forces from the Latin *centrum*, "center," and *fugere*, "to flee"), in contrast, support the natural diversity of language use, move toward the linguistic periphery, and give voice to articulations infrequently sanctioned officially. Single-mindedly teaching only nonstandard varieties of English can whittle away at centripetal forces but can simultaneously deprive students of access to socially favored ways of communicating, particularly disadvantaging students who don't have access to Standard English in their homes and communities outside school. Conversely, teaching and acknowledging only Standard English, which supports centripetal forces, reinforces its supremacy and marginalizes nonstandard varieties of English and the students who speak them. This is the reality in many public school settings. In theory, teachers' support of diverse ways of using language could serve to move students' understandings away from the idea of one legitimate language. This is not merely a pedagogical stance, but an epistemological one; it creates space for the possibility of multiple simultaneously correct language variations and the legitimacy of more than one perspective and attendant understanding.

Jane, too, made decisions about how to present language varieties:

> *Jane:* Yeah, I've taught the difference between *dog* and *dawg*.
> *Suhanthie:* Dog and *dog*?
> *Jane:* Like *dog*, D-O-G, is that sitting right there [indicating her puppy, Duff], and *dawg*, D-A-W-G, is like your friend. I thought it was just so ironic; here's me teaching the language of the kids.
> *Suhanthie:* Do you tell them specifically about language variations?
> *Jane:* I just say it's slang. It's just a popular word for your friend.
> (Jane, Interview, June 25)

What neither of us mentioned specifically is that in the context of Jane's school, with an African American population of more than 70%, the word *dawg* has associations with African American identity. In teaching "the language of the kids," therefore, Jane is actually teaching terms associated with AAVE. In the context of a school system that skirted around the connections between race and language varieties, Jane needed to find a way to explain AAVE without delegitimizing it. In teaching AAVE from her position of teacher-authority, Jane promoted its validity to her students. However, she did not identify AAVE as a language variety but rather referred to it as "slang," which might be more appropriately framed as a register than a language variety. Despite the fact that fewer than 7% of the students at her school spoke what might be defined as the standard (read White) form of English, her school system and curriculum provided no space for addressing any nonstandard form of English. The word *slang* can carry negative connotations—the second entry in *Webster's Third International Dictionary* describes slang as "vulgar or inferior"—but Jane balanced her description with the word *popular*, which is positively nuanced, thereby promoting a conception of accepted language. The equivocal representation seemed to be the most constructive framing Jane could adopt under the circumstances, an uneasy response to the oblique messages within her institutional context. Teaching and legitimating AAVE have far-reaching consequences, affecting not only AAVE speakers but all English speakers. Challenging the supremacy of Standard English can add legitimacy to all varieties of English that are not mainstream, including English spoken with a nonnative accent, thus posing a challenge to the assumed superiority of native speakers (Cook, 1999).

## CONCLUSION: PROVINCIALIZING ENGLISH

The role played by race in connecting place to language highlights for us the ways in which ESOL classrooms can contribute to the perpetuation of inequality. The deterritorialization called for by Mario Saraceni (2010) and others is a goal worth pursuing, but its admirable loftiness means that they may take many decades or even centuries to accomplish. It is likely that English will one day be seen as the language of many countries (and perhaps even of many racial identities), that the importance of nativeness will fade, that many dialects of English will be recognized as valid (even those spoken by racial minorities), and that English will be seen as capable of expressing any culture. In fact, a shift toward these states is already afoot. However, given the length of time that is likely to be necessary before English becomes deterritorialized and the resistance, primarily racial resistance, that the process encounters, I suggest that the goal of provincializing English become paramount, not instead of deterritorialization but in addition to it.

Let us consider how deterritorialization and provincialization worked in the study. It has been many centuries since the continent (place) Africa was geographically relevant to AAVE, and the idea of AAVE is now more racialized than place-based. However, what sets AAVE apart from other varieties of English is its previous association with the continent. AAVE is of course a raced construct, but it is also one that harkens back to a location. Relying solely on attempts to make AAVE placeless could be a ridiculously long-term project. Similarly, altering the social positioning of various postcolonial varieties, such as the one spoken by Jane's student Terrell, requires an undoing of centuries of habit. An alternative approach might be to shift our primary focus from deterritorialization to provincialization, promoting an awareness of the ways in which the different varieties carry meanings and why.

This chapter has engaged with the social and pedagogical processes of fashioning what we refer to as Standard English and has reflected on the consequences of these practices. It has then gone on to contemplate the invention of World Englishes and to examine teachers' negotiations of AAVE in ESOL contexts. I concluded by questioning the utility of a deterritorialization of English and propose that in addition to the project of deterritorializing English, we pursue a provincialization of the language. In the next chapter, we turn to the question of what an alternative vision might mean for teachers of English. How might their pedagogical practice be shaped by their location and by the location of English in their contexts?

## Reflection Questions

1. What form of English do I speak? How does my variety or accent position me socially?
2. What forms or varieties of English do I believe should be taught in ESOL classrooms or to ESOL students in mainstream classrooms? How do my beliefs shape what I need to do to ensure that my students are well served?
3. What do I believe about the use of multiple languages or varieties in the language classroom?
4. What do I believe about associations between English and particular countries? How do I believe that connections between English, place, and race will change in the future?
5. Do I encounter "World Englishes" in my professional context? How have I observed the teaching of English to speakers of "World English" being addressed?
6. What should students in ESOL be taught about their accents?

# CHAPTER 6

# Toward a Provincialized English

What might a provincialized English look like? How might it be achieved? What would it mean for English-teaching practice if we were to turn our attention from the pursuit of a deterritorialized English—one that conceptualizes the English language as separate from its geography—to a provincialized English, one that recognizes that the effects of empire and racialization are woven throughout the English language, the processes of teaching English, and the project of learning English? What might it mean to reconceptualize the teaching of English with a disciplinary base that no longer revolves solely around teaching methodology and language studies but instead takes as a point of departure race and empire? Embracing the notion of a provincialized English would mean that no teacher would teach English without an explicit consciousness of the hierarchies that the language is positioned within and of how the teaching of English shapes racial categories. To provincialize English would mean that inherent in the learning of English would be an intense awareness of the effects of English's colonial and racial history on current-day language, economic, political, and social practices. In recognition that consciousness is only the first step, provincializing English would furthermore examine and critique the mechanisms that sustain the invisibility of race and empire in English language teaching and would explore possibilities for transformation and agency.

## SERVANTS FOR THE EMPIRE

Teach people what will help them . . . not to become servants and bureaucrats for the empire.

—Gandhi as cited in Boggs, 2011, p. 146

While educational and linguistic researchers have examined separately the effects of race, colonialism, and language discrimination on those learning

English, a provincialized English would examine in particular the ways in which these three—race, empire, and language ideologies—come together to create a series of harmful consequences for children in schools and, consequently, for society at large. The history and contemporary situatedness of English make it a complicated language. Those of us who teach English to students of any linguistic identity are called upon to navigate our way through complex political, pedagogical, and linguistic terrain. Without the opportunity within our preservice and inservice contexts for provincializing English, for focused and intentional reflection on these patterns, we are not able to respond effectively, and we risk becoming "servants and bureaucrats for the empire." This book is designed not to tell you what to do but rather to support you as you think, to provide you with explicit and purposeful scaffolding as you consider the presence of race, empire, and language ideologies in your practice and as you make decisions about how to respond to your students, develop your curriculum, and arrange the structures of English language teaching in your institutional context.

Broad-stroke solutions to the types of dilemmas we English language practitioners face are not feasible and perhaps not even desirable. On the contrary, what becomes patently clear through the lens of the study is the importance of teachers being positioned and recognized as transformative intellectuals (Giroux, 1988) making informed, agentive, intellectual decisions in the context of their particular and situated practice. This concluding chapter will therefore not presume to outline specific recommendations or best practices for teaching practice to be dispensed broadly to teachers across contexts. Rather, it will focus on the larger questions and implications that emerge from this discussion for those who, like these four teachers, pursue an agenda of social justice in classrooms at any level, in any context, and who seek to transform and improve this nation's schools.

Similarly, it becomes clear that the heart of criticality in teaching is not to explicitly teach students to resist but rather to support their agency and to position them to make fully informed decisions about their own learning and lives with a complete understanding of the ways their decisions are meaningful within a long-term and large-scale (even global) context. U.S. schools in their current configuration are not responding adequately to the diversity of linguistic identities they represent. They are serving to track and separate students, to reinforce divisions between those who have cultural capital, including "native" mainstream monolingual English, and those who do not. They are preparing children differentially, so that minority children and English language learners are less successful in schools (National Center for Educational Statistics, 2012; Uriarte, Tung, Lavan, & Diez, 2010) than their White and native-speaking counterparts.

## CALL TO ACTION: RECONCEPTUALIZING ESOL

Taking one rhetorical approach, Contreras (2011) has pointed out the effectiveness of arguments that put equitable and just schooling into economic terms, exploring the costs of undereducating particular groups of students—including ELLs—and considering schooling in terms of human capital. She references Schultz, who in 1961 framed the individual student as a future producer of goods and services to which a price could be assigned, and she notes that "as many scholars have shown through their research findings, individual and collective investment on the front end makes sense" (p. 9). Contreras, drawing from research by, *inter alia*, Belfield and Levin (2007), Gándara (1995), and Crosnoe (2006), notes that better and more equitable schooling results in higher employment, better health, less crime, and greater economic gains not only to individuals but also to broader society.

While the effectiveness of an economic argument for improving schools is undeniable, I suggest an additional step with a different type of argument, that is, one that acknowledges that teachers and students must have an understanding of the role that English plays within the different orientations to learning and to schooling that are becoming necessary as the world is changing. A provincialized understanding of English would be strengthened by weaving wisdom from theorists who focus on civic and democratic education throughout teachings from applied linguistics and TESOL. The model of schooling promoted during the Industrial Revolution, in which the aim of schools was merely to produce individuals who could earn a paycheck, is no longer sufficient. In *The Next American Revolution,* Grace Lee Boggs (2011) suggests that "at the core of the problem is an obsolete factory model of schooling that sorts, tracks, tests, and rejects or certifies working-class children as if they were products in an assembly line" (p. 140). Rather, schools need to teach children to think for themselves, to critically analyze the worlds they live in and the relevance of English in constructing the type of future they want to live in, and to make informed decisions about how to change the world for the better. What we need, says Boggs, is a different type of schooling because "an education that gives children the freedom to exercise their powers creates the kind of socially responsible, visionary, and creative young people that we urgently need as change agents in the daily lives of our communities" (p. 141). It is not enough for schools to produce self-interested citizens involved only with their own capacity for income generation, apathetic to social justice or engagement with a broader public sphere and oblivious to the common good. This type of individual was, Walter Parker (2003) tells us, referred to by the ancient Greeks as an *idiote*, and Parker invites us to engage in "the contemporary struggle against idiocy" (p. xv). Similarly, James Banks (2005) asserts that "a thoughtful citizenry that believes in democratic ideals and is willing and able to participate in the civic life of the nation is essential for the creation and survival of a democratic nation" (p. 1).

Bringing ideas from civic education and democratic education more centrally into discussions of language acquisition and language education can help us teach children about the workings of U.S. schools and government and encourage them to take an active role in these institutions with the idea that children are being supported not only in learning English but also in understanding how they and their world are changed through the learning of English. Traditional narratives about the promises of English are not unproblematically true (Motha & Lin, 2013). We need to instead offer multiple readings of what happens when English is learned, of what happens to an individual when she or he learns English, of what happens to the world when entire populations learn English, and to more cohesively connect these understandings about English to the effects of racism, Empire, and students' political action and agency. Is it enough for schools to merely teach children language, to initiate them into the forms of English that will further them economically and equip them to make a living, disregarding the development of their first languages? Or do students need more? Suárez-Orozco and Qin-Hilliard (2004) believe so, telling us that "new and broader global visions are needed to prepare children and youth to be informed, engaged, and critical citizens in the new millennium" (p. 3). Children today are being called upon to "know" in different and more expansive ways than ever before in history. An unprecedented degree of cultural, cognitive, and linguistic flexibility will be required of them. They will need to be able to work across difference while figuring out how to preserve a sense of who they are. They will be expected to collaborate in new and complex ways while still maintaining a competitive orientation. They will be asked to interact with people who might look and sound and think quite unlike themselves. They will be asked to bring together a variety of disciplines in creative and challenging ways and to work across modalities that were completely unknown to any previous generation. And while they do this work, they will need to develop a degree of awareness and thoughtfulness in order to avoid being subsumed into the most popular, widespread ways of conceptualizing the challenges they face. "Globalization," Suárez-Orozco and Qin-Hilliard (2004) note, "is de-territorializing the skills and competencies it rewards, thereby generating powerful centripetal forces on what students the world over need to know" (p. 6). Should schools also be teaching all children, including children in ESOL, *about* what English does to English learners (how it positions and standardizes them), about the role of race in these sorting processes (how different forms of English are valued differentially), and, more important, why? Will they be served better if they are taught to think critically about the embeddedness of English in racism and Empire?

Concerns about the ability to develop a global vision and to engage critically with the processes of education are relevant not only to students but to their teachers. Is it enough for teachers to learn about how the English language works, how its grammar functions, what methods of teaching are currently most in favor, and what the latest trends in assessing, labeling, and categorizing language learners are? When teachers are adequately prepared to examine their worlds critically, they are in a better position to advocate for their students and to teach their students to advocate for themselves. When teachers are supported in thinking explicitly about the distinction between critical multiculturalism and liberal multiculturalism (Kubota, 2004), they are better positioned to craft a form of education that critiques the often Eurocentric nature of school knowledge; to recognize racial inequality, even when it is subtle and invisible; and to make decisions about whether to and how to address it head-on. How might teachers' practice be shaped by their deep understanding of the complex, racialized, and postcolonial terrain of English language teaching? In a global context in which the ELT industry has been referred to as promoting the McDonaldization of English (Block & Cameron, 2002), how should the goals and intentions of English language teaching be re-envisioned? Rather than becoming socialized into a public school system in which adults teach children to unquestioningly accept associations spun between English and opportunity, cosmopolitanism, and wealth in the social imaginary and to develop deep-seated desires for English and all that it has come to represent, and in which adults purport to be teaching neutral words, structures, and processes, our preservice and inservice education could further teach teachers to light their own lamps and to teach their young charges in turn also to light their own.

## A Rose by Any Other Name: The Language of ESOL

What language is used to describe language-minority students in the contexts you know? How are language services arranged? What limitations are imposed by state and federal laws? How are decisions made about who is in ESOL? Our school and social systems do not offer concrete ideas about what it means to speak a language. On one end of the spectrum, it can be said that students who arrived in the United States this week, never having studied English and knowing only five words of English, do *not* speak English. On the other end of the spectrum, we know that the students who speak no languages other than English and who speak forms considered to be standard can be said to speak English. However, many students fall between these two extremes—those who have lived here for some time and have acquired English but not enough to excel in school, those who were born in this country and speak some English but were raised with other home languages, and those who speak postcolonial or other varieties of English.

The mere use of the terms *NES, NNES, ESOL,* and *non-ESOL* reproduces false dichotomies inherent within these concepts, making an exploration of alternative lexicon necessary. Postcolonial theorist Homi Bhabha's (1994) concept of "fixity," the investment in keeping rigid boundaries around categories and in keeping them separate, is a helpful tool for school faculty and administrators who are seeking creative ways of lessening the space between polar constructs because it highlights the colonial roots of the tendency to try to segregate, contextualizing the broader ideological struggle at hand in something as simple as word choice. Our challenge is not to find the perfect language to describe "English learners," "ESOL students," or "nonnative speakers," but rather to reconceptualize the field to acknowledge the artificial nature of the boundaries between, for instance, "English learners" and "English speakers," "ESOL students" and "mainstream students." The concept of fixity helps us think about the many students who are in between—neither new arrivals who don't yet know any English nor monolingual English speakers who have no other languages to draw on—students who use English with varying degrees of fluency. This book argues for the forging of new school and social identities that are located in the nebulous yet immense area between these categorizations and for school practices that affirm the existence of students within these in-between spaces. Alexandra's establishment of a bridge class, an in-between class understood by students to be neither ESOL nor non-ESOL, created the theoretical possibility of space between those two groups. Another effective approach was Margaret's strategy to become involved with the learning processes of children who were not in her classes. Similarly, the acceptance by teachers who are not assigned to work with ESOL students of responsibility for the learning of those students can contribute to the development of a whole-community-based approach to education and a diluting of the boundaries between school categories—such as the various disciplinary categories (math, science, social studies) and other school categories such as ESOL, gifted and talented programs, and special education. All too often in this study, school investments in the child beyond the ESOL teacher were not easily apparent, and the ESOL teacher served as the sole liaison among the school administration, the family, and classroom teachers. While Margaret and Alexandra's solutions might not be appropriate for other classrooms, if teachers are aware of "fixity" as a site of challenge, they may be better prepared to recognize inflexibility when they see it and to respond skillfully. What was important in each of these contexts was not the actual resolution arrived at but rather the ability of the teacher to craft creative responses and solutions within her own situated practice.

Provincializing English includes problematizing the boundaries between school categories and paying close attention to possibilities that exist in the in-between spaces. Further empirical scholarship might give us a clearer idea of what these in-between identities might look like and, more importantly, might provide concrete examples of other practices that would support the development of these identities. As discussed in Chapter 3, the spaces between theoretical constructs, called "liminal spaces" by Bhabha (1994), can sometimes be fertile and exciting, providing us with a vision of what it could mean if we recognized the gray area between ESOL and non-ESOL, native speaker and nonnative speaker. Lather (2000) suggests that new concepts and understandings can be found in the "cracks," created by the "loss of mastery of the old concepts" (p. 284). Anzaldúa (1987) writes of "borderlands, *la frontera*," noting that in her experience "borders are set up to define the places that are safe and unsafe, to distinguish *us* from *them* . . . a borderland is a vague and undetermined place created by the emotional residue of an unnatural boundary" (p. 25). The boundary between ESOL and non-ESOL is drenched in emotional residue. It is not enough to condemn dichotomies, to hold up a megaphone and shout at "Western," patriarchal conventions. Rather, the task at hand is to explore alternatives by excavating these *intersticios*: "The new *mestiza* copes by developing a tolerance for contradictions, a tolerance for ambiguities" (Anzaldúa, 1987, p. 101). In terms that poignantly evoke Freire's (1998) notion of "unfinishedness," Anzaldúa says, "There is an exhilaration in being a participant in the further evolution of humankind, in being 'worked' on" (p. 38).

The teachers in this study demonstrated some inventive ways to challenge the binary nature of the categories that shaped their schooling lives. These were solutions that were appropriate for their contexts, but perhaps they wouldn't have made sense in your environment or mine. This is why it is so important that teachers not be taught simply what to do but instead be supported in thinking analytically and innovatively about solutions that are appropriate for our own immediate classrooms and in the broader context of the profession. However, it is important that we remember that we cannot depend solely on teacher-instigated versions of these strategies. These strategies need to be embraced at the school, district, and national-policy levels in order to ensure that a legitimate space exists for paradigm shifts away from racism and colonialism.

## Supporting ESOL Students' Belonging Within School Culture

The question of who truly belongs to a school community and how that belonging is shaped has important practical, theoretical, pedagogical, and policy implications. An inclusion model of teaching is more supportive of ESOL students' belonging than pull-out programs, but only if it exists while still providing necessary language support to students and if the quality of schooling it offers is not inferior to that received by other students. It could, in fact, be argued that pull-out programs are a way of circumventing the antisegregationist intent of *Castañeda v. Pickard* (1981). In terms of curriculum, the growing commitment of U.S. schools to standardization of curricula and high-stakes standardized testing compels us to see students in relation to a norm and to apply a uniform pedagogy to all children, which necessarily means that diversity is not adequately attended to. Similarly, our grading schemes need revision. Most current grading systems give us only two choices, both of which are unfair and serve to marginalize: to grade ESOL students in relation to students who are proficient in English or to simply not assign ESOL students a grade, sometimes by excluding them from assessment. ESOL students should be encouraged to participate in classroom conversations and the larger school culture. Students who speak no English at all can be paired with same-language peers in order to facilitate their communication with and entry into the school culture. School administrators need to make a special effort to ensure that ESOL students and faculty are not excluded from school activities. ESOL students should be encouraged to take an activist position within their school communities.

## Curricular Adaptations

Curriculum is an important site for transformation of epistemologies and racial and colonizing attitudes. Banks (2005) tells us that "without curriculum intervention by teachers, the racial attitudes and behaviors of students become more negative and harder to change as they grow older" (p. 202). In this section, I provide a few practical classroom-based examples of curricular efforts as examples of support for students' awareness of racism and Empire in ESOL.

It was through the process of curricular innovation around language varieties that Linda Christensen (2010) came to understand that, while creating a space for students' home resources and language practices is an effective first step, it is insufficient. She wrote:

> I started this work by intentionally inviting students to tell their stories in their home languages. I brought in August Wilson's plays, Lois Yamanaka's stories, and Jimmy Santiago Baca's poetry to validate the use of dialect and home language. But I learned that this wasn't enough. To challenge the old world order, I needed to explore why Standard English is the standard—how it came to power and how that power makes some people feel welcome and others feel like outsiders. (Christensen, 2010, p. 34)

What simply making space within classrooms for students' resources and languages omits is the recognition that outside the classroom, those spaces are constrained. Even more necessary than creating spaces is supporting students' understandings of the history of language, accent, and dialect varieties; their relationships to race; and the crucial role played by colonization in the historical evolution of the hierarchies.

It is through curricular intervention that Wayne Au (2009) seeks to disrupt representations of history that recognize the belonging of some students but not others. He has suggested, for instance, that in teaching about the U.S. war with Mexico, educators look beyond simply the actions of governments involved and also ask students about how the war was experienced and perceived by the various individuals involved, including Irish American soldiers, Mexican women in conquered territories, and Black and White abolitionists who opposed the war. Similarly, teachers could support students' examination of the ways in which wars have affected the language practices of ordinary citizens, have changed language contact patterns, and have altered national- and local-level language policies. Teachers could debate the ethics and the economic consequences of language policies arising from political conflicts with a specific eye toward the circulation of power.

ELLs at all levels could be taught about historical and contemporary restrictive language policies at state and national levels and their effects. ELLs could learn about Proposition 203 in Arizona and Proposition 227 in California, both of which restricted bilingual education, and the racializing effects of Arizona's's SB 1070, which allows police to racially profile individuals and ask them for immigration documentation. They could debate historical court cases such as *Castañeda v. Pickard* (1981), which established guidelines for adequacy of ESL programs, and the 2009 Supreme Court decision *Horne v. Flores*. Students could discuss the effects of Massachusetts Question 2, which restricted teachers' use of non-English language in ESL classes. Theresa Austin (2011) found that teachers felt disempowered by the restrictive effects of this ballot initiative. However, if teachers are supported in understanding the discriminatory effects of these and similar rulings and in connecting them to relations of Empire, both teachers and students can be positioned to be more agentive in their practice and learning. Students could be taught to use critical text analysis to consider messages about language identity telegraphed by their ESOL and other textbooks.

A class of, for instance, 6th-grade students could study the effects of Arizona's HB 2281 on the materials available to children their age living in that state. They could collectively analyze what is missed out on when they are not permitted to read *The House on Mango Street* by Sandra Cisneros, *The Tempest* by William Shakespeare, *Twelve Impossible Things Before Breakfast* by Jane Yolen, and the poetry of William Carlos Williams and Nikki Giovanni—the perspectives erased, the silences that remain, and the forms of literature and accompanying ideas that then move in to fill these gaps.

Mathematics classes offer a vast range of opportunities for examining race and empire as they relate to English. Students could develop graphing skills by learning to create and read graphs depicting differential achievement on the basis of race and language identity or by correlating factors such as poverty with immigration. Students could be taught to use mathematics to research and question incorrectly assumed correlations, such as connections between race and welfare benefits, in conjunction with teaching about the ways in which stereotypes are constructed and put into service.

Numerous other topics might support connections between English acquisition and race, empire, and language ideologies. In order to support discussions between ESOL and class divisions, students could be asked about what defines the lives and histories of those most fluent in English in countries the students are knowledgeable about (including the United States). Who is most likely to speak English—those who keep homes clean, lead the country, grow the produce you consume, own businesses, dispose of waste, study at elite universities? Are there ways to use the statistics available to correlate various social categories related to English fluency? Students could examine advertising materials for English schools in a variety of countries and analyze the types of images that are being sold. Anecdotally, students could consider questions about the number of generations that a heritage language has stayed in the families students know and could analyze reasons for heritage language loss.

Provincializing English means challenging the boundaries between, among, and around languages, varieties, and accents. Different varieties of English are often mutually intelligible and considered to belong to one language. Timothy Wellman (2013) points out that Croatian, Serbian, Bosnian, and Montenegrin are similarly mutually intelligible and in the past were considered one national language, Serbo-Croatian, but are now broadly recognized as different languages. Students might engage with questions about the political conditions that shape what constitutes a language, a variety, a dialect, or an accent. Provincializing English also necessitates problematizing monolingual habitus (Gogolin, 2013) in classrooms. Beyond simply learning English, students might critically analyze monolingualism. For instance, Nancy Bou Ayash (2013b) has her students translate a piece of traditional academic prose they have written into a variety, dialect, or genre from their own repertoire and then asks them to analyze changes in readability, intelligibility, and similar constructs that arise through the translation. Introducing the notion of mixed-language pedagogies destabilizes monolingualism and normalizes translingual practices. This type of metacognitive awareness of the interconnectedness of power and language encourages critical language awareness (Fairclough, 1992) and supports students' questioning about how language practices shape their lives.

## Stereotypes

Representations of ESOL students, nonnative speakers, immigrants, and racial minorities seem to be inescapable in the modern world, where children and adults are exposed to advertising and media more frequently than ever before. For Bhabha (1994), stereotypes are integral to relations of empire, serving as an important piece of colonial discourse by creating the appearance of stable categories and images. Stereotypes make images believable by repeating them over and over. Teachers need to take into account many factors as they decide how to address stereotypes and whether to name them aloud: Have students already been exposed to the stereotype or will the teacher be introducing it for the first time? How powerful a role does the stereotype play in the student's life? How comfortable is the student with the topic at hand (difference, race, accent)? How much agency can the student have in analyzing, recognizing, and criticizing a given stereotype?

Drawing on a variety of Disney films throughout history, Rosina Lippi-Green (2011) has demonstrated that children are taught messages about language identity through film—for instance by the disproportionate number of "bad guys" who speak with AAVE, Latino-influenced, or Middle Eastern accents (for example, *The Lion King* and *Aladdin*). Carla Chamberlin-Quinlisk (2012) recommends that beyond simply sharing damaging stereotypes with students, teachers actually equip them to recognize, identify, and analyze stereotypes they encounter in popular media. For instance, students could be asked about their favorite television shows, be asked to name characters who are nonnative speakers or racial minorities, and then name adjectives or defining characteristics to describe the characters. They could be asked about how characters are represented in relation to, for instance, responsibility, motivation, masculinity or femininity, disempowerment, work ethic, intelligence, criminality, and frequency of representation in their own living space (which Chamberlin-Quinlisk notes is rare in the case of nonnative speakers). Discussions about the roots of stereotypes could harken back to historical patterns of discrimination, exclusion, inequity, and exploitation.

## CALL TO ACTION:
## RECONCEPTUALIZING TESOL TEACHER EDUCATION

What should TESOL teacher education look like? Multiple possible approaches exist for preparing teachers to teach language-minority students, and as teacher educators develop their curricula, we are actually making decisions about which of these we privilege. We can focus on the language itself, its properties and characteristics, its phonology and structure. Or we might prioritize the processes of language acquisition from the perspective of an individual learner, attempting to model and represent the acquisition of rules and parts of speech. We can look at the different methods that have been in favor historically and in recent times and attempt to decide which are best or how they can be combined to be most effective. We could think of language learning as a process of socialization and teach the most successful ways of joining the speech community. An approach that acknowledges learners as always situated within sociocultural context is another possibility. Numerous potential approaches exist, and teacher educators make their priorities evident as they teach, whether or not they are transparent in acknowledging these. Because the history of the spread of English is a history of colonization, because English language learners globally and within the United States are overwhelmingly categorized as racial minorities, and because the ways in which we have been schooling language-minority learners have been failing them and consequently society at large, I argue for an approach to English language teaching that incorporates exposure to all of these approaches but that takes as its point of departure a race and empire approach that provincializes English. Provincializing English begins with an acknowledgment of the embeddedness of race and empire within all processes of English language learning and then maintains a persistent focus, throughout all learning, on awareness of the processes of racialization and colonial patterns with questions such as these:

1.  What position does my practice take in relation to hierarchies in social prestige and economic power among countries with different histories of colonizing and colonization?
2.  In what ways does my practice diminish and in what ways does it support racial inequality?
3.  What ideologies about languages, language varieties, accentedness, and nativeness are being carried within my practice?

In many U.S. states, teachers are not adequately prepared to attend to the needs of language-minority students. In recent years, states have begun to require all teachers to take classes in language teaching, literacy, or teaching English language learners. However, the nature of these classes should be called into question. Teacher education, both in TESOL and within other disciplines, should consistently and forcefully focus on teacher agency, applying a specific and deliberate emphasis on the role that teachers play in shaping the power relations, access to resources, and positionality of their linguistic-minority students. It is not enough for teachers to be familiar with second language acquisition theory and be able to name and identify a variety of ESL methods. Kumaravadivelu (2003) advocates for "postmethod pedagogy," which includes a sensitivity to location- and context-specific particularities and the transformative intellectual agility to craft fitting pedagogies in response to a given situation. All too often, the shaping of ESOL is taught and considered quite apart from its historical context of colonialism and its contemporary context of globalization as these relate to inequitable racial relations, the supremacy of English, and the valorization of Western culture and forms of knowledge. The inferior status of ESOL then becomes so naturalized that it is not visible without being explicitly pointed out.

## Silences Around Race

Portraying the TESOL profession as racially neutral is part of a larger social movement toward a liberal multiculturalist ideology that professes to be antiracist but actually serves to sustain racism (Bonilla-Silva, 2013). In recognition of the fact that identities shaped within the construct of ESOL are inherently racialized, the preparatory and inservice experiences of all school administrators and teachers of all disciplines should be grounded in an explicit consciousness of the implications of their practice within a broader colonial and racialized enterprise in order that they be equipped to make choices accordingly. In denying the colonial, linguistic, and racialized roots of many social practices in schools, individuals are able to justify ignoring inequalities that pervade U.S. K–12 and tertiary-level schools and indeed society at large. If all who are involved in this nation's schools, including its universities and community colleges, are adequately prepared, they will have a deliberate awareness of the processes and conditions that allow language to support discrimination, including the ways in which colorblind and no-differential-treatment arguments obscure issues of power and privilege and consequently perpetuate racial and linguistic hierarchies. An unambiguous highlighting of this distinction can equip those who teach minority children to recognize and name veiled issues of race.

Meanings of White identity are easily associated with neutrality. These associations should be questioned and deconstructed through an examination of the ways in which the invisible neutrality of Whiteness comes to be. Although antiracist work should be everyone's work, the antiracist work of teachers who are coded as White takes on different meanings from the antiracist work of teachers who are perceived to be racial minorities. Collaborative partnerships are important. White adults working with children can include racial minority adults in their antiracist work to help them avoid what might otherwise be a missionary-like positioning (Vandrick, 2002). The positions from which teachers practice are complex because teachers have authority with children. For instance, when Jane encourages Jorge to write a letter to the school paper, she is advocating against dominant discourses that fail to acknowledge the place of Latinos in the tapestry of American culture. The power of teachers, especially White native-English-speaking teachers in ESOL classrooms, should not be ignored or denied, but teachers should have a place in which to talk about what it means to use that power responsibly. More research is needed on how TESOL professionals of color are advocating for themselves and their students. How can minority faculty interrogate inequitable or discriminatory school practices?

## Multilingualism

The teachers in this study frequently encountered classroom teachers whose pedagogy was consistent with an ethic of caring, but who nonetheless reinforced ESOL students' shame about their ESOL status, were oblivious to the potential negative consequences that can result from enforcing English-only classroom policies, or underscored the supremacy of native-like English speech. When these practices are conceptualized within the context of a history of colonial and racial inequality, their consequences become more visible. Offering teachers and administrators specific guidance about how to make language choices and pedagogical decisions can support possibilities for the evolution of multilingual, multicultural identities. Menken and García (2010) make the argument that classroom practitioners are in fact policymakers, and that the ways in which teachers choose to negotiate the policies they work within are often shaped by their personal identities and prior experiences. If this is so, then teachers' ability to reflect upon their experiences and identities and to develop an explicit consciousness of the ways in which these are salient becomes an important piece of a teacher education program.

Professional development and teacher education efforts to highlight the value of multilingualism can contribute to transformation and can help prepare all faculty to specifically challenge comments that construct ESOL as deficient when they hear ESOL students speak. Mackie (2003) has suggested that we explore the ways our personal desires are shaped by everyday social texts and communities. She provides as an example the hidden messages about race within social texts (particularly movies). She proposes that we look at how desires for particular identities change when their origins and connection to cultural texts are questioned. By being able to consider and identify the relevant everyday texts and scripts that are associated with desirable identities, ESOL professionals are better positioned to help themselves and their ESOL students call into question those desires. This is the type of reflective, questioning practice that will support a critical engagement with discourses of colonialism. Social practices are shaped by language discourses

(Tollefson, 2002), so that simply introducing discourses that support "multicompetence" and "multilingualism" rather than "NNES" can change the ways in which children come to view linguistic identity. Similarly, teachers can help students position themselves regarding accentedness by redirecting language learning goals from accent or nativeness to intelligibility, all the while questioning explicitly ideologies that treat accents as pollutants of language rather than identity markers. However, it is important to be mindful that alternative discourses are not a panacea—material facts, including socioeconomic asymmetries, still persist, and the relation between discourse and materiality is not unidirectional.

## INSERVICE SUPPORT FOR ANTIRACIST, ANTICOLONIAL PRACTICE

Beyond preservice teacher education, the study highlighted the necessity of supporting teachers' exploration around issues of race during the beginning years of teaching. The need for social and intellectual support does not disappear when teachers start teaching. On the contrary, one might argue that it increases as they assume primary responsibility for young charges' learning. As teachers practice their craft, they continue to learn to teach and they continue to reconstitute their racialized selves in their teaching practice. Numerous studies have found beginning teachers who embraced liberatory ideologies during their teacher preparation programs only to become heavily socialized by conservative influences of public schooling (Kettle & Sellars, 1996; Paley, 2000). In order for teachers to remain in pursuit of an antiracist agenda, that agenda needs to be supported by their broader institutions. The silences surrounding language variation in these four public schools helped perpetuate racial inequity. The inseparability of Whiteness from Standard English both reflects and reinforces White privilege. What is constructed as mainstream English can be a valuable resource, equipping students to represent their own interests and access a broader range of identities to put into service when they are appropriate, but to learn any new language or language variety without a critical understanding of the consequences of language ideologies, of what the learning of the language is doing to the learner, can underscore racial inequity and colonial patterns. Critical literacy advocates suggest that the process of language learning be "more explicit and more situated . . . exploring the differential status and power among, and associated attitudes towards, particular language registers and language varieties" (May & Janks, 2004, p. 2).

In teacher education, teachers could be supported in recognizing silences that camouflage race. For instance, in the schools of the study where AAVE was spoken by most students, language varieties were not openly discussed.

Well-prepared teachers within school systems that use the term *World English* might be better equipped to problematize the monolithic use of the term and to avoid the practice of categorizing speakers of global language variations as *World English speakers* only if they belong to certain ethnic minority groups. Nero (2005, 2006) has called for a new paradigm for linguistic classification of multilingual students, one that takes into account the multifaceted identities that they represent.

Through Alexandra, Jane, Katie, and Margaret, I learned about the power of dialogue in community and the ways in which teacher knowledge is generated. Historically, questions about how to teach were answered by (usually White male) researchers in universities, who filtered that knowledge "down" to teachers. The teachers in this study crafted their pedagogy with the support and camaraderie of each other. Although the afternoon teas were clearly not a completely neutral space, being held in the home of their former teacher, they were separate from the faculty and administration of their public school campuses and sheltered from the surveillance of the larger school culture. In this context, the teachers could more freely negotiate texts and discourses that may not have been institutionally sanctioned or desirable—for instance, safely and openly challenging school practices that sustained inequalities regarding race, class, and other dimensions of identity.

## RACE, EMPIRE, AND MORALITY

In addition to raising profound economic and political questions, empire, colonialism, slavery, racism, and linguicism raise questions of right and wrong, morality, and character. The ideas of scholars who have considered the role of morality in education could be woven more cohesively into the disciplinary terrain of applied linguistics and TESOL to shed light on how best to teach all children. In today's schools, questions about what is right morally become easily replaced by questions about what is correct or what is appropriate, including appropriate registers and language varieties, thus obscuring the deeply moral questions raised when land is taken over, its inhabitants killed or displaced, and racism reproduced. Parker (2003) sees access to moral education as scarce in the contemporary U.S. context:

> Access to [moral education] . . . does not now widely exist, nor can it be assumed in a society where educational opportunity is so unequally allocated and where economic motives for education so often overtake liberal (mind-expanding) and public (community-building) purposes. (p. xv)

Cary Buzzelli and Bill Johnston (2002) note that given the diversity of ideas about morality by which teachers find themselves surrounded, their practice necessarily calls upon them to embrace subjectivities of morality, whether they do so explicitly or in ways that are hidden and even unwitting. The ways in which teachers negotiate the racialized and colonial tendencies of the teaching of English becomes a moral issue. Whether or not teachers acknowledge the moral choices that underpin their teaching—to challenge inequitable language hierarchies or to permit them to remain, to speak openly with students about the effects of covert ESOL segregationist practices or to leave them unproblematized—they are acting as moral agents in one direction or another. In *The Moral Life of Schools*, Jackson, Boostrom, and Hansen (1993), like Buzzelli and Johnston, argue that moral agency is embedded in all teaching:

> The moral influence schools and teachers actually have . . . extends to what teachers say and do without consciously intending to act as moral agents. It further applies to aspects of the classroom environment and the school as a whole that also are not specifically designed to achieve moral ends. (p. 237)

They suggest that teachers seek to cultivate what the authors term *expressive awareness*, an understanding and awareness of less overt, less evident forms of moral teaching. Expressive awareness might include, for instance, a more expansive critical view of the project of schooling, an intentional alertness to the ways in which power circulates in relation to race and language.

The structural arrangements of U.S. public schools support limited, simplistic, and even damaging conceptualizations of language identity. However, schools can also be a site of promise and transformation: one in which language identities can be reconceptualized, the monolingual model of identity that is so pervasive in the United States can be deconstructed, and the categories of ESOL and non-ESOL can be re-envisioned. School-based action can lead to the transformation of the peripheral status of ESOL within school culture and can radiate through to communities beyond school walls.

## CONCLUSION: "I STRIKE THE EMPIRE BACK"

Throughout this book I have shared with you examples of the ways in which ESOL as it is currently configured within U.S. public school classrooms acts unwittingly as a conduit for colonialist and racialized ways of thinking. How can ESOL be done differently? How can we, in the words of Mos Def, "strike the empire back"? The practical implications outlined in this final chapter have the potential to influence ESOL, but their effectiveness is limited if they stand alone. Teachers, educational researchers, and linguists can take practical steps to address patterns of inequity within educational arenas, but we will provoke greater change if we simultaneously push beneath the theoretical surface of race and Empire, delving deeper into a structural analysis of how TESOL as a discipline buttresses Western-based knowledges in contemporary contexts and the consequences of these practices for epistemological development in the United States and around the globe. Colonialism as a historical construct is tightly connected to the modern-day phenomenon of globalization (Kumaravadivelu, 2008; Luke, 2001). ESOL classrooms serve as channels for both local and global discourses, and we are hard-pressed to understand the postcolonial sediment that shrouds us without developing an understanding of how current shifts toward internationalization inevitably influence the teaching of English and the construction of ESOL in a world that is increasingly "flat" (Darling-Hammond, 2010) and coming to terms with simultaneously homogenizing and heterogenizing influences. An understanding of directions for the future needs to be thoroughly embedded in an analysis of local and specific sites, with connections then traced to the global. Luke (2001) suggests that "any effects of globalization can be made intelligible only by analysis of local sites where 'glocalization' is actualized, experienced, appropriated, or contested" (p. 3). The teaching lives of Katie, Alexandra, Jane, and Margaret are an example of one such local site. Because theorizing without grounding theory in classroom realities results in abstract conjecture, more data-driven studies that flesh out local experiences are necessary. In particular, in order to figure out how TESOL professionals can thoughtfully re-envision our direction, we need more intensive, ethnographic explorations of what reflective and critically minded teachers of language-minority students are doing.

How can learning communities create the possibility of new, hybrid identities? Lin et al. (2004) refer us to glocalization, which brings together the local and the global, and propose a paradigm shift from TESOL to Teaching English for Glocalized Communication (TEGCOM). They suggest that if we "reimagine the storylines underlying TESOL and its discourses, we can perhaps rework and destabilize the hegemonic relations in different settings in the world" (p. 312). A first step in this direction is the reconceptualization of ESOL within the walls of U.S. public schools, which can create possibilities for learning that recognizes multilingual students as full-fledged participants in school communities and society at large, that embraces the students' epistemologies and experiences as valuable, and that works against the numerous artifacts of colonialism embedded in the fabric of U.S. schooling.

Transformation and revolution should be joyful work. Grace Lee Boggs (2011), writing at the age of 95, deplored the United States' history of violence, exploitation, racism, and domination. She reminded us, however, that U.S. history tells multiple overlapping stories and that in the midst of horror, revolution and resistance have always been present, as much a part of the U.S. narrative as have been aggression and oppression and discrimination.

Similarly, and speaking from a comparative global perspective and, in particular, contemplating differences with Puerto Rico and Mexico, James Banks (2006) has observed that "the United States . . . is characterized by more rigid racial categories, fewer options for non-White ethnic groups, more institutional racism and discrimination, and more concern about the color of a person's skin. The United States has also experienced the most active ethnic revitalization movements and the most vigorous and sustained development in programs and practices related to multi-ethnic education and ethnic studies" (p. 178).

In forging new and hybrid identities, it is important that we consider the ideological construction of English. Educators need to have faith that ESOL learners are sophisticated enough "to manage the linguistic and ideological conflicts to their best advantage" and to engage favorably in multiple languages (Canagarajah, 1999, p. 2), but we must simultaneously be "alert to the power of dominant ideology to create illusions of freedom, clarity, and agency" (Canagarajah, 2004, p. 141). Ironically, while multilingualism, the reason for students' placement in ESOL, itself is an asset, the ways in which ESOL is constructed as a school category establish conditions for school failure among ESOL students. Furthermore, they do so in a way that is seemingly innocent: "It suited ELT to define language and teaching as a value-free cognitive activity, since in that way its material and ideological interests in spreading English globally could be conveniently ignored" (Canagarajah, 1999, p. 20). The four teachers found that in order to challenge the negative understandings of ESOL that were pervasive in their schools they needed to also challenge the global construction of NNES and to work toward changing the ways in which the institution of schooling viewed ELT. Further research that explores what ESOL teachers do in the face of imperialist and racist forces is necessary. Through their reflective and thought-provoking practice, Katie, Jane, Margaret, and Alexandra have offered numerous possibilities for exorcising the colonial and racist ghosts squatting throughout the U.S. institution of schooling and consequently for transforming the ways in which ESOL is taught.

If English represents, as asserted by Kandiah (as cited in Skutnabb-Kangas et al., 2009), a contradiction, what responsibility do we as English teachers have as we teach in the midst of this contradiction? I return to Vai Ramanathan's (2002) call for TESOL professionals to reflect upon, recognize, and address our own participation in problems within the existing conditions of our practice. What are the consequences if we ignore Kandiah's contradiction and pretend to our students that it doesn't exist? What would happen if, for some reason, the relevance of racial identity, empire, and language ideologies were somehow erased, if we as professionals stopped noticing and acknowledging the patterns of racial inequity that are sustained through English language teaching? Another way of asking this question is: What responsibility do we as TESOL professionals have for noticing and addressing the workings of race, empire, and language ideologies in our practice?

## Reflection Questions

1. What patterns of participation and belonging have I observed in the various school contexts I inhabit (or have inhabited)?
2. Who advocates for students in ESOL? With whom do students in ESOL sit in the cafeteria or dining hall? How do school practices serve to reinforce or prevent exclusion?
3. How are students categorized in my institution (e.g., gifted and talented, special education, other programs that become identities) and how do these school categories intersect with the category termed *ESOL* in this study?
4. What explicit or implicit guidelines do I follow when making decisions about how to talk about stereotypes?
5. In my teacher education experience, what knowledge is (or was) presented as most central to what teachers need to know to teach well (e.g., methods, second language acquisition theory, grammar)?
6. What will happen in the long term if U.S. schools do not respond more effectively to language-minority children? How do I feel about these consequences?
7. How would my classroom or curriculum look different if I increased my critical focus on what learning English does to my language-minority students?
8. What responsibility do I have for noticing and addressing the effects of race, empire, and language ideologies in my context?

# Telling Someone Else's Stories

The methodology that evolved during the course of this study led me on a complicated journey. I relied on multiple data sources, the three most important being audio recordings of classroom observations, interviews, and, most important, the afternoon teas, which were regular gatherings in my home every 2 or 3 weeks over a school year. I also conducted informal interviews with students, other faculty, and administrators; referred to school documents and students' work; and exchanged emails and audiotaped phone conversations with the teachers. I transcribed all recordings myself.

I developed a methodology that accentuated the qualities that I believed to be well represented by the afternoon tea data, including a foregrounding of study partner voice and power and a recognition of the ways in which teachers' ideologies and practices are shaped by their communities of practice (Wenger, 1998). I used constant comparative methodology (Glaser & Strauss, 1967) as is popular in qualitative data analysis, coding all data by hand as a matter of personal preference. I started with line-by-line analysis because it is likely to be most generative (Strauss & Corbin, 1990). However, I then took a step that was designed to privilege the afternoon tea transcriptions. I first coded the data from the afternoon teas only, identifying important themes within the afternoon tea data. I then introduced other data only in relation to the themes that emerged from the afternoon tea data. This step was intended to establish the centrality of the teachers' voices in the context of the community of practice embedded in the afternoon tea context. I considered the afternoon tea data to form the basis of the study, and I tried to avoid presenting observational data without concomitantly overlaying the lens of the teacher's perspective.

## RESEARCH FRAMING

Wong's (2005) extensive work on critical dialogic approaches to teaching, researching, and learning was influential in the framing of my research. Wong's critical dialogic approaches draw from theoretical sources as diverse as Socrates, Confucius, Paolo Freire, Mao Zedong, Lev Vygotsky, and Mikhail Bakhtin. Wong's work led me to Socrates's model of maieutic inquiry, in which wisdom is the humble assumption of one's own ignorance. Maieutic inquiry diverges from hierarchical understandings of the researcher role that have come to be accepted within most Western academia. Historically in the United States, researchers in education created knowledge in experimental settings and provided their findings to administrators, who used the information to influence and even control teachers' classroom instruction (Gitlin et al., 1992). The institutional dichotomy between research and teaching is made all the more disturbing when viewed in terms of the inequitable relationship that men and women have to power as it relates to knowledge within educational institutions, with researchers being traditionally male and teachers, even today, being predominantly female. Critical dialogic approaches serve to challenge the teacher–researcher power structure, stubbornly enduring despite recognition of its shortcomings (Fine, 1992; Lather, 1991; Wong, 2005) by listening to the teachers as experienced, knowledgeable practitioners. Without the hierarchy, the possibility arises for inquiry that is truly dialogic, in which learning is a two-way street (Wong & Motha, 2006). Wexler (1982) has criticized the dichotomy between empirical research and emancipatory pedagogy, but Lin et al. (2004) and Lather (1991) note a dearth of strategies to integrate the two. Methodologically, I sought to address that gap. Scott Kurashige (2011) has warned that "we cannot expect good ideas to hatch within an ivory tower. They instead emerge and develop through daily life and struggle, through collective study and debate among diverse entities, and through trial and errors within multiple contexts" (p. 6). Through this study, I sought to understand knowledge spawned from "daily life and struggle."

## RESEARCH AND EMPIRE

On many occasions, I sat in a classroom and recorded what I believed I was observing, only to learn with greater probing during a lunch break that my interpretations were inconsistent with the teacher's because I had missed a confrontation in the previous day's class, because I didn't understand the history with the student involved, because I hadn't been privy to a hurried and whispered conversation in the staff room that morning, or because I didn't know about the phone conversation between the teacher and a parent the previous week. The value of a humanizing (Freire, 1998) contextualization became apparent to me as the classroom observations began to appear to be disconnected from the teachers' voices and constructions of meanings. I began to revisit my questions about what I was hoping to learn in the study.

Linda Tuwahi Smith (2012) has referred to the word *research* as "one of the dirtiest words in the indigenous world vocabulary," noting that the term is "inextricably linked to European imperialism and colonialism" (p. 1). Research, say Denzin and Lincoln (2005), "is one of colonialism's most sordid legacies" (p. 1). Should researchers even be doing research? Is it possible to do research that is not dirty? How do they (we) come to terms, then, with methodological questions related to power, representation, and relationship in ethnography? How can we avoid reproducing the historical positioning of ethnographers in relation to participants, described by Behar (1996) in this way: "Somehow, out of [the] legacy born of European colonial impulse to know others in order to lambast them, better manage them, or exalt them, anthropologists have made an intellectual cornucopia" (p. 4)? In a world in which the researched has traditionally been a cultural Other, preserving a strongly delineated boundary between researcher and researched serves to reproduce the power imbalance between the two. Is it inevitable in ethnography that the researcher be positioned as a consumer of participants' experiences, using them for his or her own purposes?

Behar (1996) has written about breasts in anthropology in order to highlight the tensions facing women ethnographers studying other women. Behar noted metaphorically that bare breasts usually belong to Other women, women being observed, women under that objectifying tool of power, the gaze (Sartre, 1957), while the breasts of female anthropologists remain concealed. She comments that in hiding their breasts from view, female anthropologists can come to believe that their breasts (or gender identity) are not important, and they can be seduced into embracing detachment, objectivity, and power-neutrality. I wanted to heed Cixous's (1976) caution to all women who write about other women: "Don't denigrate woman, don't make of her what men have made of you" (p. 252). Particularly in the context of a history of "teacher-bashing" research (McLaren, 2000) conducted by (usually male) academicians on (usually female) teachers, it became important that I represent Katie, Jane, Alexandra, and Margaret's practice in a way that was respectful of them and simultaneously authentic.

I have been guided for many years by Michelle Fine's (1992) description of three possible stances that researchers can take: ventriloquy, voice, and activism. I think of *ventriloquy* as the most traditional form; in it the researcherauthor pursues objectivity at its purest, claiming to be invisible, neutral, and objective. Fine tells us that ventriloquy "can be found in all research narratives in which researchers' privileges and interests are camouflaged" (p. 214). A ventriloquist researcher would present herself as having no political agenda or underlying ideology.

It is the second category, *voices*, that is the most troubling for me because I find myself easily seduced by the idea that I can benevolently create a place for the silenced voices (and therefore knowledge) of beginning

ESOL teachers. Fine cautions us that this stance is "a subtler form of ventriloquism" and that in adopting it, while "appear[ing] to let the 'Other'
speak, just under the covers of those marginal, if now 'liberated' voices,
we hide" (p. 215). I chose to privilege one data source over all others—the
afternoon teas—because it was the data source that I believed to be closest
to the teachers' voices. In doing so, I find myself flirting with the lines that
bound the category that Fine names "voices." When I select excerpts from
transcriptions and edit them, what I choose to include or exclude is integrally linked to my research intent and my identity. To present the voices
of the four teachers as untouched by my own ideas and leanings would
be prevarication. My challenge, then, is to organize the representations of
the teachers so that I achieve a degree of candor in locating myself as a
researcher in relation to them. The afternoon teas, in particular, have both
supported and complicated my attempts to strip ventriloquism from study
partners' voices.

As a researcher concerned about antiracism, anticolonialism, and social
justice, I sought to embrace Fine's third category of researcher stance—*activism*,
referred to in her later work (1992) as activist feminist research. Activism "seeks
to unearth, disrupt, and transform existing ideological and/or institutional arrangements" (p. 220). Whether or not the researcher chooses to share her stance,
all research is positioned in relation to existing institutional arrangements, even
research that claims to be neutral. Some researchers seek to reinforce institutional power, and others, including activist researchers, seek change and disruption.
However, a desire for change in itself does not define an activist researcher.
Rather, activist researchers are characterized by their acceptance of the "deep responsibility to assess critically and continually our own, as well as informants',
changing opinions" (p. 41). As I worked with my various transcriptions and
fieldnotes, it became apparent to me that different data sources afforded me
different perspectives, and that the different sources were unequally related to
knowledge and to power. I found myself becoming increasingly uncomfortable
with and unable to escape from the objectifying nature of observations and
fieldnotes, and I began to realize that a pivotal site for the teachers' construction of meanings was their voices, rather than my record of observations. The
afternoon teas in particular allowed me intimacy with study partners' voices.
Observations are informative and very real in a positivistic sense, but they're
experienced through the eyes of the observer or researcher. I believe that there
was something about the afternoon teas that helped me disrupt the researcher–researched hierarchy by creating a distinctive space especially for teachers'
voices and in this way increasing the degree of authorship and authority in
how their teaching was interpreted. In order to be positioned to tell about their
teaching lives, they had to actually take themselves through a reflective process
and make deliberate choices about how to present the events they described.
Privileging the afternoon tea transcripts over other sources of data meant that

the teachers played a more significant role in choosing which stories to tell and were active in the construction and (re)presentation of their professional identities. It was the teachers' interpretations undergirding this study. I was therefore working not only with my interpretations of what the teachers did, but with the teachers' own retellings of what they did. For me, the afternoon teas were a marvelous educational research tool because they allowed teachers a little more agency in authoring their own experiences, a departure from a format in which researchers wrote teachers' lives.

## VALIDITY, TRUTH, AND ACCURACY

While the choice to privilege the data from afternoon teas foregrounded the teachers' voices in the narrative, it also brought to the surface complicated questions about "accuracy," which I initially perceived as presenting a challenge to validity. My concerns began to surface during the very first afternoon tea. Throughout the year, there were times when I would sit in a classroom or at a parent–teacher conference and observe an incident, then listen to it recounted at the next afternoon tea. Teachers' retellings were not always consistent with my fieldnotes. Sometimes these inconsistencies were minor, as in the time that a teacher remembered a name as "Andrew," although I had recorded it as "Anthony." At other times the differences were more significant. At first I was concerned. That little positivistic voice in my mind kept asking, "What of the incidents I hear about but do not observe? Are they valid data? What if the teacher remembered incorrectly? Misheard?" I hope that that voice never moves out of my head, and in many ways it serves me well, keeping me questioning and reflecting on many of the cornerstones of qualitative research, but it is nonetheless a voice that privileges my interpretation of events over that of study partners and hence legitimizes the historically embedded power imbalance between the researched and the researcher. Triangulation has been suggested as a way of increasing validity in qualitative research (Wolcott, 1990). In this study, triangulation would have been quite possible. I could have compared the stories told by the four teachers with my own observations, the interviews with the teachers, and interviews with students and other teachers. However, triangulation serves our purposes only when we are seeking certain forms of knowledge, usually those that are considered to be more objective and less connected to individual, personal experience. Throughout the year, it served me to repeatedly revisit the question: What is the purpose of my research? I was less interested in whether study partners told the "Truth" and more concerned with how they made meaning of their classroom events. The focus of my study was not other people's interpretations of the study partners' experiences, and shifting my emphasis from observations to afternoon teas helped me to better capture what I was trying to understand—that is, the meanings that the study partners made of their experiences.

I use the term *critical ethnography*, as distinct from *naturalistic ethnography*, to separate my efforts from the neutrality-seeking tendencies of the latter, in which the researcher purports to observe a culture without altering it by her presence. The quest for objectivity in naturalistic inquiry is a by-product of more traditional forms of research and reinforces and perpetuates the connections between ethnography and positivism. Roman and Apple (1990) in fact charge that "naturalistic ethnography constitutes an extension rather than a break from positivism" (p. 48). This is not to say that I threw caution to the wind. Rather, I acknowledge that by merely walking into a classroom I changed its climate. By turning on a tape recorder or taking notes, I affected teachers' actions. By asking certain questions, I led teachers to think differently. This did not prevent me from walking into a classroom, taking fieldnotes, turning on a tape recorder, asking a thought-provoking question. Rather, my challenge was to be mindful of my actions and their consequences and straightforward and transparent in my accounts of events. In decentering the observational data but nonetheless situating this study in ethnographic terrain, I hoped to challenge and extend definitions of ethnography and of critical ethnography by encouraging methodological experimentation that creates space for participant voice and authorship.

## PROXIMITY TO PRAXIS

A central benefit of the afternoon teas was that they offered a fertile site for studying the praxis of beginning teaching—that is, the space in which theory and practice intertwined. Beginning teaching is a fascinating area because historically, in traditionally framed teacher education programs, it was the meeting place at which theoretical knowledge amassed in academic institutions encountered the practical world of classroom teaching. In my own teacher preparation program, teacher candidates learned the theory surrounding teaching and then, at the completion of their coursework, entered schools with the intention of applying it, with minimal time spent in schools before student teaching.

Exploring the first year of teaching as a study site can therefore allow us an in-depth view into the meanings that teachers make of theory, practice, and the supposed area in between the two. (It is difficult, and perhaps not even useful, to disentangle theory and practice.) The afternoon teas permitted me greater intimacy with this terrain between knowledge and action because they became a site that nurtured the teachers' critical reflection on their practice, which Freire (1998) identifies as crucial to praxis: "Critical reflection on practice is a requirement of the relationship between theory and practice. Otherwise, theory becomes simply 'blah, blah, blah,' and practice, pure activism" (p. 30)

## COMMUNITIES OF PRACTICE AND RELATIONSHIP

All knowledge is constructed and the knower is an intimate part of the known.

—Belenky et al., 1997, p. 137

The afternoon teas allowed me to be intimate with participants' voices, but then again so did the interviews. A further ingredient that made the afternoon teas such a rich data source, in a way that interviews were not, was the element of community, which helped move my exploration beyond understandings of individual identity in isolation to the richness and complexity of how identities construct each other. Community became important, not only emotionally but also methodologically, because power is integrally related to intimacy and relationship.

My history and intimacy with Jane, Katie, Margaret, and Alexandra affected the way I structured the study and the methodological choices and changes I made throughout. Because I was in relation with the four women, I cared about their teaching practice and their personal lives, about how I represented them, and about what they thought of me and my work. As I wrote and rewrote their stories, I struggled incessantly with the daunting challenge of telling their stories in a way that had integrity. I recognized that my truth would be only a rendering, but this knowledge did not absolve me of the responsibility to tell stories in a way that was candid and compatible with my truth and yet did not represent the teachers negatively. I wanted to tell stories in a way that was geniune but that didn't exploit or break faith with them.

## CONCLUSION: TELLING SOMEONE ELSE'S STORY

Regardless of the steps I took to disrupt the traditional structures of power in educational research, and regardless of what I hope is an elevated presence of the teachers' voices in my study, this work remains my interpretation of what I saw. I wrote it sitting alone at my computer. Spivak (1990) says that "we cannot but narrate, but when a narrative is constructed, something is left out" (pp. 18–19). Even when a teacher's words were quoted directly, I chose which words to include and also which to exclude. Weedon (1999) cautions, "It is important not to speak on behalf of others in ways which silence them and obscure real material differences" (p. 109). This work can be viewed only as my adulterated and personal version of reality, my representation of someone else's story, ultimately only one of countless possible representations of the study year. Within these pages are many stories that I am not telling, including some that were not mine to tell (for instance, those that the teachers asked me not to transcribe) and some that that I do not know (because the teachers did not tell them to me). These stories exist, interwoven around those that I am telling. This is not reality, just the temporary account that I've managed to stretch and trim over this particular textual surface at this particular moment.

The quest for understanding is endless. One methodological lesson I learned is that there is no perfect method, and there isn't even a right method. Patti Lather (personal communication, 2003) calls on us to face the non-innocence of our work. In doing so I'm compelled to acknowledge that I embarked on this study reifying method, believing that if I could only find the "right" way to gather and analyze, my representations of my study partners would do them justice. Dale Spender (1985) cautions that there is "no one truth, no one authority, no objective method which leads to the production of true knowledge" (p. 5). What I'm learning to accept is that this work is still me telling someone else's story.

Freire (1998) wrote of the *unfinishedness* of the human condition, telling us that "it is in our incompleteness, of which we are aware, that education as a permanent process is grounded. Women and men are capable of being educated only to the extent that they are capable of seeing themselves as unfinished. Education does not make us educable. It is our awareness of being unfinished that makes us educable. And the same awareness in which we are inserted makes us eternal seekers. Eternal because of hope. Hope is not just a question of grit or courage. It's an ontological dimension of our human condition" (p. 58).

Unfinishedness is a liberating concept. Recognizing the unfinished nature of all research frees me to view this work as part of a larger ongoing research process. The methodology I explored through this study may not be for all researchers, all studies, or all questions, but the process of experimenting with and even challenging orthodoxies in research methods was generative. I embrace Freire's connection between unfinishedness and scholarly community: "I like being human because I am involved with others in making history out of possibility" (p. 54).

# References

Adelman, L. (Executive Producer). (2003). *Race: The power of an illusion*. San Francisco, CA: California Newsreel.

Ahmed, S. (2010). *The promise of happiness*. Durham, NC: Duke University Press.

Alba, R., Logan, J., Lutz, A., & Stults, B. (2002). Only English by the third generation? Loss and preservation of the mother tongue among the grandchildren of contemporary immigrants. *Demography, 39*(3), 467–484.

Alim, H. S. (2009). Straight outta Compton, straight aus München. In H. S. Alim, A. Ibrahim, & A. Pennycook (Eds.), *Global linguistic flows: Hip hop cultures, youth identities, and the politics of language* (pp. 1–24). New York, NY: Routledge.

Amin, N. (1997). Race and the identity of the nonnative ESL teacher. *TESOL Quarterly, 31*(3), 580–583.

Amin, N., & Kubota, R. (2004). Native speaker discourses: Power and resistance in postcolonial teaching of English to speakers of other languages. In P. Ninnes & S. Mehta (Eds.), *Re-imagining comparative education: Postfoundational ideas and applications for critical times* (pp. 107–127). New York, NY: Routledge Falmer.

Anzaldúa, G. (1987). *Borderlands/La frontera: The new mestiza*. San Francisco, CA: Spinsters/Aunt Lute.

Appadurai, A. (1990). Disjuncture and difference in the global cultural economy. In M. Featherstone (Ed.), *Global Culture* (pp. 295–310). London, England: Sage.

Appadurai, A. (1996). *Modernity at large: Cultural dimensions of globalization*. Minneapolis: University of Minnesota Press.

Apple, M. W. (1999). *Power, meaning, and identity: Essays in critical educational studies*. New York, NY: P. Lang.

Appleby, R. (2013). Desire in translation: White masculinity and TESOL. *TESOL Quarterly, 47*(1), 122–147.

Ashcroft, B., Griffiths, G., & Tiffin, H. (1989). *The empire writes back: Theory and practice in post-colonial literatures*. London, England: Routledge.

Au, W. (2009). *Rethinking multicultural education: Teaching for racial and cultural justice*. Milwaukee, WI: Rethinking Schools.

August, D., & Shanahan, T. (2008). *Developing reading and writing in second-language learners*. New York, NY: Taylor and Francis.

Austin, T. (2011). Language learner-teachers: Evolving insights. *International Journal of the Sociology of Language, 2011*(208), 119–137. doi:10.1515/IJSL.2011.015

Bakhtin, M. M. (1981). *The dialogic imagination: Four essays*. Austin: University of Texas Press.

Banks, J. A. (2005, March 3). Democracy, diversity and social justice: Education in a global age. The 29th annual faculty lecture, University of Washington, Seattle, WA.

Banks, J. A. (2006). *Race, culture, and education: The selected works of James A. Banks*. London, England: Routledge.

Banks, J. A. (2013). *An introduction to multicultural education*. Upper Saddle River, NJ: Pearson

Banks, J. A., & Banks, C. A. M. (Eds.). (2004). *Handbook of research on multicultural education* (2nd ed.). San Francisco, CA: Jossey-Bass.

Banks, J. A., & Banks, C. A. M. (2013). *Multicultural education: Issues and perspectives* (8th ed.). Hoboken, NJ: Wiley.

Bannerji, H. (2001). *Inventing subjects: Studies in hegemony, patriarchy, and colonialism*. New Delhi, India: Tulika.

Bayley, R., & Schecter, S. R. (2003). *Language socialization in bilingual and multilingual societies*. Clevedon, England: Multilingual Matters.

Behar, R. (1996). *The vulnerable observer: Anthropology that breaks your heart*. Boston, MA: Beacon Press.

Belenky, M. F., Clinchy, B. M., Goldberger, N. R., & Tarule, J. M. (1997). *Women's ways of knowing: The development of self, voice, and mind* (10th anniv. ed.). New York, NY: Basic Books.

Belfield, C. R., & Levin, H. M. (2007). *The price we pay: Economic and social consequences of inadequate education*. Washington, DC: Brookings Institution Press.

Belluscio, S. J. (2006). *To be suddenly white: Literary realism and racial passing*. Columbia: University of Missouri Press.

Bhabha, H. K. (1994). *The location of culture*. London, England: Routledge.

Bhatt, R. (2005). Expert discourses, local practices, and hybridity: The case of Indian Englishes. In A. S. Canagarajah (Ed.), *Reclaiming the local in language policy and practice* (pp. 25–54). Mahwah, NJ: Lawrence Erlbaum.

Blackledge, A. (2002). The discursive construction of national identity in multilingual Britain. *Journal of Language, Identity & Education, 1*(1), 67–87.

Blackledge, A., & Creese, A. (2010). *Multilingualism: A critical perspective*. London, England: Continuum.

Block, D., & Cameron, D. (2002). *Globalization and language teaching*. London, England: Routledge.

Block, D., Gray, J., & Holborow, M. (2012). *Neoliberalism and applied linguistics*. London, England: Routledge.

Boggs, G. L. (2011). *The next American revolution: Sustainable activism for the twenty-first century*. Berkeley: University of California Press.

Bonilla-Silva, E. (2013). *Racism without racists: Color-blind racism and the persistence of racial inequality in the United States* (4th ed.). Lanham, MD: Rowman & Littlefield.

Bou Ayash, N. (2013a). Hi-ein, Hi بين or بين Hi? Translingual practices from Lebanon and mainstream literacy education. In A. S. Canagarajah (Ed.), *Literacy as translingual practice: Between communities and classrooms* (pp. 96–103). New York, NY: Routledge.

Bou Ayash, N. (2013b). An investigation of translation. Assignment sheet for ENGL 131, Fall 2013.

Bourdieu, P. (1984). *Distinction: A social critique of the judgement of taste*. Cambridge, MA: Harvard University Press.

Braine, G. (1999). *Non-native educators in English language teaching*. Mahwah, NJ: Lawrence Erlbaum.

Brenner, A. (2006). Too White to teach race? In R. Moore (Ed.), *African Americans and Whites: Changing relationships on college campuses* (pp. 19–35). Lanham, MD: University Press of America.

Britzman, D. (1991). *Practice makes practice*. Albany: State University of New York Press.

Brodkin, K. (1998). How Jews became white folks and what that says about race in America. New Brunswick, NJ: Rutgers University Press.

Brown, M. S., & Silberstein, S. (2012). Contested diaspora: A century of Zionist and Anti-Zionist rhetorics in America. *Journal of Language, Identity & Education, 11*(2), 85–95.

Brutt-Griffler, J. (2002). *World English: A study of its development*. Clevedon, England: Multilingual Matters.

Brutt-Griffler, J., & Samimy, K. K. (1999). Revisiting the colonial in the postcolonial: Critical praxis for nonnative-English-speaking teachers in a TESOL Program. *TESOL Quarterly, 33*(3), 413–431.

Bush, M. E. L. (2011). Everyday forms of whiteness: Understanding race in a "post-racial" world. Lanham, MD: Rowman & Littlefield.

Butler, J. (1997). *Excitable speech: A politics of the performative*. New York, NY: Routledge.

Buzzelli, C. A., & Johnston, B. (2002). *The moral dimensions of teaching: Language, power, and culture in classroom interaction*. New York, NY: Routledge Falmer.

Canagarajah, A. S. (1999). *Resisting linguistic imperialism in English teaching*. Oxford, England: Oxford University Press.

Canagarajah, A. S. (2004). Language rights and postmodern conditions. *Journal of Language, Identity & Education, 3*(2), 140–145.

Canagarajah, A. S. (2006). The place of world Englishes in composition: Pluralization continued. *College Composition and Communication, 57*(4), 586–619.

Canagarajah, A. S. (2008). Language shift and the family: Questions from the Sri Lankan Tamil diaspora. *Journal of Sociolinguistics, 12*(2), 143–176.

Canagarajah, A. S. (2011). Codemeshing in academic writing: Identifying teachable strategies of translanguaging. *The Modern Language Journal, 95*(3), 401–417.

Canagarajah, A. S. (2013). *Translingual practice: Global Englishes and cosmopolitan relations*. London, England: Routledge

Canagarajah, S., & Silberstein, S. (2012). Diaspora identities and language. *Journal of Language, Identity and Education, 11*(2), 81–84.

Carroll, S, Motha, S., & Price, J. (2008). Accessing imagined communities, reinscribing regimes of truth. *Critical Inquiry in Language Studies, 5*(3), 165–191.

Carspecken, P. (1996). *Critical ethnography in educational research*. New York, NY: Routledge.

Castañeda v. Pickard, 648 F. 2d 989 (Ct. App., 5th Cir. 1981)

Center for Educational Statistics. (2012). *The condition of education*. Alexandria, VA: U.S. Department of Education.

Césaire, A. (1972). *Discourse on colonialism*. New York, NY: Monthly Review Press.

Chakrabarty, D. (2000). Provincializing Europe: Postcolonial thought and historical difference. Princeton, NJ: Princeton University Press.

Chamberlin-Quinlisk, C. (2012). TESOL and media education: Navigating our screen-saturated worlds. *TESOL Quarterly, 46*(1), 152–164.

Chowdhury, R., & Ha, P. L. (2008). Reflecting on Western TESOL training and communicative language teaching: Bangladeshi teachers' voices. *Asia Pacific Journal of Education, 28*(3), 305–316.

Christensen, L. (2010). Putting out the linguistic welcome mat. *Wisconsin English Journal, 52*(1), 33–37.

Chun, C. W. (2009). Contesting neoliberal discourses in EAP: Critical praxis in an IEP classroom. *Journal of English for Academic Purposes, 8*(2), 111–120.

Cixous, H. (1976). The laugh of the Medusa (K. Cohen, Trans.). *Signs, 1*(4), 875–893.

Contreras, F. (2011). Achieving equity for Latino students: Expanding the pathway to higher education through public policy. New York, NY: Teachers College Press.

Cook, V. (1991). The poverty-of-the-stimulus argument and multicompetence. *Second Language Research, 7*(2), 103–117.

Cook, V. (1999). Going beyond the native speaker in language teaching. *TESOL Quarterly, 33*(2), 185–209.

Cook, V., & Bassetti, B. (Eds.). (2011). *Language and bilingual cognition.* New York, NY: Psychology Press.

Crawford, J. (2000). *At war with diversity: US language policy in an age of anxiety.* Clevedon, England: Multilingual Matters.

Crosnoe, R. (2006). *Mexican roots, American schools: Helping Mexican immigrant children succeed.* Stanford, CA: Stanford University Press.

Cummins, J., & Swain, M. (1986). *Bilingualism in education: Aspects of theory, research, and practice.* London, England: Longman.

Curtis, A., & Romney, M. (2006). *Color, race, and English language teaching.* Mahwah, NJ: Lawrence Erlbaum.

Darling-Hammond, L. (2010). *The flat world and education: How America's commitment to equity will determine our future.* New York, NY: Teachers College Press.

Dei, G. J. S., Karumanchery, L. L., & Karumanchery-Luik, N. (2004). *Playing the race card: Exposing white power and privilege.* New York, NY: P. Lang.

Deleuze, G., & Guattari, F. (1986). *Kafka: Toward a minor literature* (D. Polan, Trans.). Minneapolis: University of Minnesota Press.

Denzin, N. K., & Lincoln, Y. S. (2005). *The Sage handbook of qualitative research.* Thousand Oaks, CA: Sage.

DuBois, W. E. B. (1989). *The souls of Black folk.* New York, NY: Penguin Books.

Dyer, R. (1997). *White: Essays on race and culture.* London, England: Routledge.

Edge, J. (2008). *(Re)locating TESOL in an age of empire.* New York, NY: Palgrave and MacMillan.

Ellwood, C. (2009). Uninhabitable identifications: Unpacking the production of racial difference in a TESOL classroom. In R. Kubota, & A. M. Y. Lin (Eds.), *Race, culture, and identities in second language education: Exploring critically engaged practice* (pp. 101–117). New York, NY: Routledge.

Eugenides, J. (2011). *The marriage plot.* New York, NY: Farrar, Straus and Giroux.

Fairclough, N. (1992). *Critical language awareness.* London, England: Longman.

Fanon, F. (1967). *Black skin, white masks.* New York, NY: Grove Press

Feagin, J. R., & Vera, H. (1995). *White racism: The basics.* New York, NY: Routledge.

Ferguson, A. A. (2000). *Bad boys: Public schools in the making of Black masculinity.* Ann Arbor: University of Michigan Press.

Fine, M. (1992). *Disruptive voices: The possibilities of feminist research*. Ann Arbor: University of Michigan Press.

Fine, M. (2004). Witnessing Whiteness, gathering intelligence. In L. Weis, L. Powell Pruitt, A. Burns, & M. Fine (Eds.), *Off White: Readings on power, privilege, and resistance* (pp. 245–256). New York, NY: Routledge.

Foerster Luu, A. (2013, March 20). Best practices for ELT excellence. Paper presented at the TESOL International convention, Dallas, TX.

Fordham, S. (1996). *Blacked out*. Chicago, IL: University of Chicago Press.

Fordham, S. (2010). Passin' for Black: Race, identity, and bone memory in postracial America. *Harvard Educational Review, 80*, 4–30.

Foucault, M. (1972). *The archaeology of knowledge*. New York, NY: Pantheon Books.

Foucault, M. (1977). *Discipline and punish: The birth of the prison*. New York, NY: Pantheon Books.

Frankenberg, R. (1993). *White women, race matters: The social construction of whiteness*. Minneapolis: University of Minnesota Press.

Freeborn, D. (2006). From Old English to Standard English: A course book in language variations across time. New York, NY: Palgrave Macmillan.

Freire, P. (1998). *Pedagogy of freedom: ethics, democracy, and civic courage*. Lanham, MD: Rowman and Littlefield.

Gándara, P. C. (1995). *Over the ivy walls: The educational mobility of low-income Chicanos*. Albany: State University of New York Press.

Gándara, P., & Orfield, G. (2012). Segregating Arizona's English learners: A return to the "Mexican room"? *Teachers College Record, 114*(9), 2.

García, O., & Mason, L. (2009). Where in the world is U.S. Spanish? Creating a space of opportunity for U.S. Latinos. In W. Harbert, S. McConnell-Ginet, A. Miller, & J. Whitman, *Language and Poverty* (pp. 78–101). Bristol, England: Multilingual Matters..

García, O., & Wei, L. (2014). *Translanguaging: Language, bilingualism and education*. New York, NY: Palgrave.

Gay, G. (2000). *Culturally responsive teaching: Theory, research, and practice*. New York, NY: Teachers College Press.

Giddens, A. (1990). *The consequences of modernity*. Stanford, CA: Stanford University Press.

Giroux, H. A. (1988). *Teachers as intellectuals: Toward a critical pedagogy of learning*. Granby, MA: Bergin & Garvey.

Gitlin, A., Bringhurst, K., Burns, M., Cooley, V., Myers, B., Price, K., . . . Tiess, P. (1992). *Teachers' voices for school change*. New York, NY: Teachers College Press.

Glaser, B. G., & Strauss, A. (1967). *Discovery of grounded theory: Strategies for qualitative research*. Mill Valley, CA: Sociology Press.

Gogolin, I. (2013). The "monolingual habitus" as the common feature in teaching in the language of the majority in different countries. *Per Linguam, 13*, 2.

Gramsci, A. (1972). *Selections from the prison notebooks of Antonio Gramsci*. New York, NY: International Publishers.

Grant, R. A., & Wong, S. D. (2004). Forging multilingual communities: School-based strategies. *Multicultural Perspectives, 6*(3), 17–23.

Grant, R. A., & Wong, S. D. (2005). Barriers to literacy for language-minority learners: An argument for change in the literacy education profession. In P. Shannon

& J. Edmondson (Eds.), *Reading education policy: A collection of articles from the International Reading Association* (pp. 214–227) Newark, DE: International Reading Association.

Grant, R. A., & Wong, S. D. (2008). Critical race perspectives, Bourdieu and language education. In J. Albright & A. Luke (Eds.), *Pierre Bourdieu and literacy education* (pp. 162–184). New York, NY: Routledge.

Grin, F. (2001). English as economic value: Facts and fallacies. *World Englishes, 20*(1), 65–78.

Guo, Y., & Beckett, G. H. (2007). The hegemony of English as a global language: Reclaiming local knowledge and culture in China. *Convergence, 40,* 117–132.

Haque, E., & Morgan, B. (2009). Un/marked pedagogies: A dialogue on race in EFL and ESL settings. In R. Kubota & A. M. Y. Lin (Eds), *Race, culture, and identities in second language education: Exploring critically engaged practice.* (pp. 271–285). New York, NY: Routledge.

Harbert, W., McConnell-Ginet, S., Miller, A., & Whitman, J. (2008). *Language and poverty.* Bristol, England: Multilingual Matters.

Harding, S. (Ed.). (1987). *Feminisms and methodology.* Bloomington: Indiana University Press.

Hardt, M., & Negri, A. (2000). *Empire.* Cambridge, MA: Harvard University Press.

Hardt, M., & Negri, A. (2004). *Multitude: War and democracy in the age of Empire.* New York, NY: Penguin.

Hardt, M., & Negri, A. (2009). *Commonwealth.* Cambridge, MA: Belknap Press of Harvard University Press.

Harklau, L. (2000). From the "good kids" to the "worst": Representations of English language learners across educational settings. *TESOL Quarterly, 34*(1), 35–67.

Hassanpour, A. (2000). The politics of a-political linguistics: Linguists and linguicide. In T. Skutnabb-Kangas & R. Phillipson (Eds.), *Rights to language: Equity, power, and education. Celebrating the 60th birthday of Tove Skutnabb-Kangas* (pp. 33–39). Mahwah, NJ: Lawrence Erlbaum

Hill, J. H. (2008). *The everyday language of white racism.* Chichester, England: Wiley-Blackwell.

Holliday, A. (2005). *The struggle to teach English as an international language.* Oxford: Oxford University Press.

Howard, G. R. (1999). *We can't teach what we don't know: White teachers, multiracial schools.* New York, NY: Teachers College Press.

Hudley, A. H. C., & Mallinson, C. (2011). *Understanding English language variation in U.S. schools.* New York, NY: Teachers College Press.

Hughes, C., Newkirk, R., & Stenhjem, P. H. (2010). Addressing the challenge of disenfranchisement of youth: Poverty and racism in the schools. *Reclaiming Children and Youth, 19*(1), 22–26.

Ibrahim, A. (1999). Becoming Black: Rap and hip hop, race, gender, identity, and the politics of ESL learning. *TESOL Quarterly, 33*(3), 349–369.

Ibrahim, A. (2009). Takin hip hop to a whole nother level: Métissage, affect, and pedagogy in a global hip hop nation. In H. S. Alim, A. Ibrahim, & A. Pennycook (Eds.), Global linguistic flows: Hip hop cultures, youth identities, and the politics of language (pp. 231–248). New York, NY: Routledge.

Ignatiev, N. (1995). *How the Irish became White.* New York, NY: Routledge.

Jackson, P. W., Boostrom, R. E., & Hansen, D. T. (1993). *The moral life of schools.* San Francisco, CA: Jossey-Bass.

Jacobson, M. F. (1998). *Whiteness of a different color: European immigrants and the alchemy of race.* Cambridge, MA: Harvard University Press.

JanMohammed, A. R. (1985). The economy of Manichean allegory: The function of racial difference in colonialist literature. *Critical Inquiry, 12*(1), 59–87.

Jenkins, J. (2009). *World Englishes: A resource book for students.* London, England: Routledge.

Joseph, R. L. (2013). *Transcending Blackness: From the new millennium Mulatta to the exceptional multiracial.* Durham, NC: Duke University Press.

Kachru, B. B. (1988). Teaching world Englishes. *ERIC/CLL News Bulletin, 12*(1), 1, 3–4, 8.

Kachru, B. B. (1990). World Englishes and applied linguistics. *World Englishes, 9*(1), 3–20.

Kachru, B. B. (1992). *The other tongue: English across cultures.* Urbana: University of Illinois Press.

Kanno, Y., & Cromley, J. G. (2013). English language learners' access to and attainment in postsecondary education. *TESOL Quarterly, 47*(1), 89–121.

Kanno, Y., & Norton, B. (2003). Imagined communities and educational possibilities: Introduction. *Journal of Language, Identity & Education, 2*(4), 241–249.

Kaplan, A. (2002). *The anarchy of empire in the making of U.S. culture.* Cambridge, MA: Harvard University Press.

Kettle, B., & Sellars, N. (1996). The development of student teachers practical theory of teaching. *Teaching and Teacher Education, 12*(1), 1–24.

Kirkpatrick, A. (2007). *World Englishes: Implications for international communication and English language teaching.* Cambridge, England: Cambridge University Press.

Krishnaswamy, R. (1998). *Effeminism: The economy of colonial desire.* Ann Arbor: University of Michigan Press.

Kroeger, B. (2005). *Passing: When people can't be who they are.* New York, NY: Public Affairs.

Kouritzin, S. (2000). Immigrant mothers redefine access to ESL classes: Contradiction and ambivalence. *Journal of Multilingual and Multicultural Development, 21*(1), 14–32.

Kubota, R. (2004). Critical multiculturalism and second language education. In B. Norton & K. Toohey (Eds.), *Critical pedagogies and language learning* (pp. 30–52). Cambridge, England: Cambridge University Press.

Kubota, R. (2011a). Learning a foreign language as leisure and consumption: Enjoyment, desire, and the business of *eikaiwa*. *International Journal of Bilingual Education and Bilingualism, 14,* 473–488.

Kubota, R. (2011b). Questioning linguistic instrumentalism: English, neoliberalism, and language tests in Japan. *Linguistics and Education, 22,* 248–260.

Kubota, R., & Lin, A. M. Y. (2006). Race and TESOL: Introduction to concepts and theories. *TESOL Quarterly, 40*(3), 471–493.

Kubota, R., & Lin, A. M. Y. (2009). *Race, culture, and identities in second language education: Exploring critically engaged practice.* New York, NY: Routledge.

Kumaravadivelu, B. (2003). *Beyond methods: Macrostrategies for language teaching.* New Haven, CT: Yale University Press.

Kumaravadivelu, B. (2008). *Cultural globalization and language education*. New Haven, CT: Yale University Press.

Kurashige, S. (2011). Introduction. In G. L. Boggs (Ed.), *The next American revolution: Sustainable activism for the twenty-first century* (pp. 1–27). Berkeley: University of California Press.

Lareau, A. (2000). *Home advantage*. Lanham, MD: Rowman and Littlefield.

Larsen, N. (1997). *Passing*. New York, NY: Penguin. (Original work published 1929)

Lather, P. (1991). *Getting smart: Feminist research and pedagogy with/in the postmodern*. New York, NY: Routledge.

Lather, P. (2000). Drawing the line at angels: Working the ruins of feminist ethnography. In E. St. Pierre & W. S. Pillow (Eds.), *Working the ruins: Feminist poststructural theory and methods in education*, (pp. 284–312). New York, NY: Routledge.

Lau v. Nichols, 414 U.S. 56 (1973)

Lave, J., & Wenger, E. (1991). *Situated learning: Legitimate peripheral participation*. Cambridge, England: Cambridge University Press.

Lee, S. J. (2005). *Up against whiteness: Race, school, and immigrant youth*. New York, NY: Teachers College Press.

Liggett, T. (2009). Unpacking White racial identity in English language teacher education. In R. Kubota & A. M. Y. Lin (Eds.), *Race, culture, and identities in second language education: Exploring critically engaged practice* (pp. 27–43). New York, NY: Routledge.

Lin, A., Grant, R., Kubota, R., Motha, S., Tinker Sachs, G., Vandrick, S., & Wong, S. (2004). Women faculty of color in TESOL: Theorizing our lived experiences. *TESOL Quarterly, 38*(3), 487–504.

Lin, A., & Luke, A. (2006). Coloniality, postcoloniality, and TESOL . . . Can a spider weave its way out of the web that it is being woven into just as it weaves? *Critical Inquiry in Language Studies, 3*(2 & 3), 65–73.

Lin, A. M. Y. (1999). Doing-English-lessons in the reproduction or transformation of social worlds? *TESOL Quarterly, 33*(3), 393–412.

Lin, A. M. Y. (2008). *Problematizing identity: Everyday struggles in language, culture, and education*. New York, NY: Lawrence Erlbaum.

Lin, A. M. Y., & Luke A. (Eds.). (2006). Postcolonial approaches to TESOL. *Critical Inquiry in Language Studies, 3*(2 & 3), 65–200.

Lin, A. M. Y. , & Martin, P. W. (2005). *Decolonisation, globalisation: Language-in-education policy and practice*. Clevedon, England: Multilingual Matters.

Lindemann, S. (2005). Who speaks "broken English"? US undergraduates' perceptions of non-native English. *International Journal of Applied Linguistics, 15*(2), 187–212.

Lippi-Green, R. (2011). *English with an accent: Language, ideology, and discrimination in the United States* (2nd. ed.). London, England: Routledge.

Llurda, E. (2004). Non-native-speaker teachers and English as an international language. *International Journal of Applied Linguistics, 14*, 314–323.

López, A. J. (2005). *Postcolonial whiteness: A critical reader on race and empire*. Albany: State University of New York Press.

Lorenz, E. N. (1993). *The essence of chaos*. Seattle: University of Washington Press.

Lu, M., & Horner, B. (2013). Translingual literacy and matters of agency. In A. S. Canagarajah (Ed.), *Literacy as translingual practice: Between communities and classrooms* (pp. 26–38). New York, NY: Routledge.

Luke, C. (2001). *Globalization and women in academia: North/west south/east.* Mahwah, NJ: Lawrence Erlbaum.

Mackie, A. (2003). Race and desire: Toward critical literacies for ESL. *TESL Canada Journal, 20*(2), 23–37.

MacPherson, S. (2003). TESOL for biolinguistic sustainability: The ecology of English as a lingua mundi. *TESL Canada Journal, 20*(2), 1–22.

Madison, S. (2012). *Critical ethnography: Methods, ethics, and performance* (2nd ed.). Thousand Oaks, CA: Sage.

Makoni, S., & Pennycook, A. D. (Eds.). (2007). *Disinventing and reconstituting languages.* Clevedon, England: Multilingual Matters.

Maldonado-Torres, N. (2007). On coloniality of being: Contributions to the development of a concept. *Cultural Studies, 21*(2/3), 240–270.

Matsuda, A., & Duran, C. S. (2013). Problematizing the construction of Americans as monolingual English speakers. In V. Ramanathan (Ed.), *Language policy, pedagogic practices: Rights, access, citizenship* (pp. 35–51). Bristol, England: Multilingual Matters.

May, S. (2008). *Language and minority rights: Ethnicity, nationalism and the politics of language.* New York, NY: Routledge.

May, S. (2010). Critical multiculturalism and education. In J. A. Banks (Ed.), *The Routledge international companion to multicultural education* (pp. 33–48). New York, NY: Routledge.

May, S. (2012). *Language and minority rights: Ethnicity, nationalism and the politics of language.* New York, NY: Routledge.

May, S., & Janks, H. (2004). Editorial: The challenge of teaching English in diverse contexts. *English Teaching: Practice and Critique, 3*(1), 1–4.

Mbembe, A. (2006). What is postcolonial thinking? An interview with Achille Mbembe (J. Fletcher, Trans.). *Espirit.* Retrieved from http://www.eurozine.com/articles/2008-01-09-mbembe-en.html

McIntosh, P. (1997). White privilege: Unpacking the invisible knapsack. In B. Schneider (Ed.), *Race: An anthology in the first person* (pp. 120–126). New York, NY: Crown Trade Paperbacks.

McLaren, P. (2000). Critical pedagogy: A look at the major concepts. In A. Darder et al. (Eds.), *The critical pedagogy reader* (pp. 69–96). Philadelphia, PA: Routledge Falmer.

Melchers, G., & Shaw, P. (2003). *World Englishes: An introduction.* London, England: Arnold.

Menken, K., & García, O. (2010). *Negotiating language policies in schools: Educators as policymakers.* Hoboken, NJ: Taylor & Francis.

Michael-Luna, S. (2008). Todos somos blancos/We are all White: Constructing racial identities through texts. *Journal of Language, Identity & Education, 7,* 3–4.

Mignolo, W. (1995). The darker side of the Renaissance: Literacy, territoriality, and colonization. Ann Arbor: University of Michigan Press.

Mignolo, W. (2011). *The darker side of Western modernity: Global futures, decolonial options.* Durham, NC: Duke University Press.

Mohanty, C. T. (1991). Under Western eyes: Feminist scholarship and colonial discourses. In C. T. Mohanty, A. Russo, & L. Torres (Eds.), *Third world women and the politics of feminism* (pp. 51–80). Bloomington: Indiana University Press.

Morgan, B. (2004). Teacher identity as pedagogy: Towards a field-internal concep-
tualisation in bilingual and second language education. *International Journal of
Bilingual Education & Bilingualism, 7*, 172–188

Motha, S. (2006a). Racializing ESOL teacher identities in U.S. K–12 public schools.
*TESOL Quarterly, 40*(3), 495–518.

Motha, S. (2006b). Decolonizing ESOL: Negotiating linguistic power in U.S. public
school classrooms. *Critical Inquiry in Language Studies, 3*(2 & 3), 75–100.

Motha, S. (2006c). Out of the safety zone. In A. Curtis & M. Romney (Eds.), *Color,
race and English language teaching: Shades of meaning* (pp. 161–172). Mahwah,
NJ: Lawrence Erlbaum.

Motha, S. (2009). Afternoon tea at Su's: Participant voice and community in criti-
cal feminist ethnography. In S. Kouritzin, N. Piquemal, & R. Norman (Eds.),
*Qualitative research: Challenging the orthodoxies* (pp. 103–119). New York,
NY: Routledge.

Motha, S., Jain, R., & Tecle, T. (2011). Translinguistic Identity-As-Pedagogy: Implications for Teacher Education. *International Journal of Innovation in English
Language Teaching & Research, 1*(1), 13–28.

Motha, S., & Lin, A. (2013, August 1). Non-coercive rearrangements: Theorizing
desire in English language teaching. *TESOL Quarterly*. Advance online publication. doi: 1002/tesq.126

Moussu, L., & Llurda, E. (2008). Non-native English-speaking English language teachers: History and research. *Language Teaching: Surveys and Studies, 41*(3), 315–348.

Mufwene, S. S. (2001). *The ecology of language evolution*. Cambridge, England:
Cambridge University Press.

National Center for Educational Statistics. (2012). *The condition of education 2012*.
Retrieved from http://nces.ed.gov/pubs2012/2012045_2.pdf

Nero, S. (2005). Language, identities, and ESL pedagogies. *Language and Education,
19*(3), 194–211.

Nero, S. (2006). *Dialects, Englishes, creoles, and education*. Mahwah, NJ: Lawrence
Erlbaum.

Nesteruk, O. (2010). Heritage language maintenance and loss among the children
of Eastern European immigrants in the USA. *Journal of Multilingual and Multicultural Development, 31*(3), 271–286.

Ng, R. (1993). A woman out of control: Deconstructing racism and sexism in the
university. *Canadian Journal of Education, 18*, 189–205.

Nieto, S. (2002). *Language, culture, and teaching: Critical perspectives for a new
century*. Mahwah, NJ: Lawrence Erlbaum.

Noddings, N. (1984). *Caring: A feminine approach to ethics and moral education*.
Berkeley: University of California Press.

Norton, B. (2000). *Identity and language learning: Gender, ethnicity and educational
change*. Harlow, England: Longman.

Olsen, L. (2008). *Made in America: Immigrant students in our public scho
ols* (10th anniversary ed.). New York, NY: New Press.

Otsuji, E., & Pennycook, A. (2010). Metrolingualism: Fixity, fluidity and language
in flux. *International Journal of Multilingualism, 7*(3), 240–254.

Paley, V. G. (2000). *White teacher*. Cambridge, MA: Harvard University Press.

Pandey, A. (2013). When "second" comes first—हिंदी to the eye? Sociolinguistic hybridity in professional writing. In A. S. Canagarajah (Ed.), *Literacy as

*translingual practice: Between communities and classrooms* (pp. 215–227). New York, NY: Routledge.

Park, H., Tsai, K. M., Liu, L. L., & Lau, A. S. (2012). Transactional associations between supportive family climate and young children's heritage language proficiency in immigrant families. *International Journal of Behavioral Development, 36*(3), 226–236.

Park, J. S.-Y. (2009). *The local construction of a global language: Ideologies of English in South Korea.* Berlin, Germany: Walter de Gruyter.

Park, J. S.-Y. (2011). The promise of English: Linguistic capital and the neoliberal worker in the South Korean job market. *International Journal of Bilingual Education and Bilingualism, 14*(4), 443–455.

Park, S. J., & Abelmann, N. (2004). Class and cosmopolitan striving: Mothers' management of English education in South Korea. *Anthropological Quarterly, 77*(4), 645–672.

Parker, W. (2003). *Teaching democracy: Unity and diversity in public life.* New York, NY: Teachers College Press.

Paton, G. (2008, October 24). Standard English in decline among teenagers. *Daily Telegraph.* Retrieved from http://www.telegraph.co.uk/education/3254407/Standard-English-in-decline-among-teenagers.html

Pattanayak, D. P. (1996). Chance, language and the developing world. In H. Coleman & L. Cameron (Eds.), *Change and language* (pp. 143–152). Clevedon, England: BAAL/Multilingual Matters.

Pavlenko, A. (2001). In the world of the tradition, I was unimagined: Negotiation of identities in cross-cultural autobiographies. *International Journal of Bilingualism, 5*(3), 317–344.

Pavlenko, A. (2006). *Bilingual minds: Emotional experience, expression, and representation.* Clevedon, England: Multilingual Matters

Payne, R. K. (2005). *A framework for understanding poverty.* Highlands, TX: Aha! Process.

Pennycook, A. (1998). *English and the discourses of colonialism.* London, England: Routledge.

Pennycook, A. (2001). *Critical applied linguistics: A critical introduction.* Mahwah, NJ: Lawrence Erlbaum.

Pennycook, A. (2002). Mother tongues, governmentality, and protectionism. *International Journal of the Sociology of Language, 154*(1), 11–28.

Pennycook, A., & Mitchell, T. (2009). Hip hop as dusty foot philosophy: Engaging locality. In H. S. Alim, A. Ibrahim, & A. Pennycook (Eds.), *Global linguistic flows: Hip hop cultures, youth identities, and the politics of language* (pp. 25–42). New York, NY: Routledge.

Pennycook, A. D. (2007). *Global Englishes and transcultural flows.* London, England: Routledge.

Pfeiffer, K. (2003). *Race passing and American individualism.* Amherst: University of Massachusetts Press.

Phillipson, R. (1992). *Linguistic imperialism.* Oxford, England: Oxford University Press.

Phillipson, R. (2008). The linguistic imperialism of neoliberal empire. *Critical Inquiry in Language Studies, 5*(1), 1–43.

Phillipson, R. (2009). *Linguistic imperialism continued.* New York, NY: Routledge.

Piller, I. (2002). Passing for a native speaker: Identity and success in second language learning. *Journal of Sociolinguistics, 6*(2), 179–208.

Piller, I., Takahashi, K., & Watanabe, Y. (2010). The dark side of TESOL: The hidden costs of overconsumption of English. *Cross-Cultural Studies, 20,* 183–201.

Portes, A., & Rumbaut, R. G. (2001). *Legacies: The story of the immigrant second generation.* Berkeley: University of California Press.

Portes, A., & Rumbaut, R. G. (2006). *Immigrant America: A portrait.* Berkeley: University of California Press.

Ramanathan, V. (2002). The politics of TESOL education: Writing, knowledge, critical pedagogy. New York, NY: Routledge Falmer.

Ramanathan, V. (2006). The vernacularization of English: Crossing global currents to re-dress West-based TESOL. *Critical Inquiry in Language Studies, 3,* 131–146.

Rampton, B. (1999). Styling the other. *Journal of Sociolinguistics, 3*(4), 421–556.

Reagan, T. G. (2002). Language, education, and ideology: Mapping the landscape of U.S. schools. Westport, CT: Praeger.

Reagan, T. G. (2005). Non-Western educational traditions: Indigenous approaches to educational thought and practice. Mahwah, NJ: Lawrence Erlbaum.

Reinharz, S. (1992). *Feminist methods in social research.* New York, NY: Oxford University Press.

Rios-Aguilar, C., & Gándara, P. (2012). *Horne v. Flores* and the future of language policy. *Teachers College Record, 114*(9), 2.

Roman, L., & Apple, M. W. (1990). Is naturalism a move away from positivism? In E. W. Eisner & A. Peshkin (Eds.), *Qualitative inquiry in education: The continuing debate* (pp. 38–73). New York, NY: Teachers College Press.

Rubin, D. L. (1992). Nonlanguage factors affecting undergraduates' judgments of non-native English speaking teaching assistants. *Research in Higher Education, 33,* 511–531.

Ruecker, T. (2011). Challenging the native and nonnative English speaker hierarchy in ELT: New directions from race theory. *Critical Inquiry in Language Studies, 8*(4), 400–422.

Ruiz-de-Velasco, J., & Fix, M. (2000). *Overlooked and underserved: Immigrant students in U.S. secondary schools.* Washington, DC: Urban Institute. Retrieved from www.urban.org/UploadedPDF/overlooked.pdf

Said, E. W. (1978). *Orientalism.* New York, NY: Vintage Books.

Sandhu, P. (2013). Constructing normative and resistant societal discourses about Hindi and English in an interactional narrative. *Applied Linguistics.* Advance online publication. doi: 10.1093/applin/ams075

Santelices, M. V., & Wilson, M. (2010). Unfair treatment? The case of Freedle, the SAT, and the standardization approach to differential item functioning. *Harvard Educational Review, 80*(1), 106–134.

Saraceni, M. (2010). *The relocation of English: Shifting paradigms in a global era.* Basingstoke, England: Palgrave Macmillan.

Sartre, J. P. (1957). *Being and nothingness: An essay on existential ontology* (H. E. Barnes, Trans.). London, England: Methuen.

Sarup, M. (1991). *Education and the ideologies of racism.* Stoke-on-Trent, England: Trentham.

Scholte, J. A. (2000). *Globalization: A critical introduction.* New York, NY: St. Martin's Press.

Schueller, M. J. (2009). *Locating race: Global sites of post-colonial citizenship.* Albany: State University of New York Press.

Selinker, L. (1972). Interlanguage. *International Review of Applied Linguistics in Language Teaching, 10,* 1–4.

Sellami, A. (2006). Slaves of sex, money, and alcohol: (Re-)locating the target culture of TESOL. In J. Edge (Ed.), *(Re-)locating TESOL in an age of empire* (pp. 171–194). Basingstoke, England: Palgrave Macmillan.

Shin, H. (2006). Rethinking TESOL from a SOL's perspective: Indigenous epistemology and decolonizing praxis in TESOL. *Critical Inquiry in Language Studies, 3*(2 & 3), 147–167.

Shuck, G. (2006). Racializing the nonnative English speaker. *Journal of Language, Identity & Education, 5*(4), 259–276.

Skutnabb-Kangas, T., Phillipson, R., Mohanty, A., & Panda, M. (Eds). (2009). *Social justice through multilingual education.* Bristol, England: Multilingual Matters.

Sleeter, C. E. (2005). *Un-standardizing curriculum: Multicultural teaching in the standards-based classroom.* New York, NY: Teacher College Press.

Sleeter, C. E., & Delgado Bernal, D. (2004). Critical pedagogy, critical race theory, and antiracist education: Implications for multicultural education. In J. A. Banks & C. A. M. Banks (Eds.), *Handbook of research on multicultural education* (2nd ed., pp. 240–259). San Francisco, CA: Jossey-Bass.

Smith, L. T. (2012). *Decolonizing methodologies: Research and indigenous peoples* (2nd ed.). London, England: Zed Books.

So, C. (2008). *Economic citizens: A narrative of Asian American visibility.* Philadelphia, PA: Temple University Press.

Spender, D. (1992). *For the record: The making and meaning of feminist knowledge.* London, England: The Women's Press.

Spivak, G. (1990). Gayatri Spivak on the politics of the subaltern. *Socialist Review, 20*(3), 85–97.

Spradley, J. (1980). *Participant observation.* New York, NY: Holt, Rineheart, and Winston.

Spring, J. H. (2004). Deculturalization and the struggle for equality: A brief history of the education of dominated cultures in the United States. Boston, MA: McGraw-Hill.

Strauss, A., & Corbin, J. (1990). *Grounded theory in practice.* Thousand Oaks, CA: Sage.

Suárez-Orozco, M. M., & Qin-Hilliard, D. (2004). *Globalization: Culture and education in the new millennium.* Berkeley: University of California Press.

Suárez-Orozco, M. M., & Sattin, C. (2007). Introduction: Learning in the global era. In M. M. Suárez-Orozco (Ed.), *Learning in the global era: International perspectives on globalization and education* (pp. 1–43). Berkeley: University of California Press.

Takahashi, K. (2013). *Language learning, gender and desire: Japanese women on the move.* Bristol, England: Multilingual Matters.

Tamim, T. (2013). Higher education, languages, and the persistence of inequitable structures for working-class women in Pakistan. *Gender and Education, 25*(2), 155–169.

Thomas, W. P., & Collier, V. P. (2003). The multiple benefits of dual language. *Educational Leadership, 61*(2), 61–64.

Tinker Sachs, G. (2006). The world away from home. In A. Curtis & M. Romney (Eds.), *Color, race, and English language teaching* (pp. 121–135). Mahwah, NJ: Lawrence Erlbaum.

Tinker Sachs, G., & Li, D. C. S. (2007). Cantonese as an additional language in Hong Kong: Problems and prospects. *Multilingua, 26*(1), 95–130.

Tollefson, J. W. (2002). *Language policies in education: Critical issues*. Mahwah, NJ: Lawrence Erlbaum.

Toohey, K. (1998). "Breaking them up, taking them away": ESL Students in grade 1. *TESOL Quarterly, 32*(1), 61–84.

Uriarte, M., Tung, R., Lavan, N., & Diez, V. (2010). Impact of restrictive language policies on engagement and academic achievement of English language learners in Boston public schools. In P. C. Gándara & M. Hopkins (Eds.), *Forbidden language: English learners and restrictive language policies* (pp. 65–85). New York, NY: Teachers College Press.

U.S. Department of Education. (1991, September 27). Developing programs for English language learners: OCR memorandum. Retrieved from http://www2.ed.gov/about/offices/list/ocr/ell/september27.html

Valdés, G. (1996). *Con respeto: Bridging the distances between culturally diverse families and schools—An ethnographic portrait*. New York, NY: Teachers College Press.

Valdés, G. (2001). *Learning and not learning English*. New York, NY: Teachers College Press.

Valdés, G. (2010). *Latino children learning English*. New York, NY: Teachers College Press.

Valenzuela, A. (1999). *Subtractive schooling: U.S.-Mexican youth and the politics of caring*. Albany: State University of New York Press.

Valli, L., & Rennert-Ariev, P. L. (2000). Identifying consensus in teacher education reform documents: A proposed framework and action implications. *Journal of Teacher Education, 51*(1), 5–17.

Van Ausdale, D., & Feagin, J. R. (2001). *The first R: How children learn race and racism*. Lanham, MD: Rowman & Littlefield.

Van Dijk, T. (2000). Discourse and access. In R. Phillipson (Ed.), *Rights to language: Equity, power, and education* (pp. 73–78). Mahwah, NJ: Lawrence Erlbaum.

Vandrick, S. (2002). ESL and the colonial legacy: A teacher faces her "missionary kid" past. In V. Zamel & R. Spack (Eds.), *Enriching ESOL pedagogy: Readings and activities for engagement, reflection, and inquiry* (pp. 411–422). Mahwah, NJ: Lawrence Erlbaum.

Vandrick, S. (2009). *Interrogating privilege: Reflections of a second language educator*. Ann Arbor: University of Michigan Press.

Varghese, M. M., & Johnston, B. (2007). Evangelical Christians and English language teaching. *TESOL Quarterly, 41*(1), 5–31.

Wald, G. (2000). *Crossing the line: Racial passing in twentieth-century U.S. literature and culture*. Durham, NC: Duke University Press.

Wallerstein, I., Amin, S., Arrighi, G., & Frank, A. (1982). *Dynamics of global crisis*. London, England: Macmillan.

Warschauer, M., El Said, G. R., & Zohry, A. (2004). Language choice online: Globalization and identity in Egypt. In F. E. Jandt (Ed.), *Intercultural communication* (pp. 160–172). Thousand Oaks, CA: Sage.

Webb, P. T. (2002). Teacher power: The exercise of professional autonomy in an era of strict accountability. *Teacher Development, 6*(1), 47–62.

Wee, L. (2008). Linguistic instrumentalism in Singapore. In P. K. W. Tan & R. Rubdy (Eds.), *Language as commodity: Global structures, local market places* (pp. 31–43). London, England: Continuum.

Weedon, C. (1999). *Feminism, theory and the politics of difference*. Malden, MA: Blackwell.

Wellman, T. (2013). *Better outcomes in learning a new language through investment and agency in negotiating identity*. Term paper for ENGL 571, Fall 2013.

Wenger, E. (1998). *Communities of practice: Learning, meaning, and identity*. London, England: Cambridge University Press.

Wexler, P. (1982). Ideology and education: From critique to class action. *Interchange, 13*(3), 53–68.

Widin, J. (2010). *Illegitimate practices: Global English language education*. Bristol, England: Multilingual Matters.

Wildman, S. M., & Davis, A. (1996). Making systems of privilege visible. In S. M. Wildman (Ed.), *Privilege revealed: How invisible preference undermines America* (pp. 7–24). New York, NY: New York University Press.

Williams, P., & Chrisman, L. (1994). *Colonial discourse and post-colonial theory: A reader*. New York, NY: Columbia University Press.

Willinsky, J. (1998). *Learning to divide the world: Education at empire's end*. Minneapolis: University of Minnesota Press.

Wolcott, H. F. (1990). On seeking—and rejecting—validity in qualitative research. In E. W. Eisner & A. Peshkin (Eds.), *Qualitative inquiry in education: The continuing debate* (pp. 121–152). New York, NY: Teachers College Press.

Wong, S. (2005). *Dialogic approaches to teaching English to speakers of other languages: Where the ginkgo tree grows*. Mahwah, NJ: Lawrence Erlbaum.

Wong, S., & Motha, S. (2007). Multilingualism in post-9/11 schools: Implications for engaging empire. *Peace and Change: A Journal of Peace Research, 32*(1), 62–77.

Wong, S., & Motha, S., with Frye, D., Roberts, W., & Wang, C. (2006). Collaborative research with student teachers: Tool and mediation in classroom interaction. In S. Wong (Ed.), *Dialogic approaches to TESOL: Where the gingko tree grows* (pp. 98–109). Mahwah, NJ: Lawrence Erlbaum.

Yin, R. (1994). *Case study research: Design and methods* (2nd ed.). Beverly Hills, CA: Sage.

Young, R. (2001). *Postcolonialism: An historical introduction*. Oxford, England: Blackwell Publishers.

Young, V. A. (2013) Keep code-meshing. In Canagarajah, A. S. (Ed.), *Literacy as translingual practice: Between communities and classrooms* (pp. 139–146). New York, NY: Routledge.

Young, V. A., Martinez, A. Y., & National Council of Teachers of English. (2011). *Code-meshing as World English: Pedagogy, policy, performance*. Urbana, IL: National Council of Teachers of English.

Zheng, X. (2010). Re-interpreting silence: Chinese international students' verbal participation in U.S. universities. *International Journal of Learning, 17*(5), 451–464.

# Index

# About the Author

**Suhanthie Motha** is an assistant professor in the Department of English at the University of Washington in Seattle, where she teaches graduate classes in TESOL and applied linguistics. While she frequently feels conflicted about her participation in the project of teaching English, she more often than not believes in and holds hope for the possibility of teaching English in responsible and ethical ways. She was born in Sri Lanka and raised in various countries with complicated colonial histories, most notably Australia and Nouvelle Calédonie. Her work has been published in journals including *TESOL Quarterly*, *Modern Language Journal*, *Critical Inquiry in Language Studies*, *TESL Canada Journal*, *Educational Practice and Theory*, *Language Teaching*, and *Peace and Change Journal* and as chapters in several books. She serves on the editorial review board of *TESOL Quarterly*. Her next book theorizes the concept of desire in relation to English, race, and coloniality.